the guide

the guide

Dr William Holden

© Dr William Holden, 2009

Published by Forecast Publishing

www.forecastpublishing.co.uk
www.sewells.com

February 2009

Reprinted October 2009

Reprinted April 2010

Reprinted December 2010

ISBN 978-0-9561891-0-3 Paperback
ISBN 978-0-9561891-1-0 Hardback

A CIP catalogue record for this book is available from the British Library.

Cover designed by: Ben Holden at Cahoona Ltd
Photo by Ben Holden

www.cahoona.co.uk

www.theguide.info

Prepared and printed by:

York Publishing Services Ltd
64 Hallfield Road
Layerthorpe
York YO31 7ZQ
Tel: 01904 431213
Website: www.yps-publishing.co.uk

Reviews

Press Reviews

"A book that makes sense. It gives explanations of why things happen, but also gives practical ways to change and reach your true potential. A must-read."

Avril Cadden, Sunday Mail Scotland

"If you only ever buy one personal development book in your lifetime, I whole-heartedly suggest you make it this one."

Peter Morrell, AboutMyGeneration.com

"So many things have already changed ... I'm totally up for world domination now!"

Sarah Cawood, TV Presenter and columnist

Five Star Reviews

*******the guide** – Much better than The Secret!!

After reading both **the guide** and The Secret by Rhonda Byrne, I would definitely recommend **the guide** out of the two. I enjoyed reading **the guide** because it offers further explanation on the ideas suggested about being successful. Within the explanations given, it shows you how to apply the ideas to everyday life; The Secret doesn't do this.

*****Inspirational

Will is one of THE most inspirational people I have met in business. His book is a must have for every home and business. Buy it, read it ... let Will help you to brighten up your day and your life!

Reader Reviews

Easy to read - made sense - and great strategies for every day life - personally and professionally. A number of my family members have since read the book and have felt as uplifted as I did. I would really recommend it and also if you get the opportunity to see Will speak - take it!"

H K, Lytham.

"I thought **the guide** was excellent in respect of what I was looking for and the approach taken by Dr Holden was fantastically creative. His advice to suspend all critical judgment and try out the methods for yourself is very sound."

G.H, Ireland

Business Reviews

"**the guide** made me more positive. Suddenly some of the little stones I had in the way started to disappear and day to day life became happier, lighter, easier".

European Marketing Manager, KFC

"A must buy book wherever your life is right now. Take these principles on board and it will change your life forever."

Field Sales Manager, Yell.com

"Thought provoking without the usual condescending tosh for the emotional illiterate you normally find in this genre of books. I'm now on my second read".

Managing Director, Fragrance Oils

To the reader

This book has been a long time coming.

It is the result of an obsession. It's one I've had for as long as I can remember and has two linked elements. Firstly, it's about understanding how people can get the best out of life; and secondly, it's about explaining in simple terms what people need to do to make it work for themselves.

This is not a book to be rushed. It's to be studied and savoured. Stories of ordinary people reaching extraordinary levels of achievement, joy, success, health and wealth are designed to inspire people to know that they too can change. Some of the principles are deliberately repeated to enhance and deepen the learning.

Another motivation for writing this book is borne of frustration with other self-fulfilment communications. Many merely describe **what** to do, but don't explain **why** it works and **how** to do it.

You are encouraged to study these pages carefully and at your own pace. It takes time for some of the powerful principles and practices to sink in to your very core. Read and re-read the words until the meaning has been absorbed. If you need a couple of days to contemplate and consider your own ideas on how this all works, take the time.

The timeless, tried and tested principles and practices, which are well within the capability of any human being, when applied, give people complete control over the circumstances and situations in life. The power contained within these pages has been proven time and time again by people who have followed its wisdom.

The step-by-step process of learning to take control of your life is more akin to a tide than a wave. It comes and comes and comes. Let it.

For the sceptics, all I ask you to do is temporarily suspend all critical judgement and try the methods out for yourself. This will allay your scepticism. This stuff works. Let it.

Chapter One

Paul and Maya were great friends. They had been since they were at school together. In their teens they had tried the romance thing, but it didn't work out for them. They were 'soul mates', with a relationship that transcended the physical.

Their upbringing was, for the most part, normal. They both grew up in a slightly run-down area of town. They didn't go to a particularly good school, and neither of them did particularly well academically. They both married solid and steady partners; Paul and his wife, Jackie, had three children, while Maya and her husband, Andy, after many years of trying, had one child.

They both worked hard in jobs that they enjoyed, but constantly struggled to get the life–work balance correct. There always seemed to be a restructure, or a reorganisation, in their respective working environments that demanded more and more of their time. This created problems at home for them both: they did not see enough of their children, and spent very little, if any, quality time with their partners. And money always seemed to be an issue for both families. They would just be making progress when something would knock them back again: an expensive school trip, or the car needing emergency repair work to keep it going.

Neither Paul nor Maya complained at all; they were a lot better placed than many people they knew. They also both knew people who, on the surface, appeared to have it all, money, health, happy family; but, upon digging deeper, their situation was no better than their own. These people were just very good at presenting the right image to a watching world.

Now Paul and Maya were in their 40s, their health and vitality were beginning to show the strain. Maya was very ill for a few months and eventually had to have a hysterectomy, which she never really got over. She also put on 20 lbs in weight. Paul was suffering from stress, with the constant threat of redundancy hanging over him and the many restructures at work. He had promised himself that he would leave and find a more secure job, but such a job didn't seem to exist. Many of Paul's friends had set up their own businesses in an attempt to gain security. Each one of them had worked all the hours God sent, struggling like crazy just to make ends meet, and some had failed.

Paul and Maya shared a strong belief that there must be more to life than this. Why should life be such a struggle for them and so many others? This belief was strengthened by the odd glimpse, a rare glimpse, of men and women making a real success of life. These people genuinely possessed an abundance of wealth, health, happiness and success in every aspect of their lives, at work and at home.

For hours, either face to face or on the phone, Paul and Maya would discuss the latest 'success guaranteed' theories and practices. They both tried this and that; they both invested as much time and money as they dared on books, tapes and attending seminars, all promising to deliver '*the answer*'. But everything they tried fell short.

Many of their friends were fascinated and intrigued by their search, because they, too, had been looking, with no success. Paul and Maya had in fact concluded that, deep down, it was in everyone's nature to desire the key to delivering abundant health, wealth, happiness and success; an unsatisfied longing to know the truth, not only of success, but of life itself.

Paul and Maya had independently searched for the truth via the religious route, trying traditional religions as well as new-age ones. Paul, in his late 20s, even dabbled in a crazy 'cult' type religion. For them both, no answers were forthcoming; rather than supplying answers, the more they searched, the more conflicting the ideas were and the more confused they became.

By the time Maya moved away, to take up a new job in new corporate headquarters after yet another restructure within the organisation she worked for, she and Paul had both arrived at the same conclusion. Their conclusion was this: life is a mystery that is not meant to be understood or taken control of; life is one long fight against poverty, unhappiness, ill health and failure, and, one day, probably on their death beds, all may be revealed so that they can enjoy the afterlife, if there is one.

Maya moved more than a hundred miles away and, for the first few weeks, stayed in touch with Paul regularly. Then, because of work pressure and general crises of day-to-day living, she didn't speak to Paul for more than 12 months. When Maya eventually phoned Paul, she sounded like a different person.

"We've got to meet up. I've found it: I've found what we've both been looking for. In fact, I've found what the whole of the human race has been looking for. It's so wonderful. When can we meet?"

Paul was astonished. Maya had never sounded so self-assured and genuine. She'd always been enthusiastic, but this was different; this was more than enthusiastic, this was total conviction. There was no hint of doubt. Something very profound had happened to Maya, and he was keen to discover what it was.

"Let's meet tomorrow at The Old Fox 'gastro' pub," Paul suggested, "I'll see you there at 7 o'clock." Maya agreed adding "Prepare to be amazed. I now know what is responsible for every success and every failure in people's lives. And, more importantly, how to consciously take control. I can't wait to tell you what has happened in my life and to share it with you, so that you can begin to obtain anything you desire in life without limit. Believe me, it is mind-blowing." "I can't wait", said Paul, more than a little intrigued.

Paul was consumed with this news; he could not think of anything else, at home or at work; he couldn't sleep with anticipation. 'Maya is no fool,' he thought, 'If she says she's found something that answers our life-long searching, well, she must have done. And if she says she is going to share it, whatever she has discovered is transferable to others; it can't be a specific thing that only suits one person or one group of people.'

For Paul, time seemed to stand still while he waited for his meeting with Maya.

Chapter Two

Paul arrived 15 minutes early and found a quiet corner of the pub where he and Maya could talk without being disturbed. He went to the bar and bought a large bottle of sparkling water and carried it and two glasses containing ice and lemon back to the table.

Casting a glance over his shoulder, Paul nearly dropped the lot at the sight of Maya, who had arrived while he had been at the bar. "Good heavens!" he cried, "you look sensational." Sensational did not even come close to an accurate description. Maya was glowing; her eyes sparkled; her smile would have melted polar ice caps; she was slim, dressed beautifully and when she greeted him she had a cheeky little intonation in her voice. Everyone in the pub was drawn to her. Paul felt a warmth and assuredness flowing from her that totally disarmed him yet put him at ease.

"It's pretty clear you've got something significant to tell me," Paul said, "and I'm not even going to ask how you are: it's oozing out of every pore in your body! You've clearly found the key to something special."

"I've found more than that," Maya said, "but tell me how you have been doing lately."

"Oh, much of the same as always: working too hard; not getting paid enough; the kids driving me mad wanting this and that; the arguments; and I've been to the doctor again with stress. You know, life goes on ... but it never seems to go the way you want it to!"

Maya replied, "Well, that's why I was so keen to meet you and let you discover for yourself what I've found. How would you like to know how, as you said, life goes on, but *always* the way you want it to?"

Paul was reflective, "Well, isn't that what we've been looking for all our lives? And didn't we come to the conclusion that it was all 'pie in the sky' stuff?"

"Well, yes, we did," said Maya, "but something truly amazing has happened to me in the last 12 months that has changed my life positively and dramatically for the better. And forever."

"It certainly has," Paul said, "you've really fallen on your feet, I can tell. Did you win the lottery or something?"

"No, no, nothing like that. But let me tell you something: it got a lot worse before it started getting better." Maya paused for a moment. "It got a lot, lot worse." Even though Maya was recalling hurtful memories, her radiance never diminished. "Let me explain what happened.

"After we moved it was OK for a while, when we were still keeping in touch. My son, Tom, was settling nicely into school and all was going well. Then it all changed, as one crisis after another hit." There was a vitality and compassionate countenance about the way she spoke that made Paul know that whatever problems she was going to tell him, she had discovered a solution to them. And she was going to tell him how she overcame them.

Maya went on to say that the company she worked for, and had moved for, was taken over by a larger organisation and her position was made redundant. Her husband, Andy, left her for her best friend. Her son, Tom, blamed himself for the break-up and became unruly at school, and was asked to leave. With all the stress and strains, Maya had become very ill and, if it hadn't been for Tom, she wouldn't have had the courage or conviction to carry on. "I was below rock-bottom," she said. "Everyone and everything was going wrong, and the harder I tried to put it right, the worse it seemed to get. Nothing was working. Nothing at all. I was drinking myself into oblivion night after night, but even that didn't deaden the pain. My parents, God bless them, helped me to keep my head above water, just. Without their love and support, I could easily have slipped away without a trace."

Paul asked, "Why didn't you call me? You know I would have been there for you." "Yes I know that," she said, "but I couldn't think straight. I was lost. I was helpless and still sliding deeper into an emotional abyss. I wanted to have the worst behind me before contacting you." "OK," said Paul, "I understand: you've always been an independent so-and-so."

Maya laughed, "Yes, yes, I've always been an independent 'I'll sort it out for myself' type of person, haven't I? However, on this occasion, I could only sort it out myself to a certain extent. In the depths of my despair, it hit me like a board: I hadn't had a single positive or enjoyable thought run through my mind for months. My situation was pitiful. This realisation served as a real wake-up call. Whilst there were some awful challenges in my life, they did not make my life awful. I'd made my life awful all on my own, by wallowing in my own self pity.

"I decided to get a grip. After all, no one had died! And even if they had, life goes on. I changed my approach to life; rather than focus on everything that I didn't have and being bitter and resentful, I learnt to focus on what I did have, and to become truly grateful and appreciative. It was not easy at first, not at all. It required a lot of discipline. Tom was healthy, and I was grateful for that. My parents and a few friends came through for me big time, especially when it came to looking after Tom during my darkest days. I was doubly appreciative of that, because I was not the easiest person to deal with. My mood swings gave me a Jekyll and Hyde character. However, I worked hard on building gratitude and genuine appreciation for everything in my life.

"I became grateful for being able to walk, so I walked. And I walked and walked and walked and walked! I was appreciative that I could walk so far that I got tired out! I was truly grateful that my strength was coming back to me. In my walks in the park, my heart sang with appreciation and gratitude for the flowers, shrubs, trees, birds, ducks, rabbits and squirrels. Even the cafe by the boating lake received heart-felt appreciation, as a welcome oasis for rest and refreshment after my long walks.

"I would sit in the cafe for what seemed like hours, sipping tea and drinking in gallons of gratitude. I'd never considered it before, but sight is a wonderful gift: it's incredible what you can see when you really look. Hearing is the same, and our sense of touch is magical. I learned to love all my senses; my skin tingled when it was cold and glowed when it was warm. I particularly appreciated my positive feelings, because my heart had been broken into so many pieces. The world seemed to be different, but did it seem different because I was viewing it through different eyes? My mind was consumed in a different way. I was trying to figure out consciously what was happening to me, as it was happening to me. It was tough.

"It was in the cafe by the boating lake that I first spoke to him. I'd seen him a few times walking in the park. There was just something about him."

Paul interrupted, "Oh Maya, you've got a new man in your life! How wonderful for you, after all the grief Andy put you through."

Maya smiled at Paul, "No, no, there is no new man in my life, but there has been a new life in my life, after I met this man. As I was saying, I'd noticed him in the park before. He looked to be in his 50s, but someone told me that he was 85. He was 6 feet tall, sprightly and fit. His facial features were well composed. His clothes were nothing special, but there was something very special about him. He had a certain presence. His expression, smile and courteous demeanour made it obvious that he was at peace with everyone and everything. His presence infected everyone positively.

"We started saying 'good morning' and 'afternoon' to each other, if our paths crossed during my walks, but no more than that. Then, one day in the cafe, I was sitting at a table overlooking the boating lake. It was an overcast, drizzling April day and I was lost in thought. I'd been watching the ducks, fighting like crazy one second, and then serenely swimming the next, as if nothing had gone on before! 'Oh, to be like a duck', I thought to myself, wondering what it would be like not to carry every disagreement we've ever had around in our minds for the rest of our lives.

"Even though I was the only customer in the cafe, the atmosphere suddenly became charged with energy, a benevolent, positively charged energy that made me tingle and feel calm at the same time. Someone sat down at the table next to me. I saw them out of the corner of my eye because they also chose to sit overlooking the boating lake. I could not see who it was and, out of politeness and courtesy, I did not look straight away; I thought I'd let them settle down first. I then turned to catch their eye to say 'good morning' and make some comment about the weather; at the same time, they turned to catch my eye. It was the man with presence I had passed occasionally on my walks. Before I had a chance to speak, he'd said, 'good morning' and nodded knowingly, 'isn't life wonderful!' His eyes were kind, his expression full of wisdom and his voice full of certainty.

"I muttered something in reply that didn't make much sense to me, so he must have been bewildered! It was something like: 'Er, well, er, yes it is wonderful sometimes, but most of the time it can be a real struggle, but then, if you choose to see things differently, it can change the way things turn out, but most of the time we can't choose, and life grinds us into the ground … and …' I think I ran out of breath, rather than words. His genuine compassion for me and my confusion was tangible. Already I felt safe next to him; I somehow felt valued and respected. 'It sounds to me that life has dealt you some pretty severe blows', he said. Before he'd finished the sentence, woosh …, I was off, and, within 25 minutes, I'd told him my whole life story. To a virtual stranger! I don't know why: it just felt right to do that and, do you know what?" Paul shook his head, "No, what?"

"He listened," Maya replied, "he really, really listened. He listened with such sincerity and intensity, it was almost therapeutic. No, no: it was therapeutic! He wasn't judgmental about anything anyone had said or done; he just listened. He wanted to know the details of everyone affected, including Andy, Tom and my Mum and Dad. There were no comments like, 'Oh, that's terrible', 'He shouldn't have done that', 'You poor thing'. He just wanted to understand the circumstances and the situations. Also, it was a real joy not having someone say, 'Well, if I were you, I'd have done this', or 'I'd have done that'. It was real empathy; making an effort to see it from my point of view, not his, and understand my approaches and options to what was unfolding before me. I finished by explaining where I was now and how much better I felt, and how much more 'in control' I was, now that I was in gratitude and appreciation mode.

"He nodded in a discerning way and asked, 'Are you surprised by that, by how much better you feel and in control you are, now your approach to life has changed?' I told him that, at one level, I was, and that at another level, I wasn't. 'Consciously, I was surprised,' I said, 'intuitively, I wasn't. I guess I always knew, deep down, that there was a link.' That answer seemed to open the floodgates to his and my connectivity. I've never felt anything like that in my life before. Our souls from that moment on were well and truly connected.

"He asked calmly, 'Would you like to understand consciously what you know intuitively? Would you like to know the secrets behind everything that happens to us in life?' I gave a very simple nod of my head. 'Yes, I would', I said. He continued, 'Would you like to know where joy and sorrow come from, where health and disease originate, and where happiness and despair have their source? And would you like me to be your guide, and teach you some practical lessons on how to connect with, and channel, a great creative and universal power that can help you, and anyone else, overcome any challenges, in order to achieve any right and proper desire you may have in life?' His voice was utterly sincere and truthful. His face revealed the authenticity of the power of the philosophy and techniques he was willing to share with me.

"'Of course I would. In fact, I would be honoured, grateful and truly appreciative if you became my guide. What would it involve? How long will it take, and why would you want to guide me?' His response was strong and calm, 'Whoa! Let's take those questions one at a time!' He went on to explain that it would take a number of meetings together, always in public places, where lessons on taking control of life would be discussed, followed by an opportunity to practise and perfect them in my own time and in my own way. It would take as long as it would take, as different people learn to master the techniques at different speeds. However, he did reassure me that, without any shadow of doubt, I would be able to master the techniques, as could anyone. He went on to say that the only thing that would be required was my passionate commitment to master the simple, yet life-changing, principles and practices that would govern the creation of a life that worked for me, and to share those principles and practices with others when the time was right. I made that commitment there and then, and my life has been transformed."

Paul was open-mouthed, "I can see that!"

Maya continued, "Paul, you can transform your life, too. Anyone can, and I mean anyone. As to the question about why he would want to guide me, he explained that he regarded our purpose in life, as human beings, was to make the world a better place for everyone in it. Because I wasn't in the best place I could be, he said he would consider it an honour and a privilege to be my guide. I was moved to tears of gratitude and appreciation. Then I remembered something you once told me 'when the student is ready, the teacher will appear!' I'd never really understood it until that moment."

Paul confessed: "I got that quote from a philosopher called Goethe, and I've never really understood it either!" They both laughed heartily; their laughter was time spent with the gods, as their souls connected.

"Paul, I want to be your guide and to share with you what I have learnt: the power we have at our disposal, the control we have, the limitlessness of our being. You are not currently where you want to be, and I can help guide you there, if you want me to and if you will let me."

"Maya, you've got yourself the number 1 dedicated and committed supporter here! Guide away!"

"Do you passionately commit to share what you learn with others?" Maya enquired. "Because, if you don't, the connection to the great universal power available to you will fade and eventually stop all together. That is one of the first lessons to learn: we can have all the right and proper things that we want in life if we help enough other people get those things for themselves. What you hoard you lose; what you share multiplies. It's as simple as that. You'll understand it more as I guide you through the lessons.

"Let's start with an essential principle: this great fundamental universal law, governing and controlling health, happiness and material abundance, has no respect for a person's position or circumstances, because it operates with perfect precision in every human life. Isn't that what we've always believed, but have never been able to find? Remember our discussions?" Maya said excitedly, "That in a universe that follows natural laws, surely there must be laws that govern the human condition? These, once discovered and used properly, could be the answer to removing and replacing all the undesirable conditions in life?

"In fact, I've come to realise that all the undesirable conditions we face only manifest themselves through ignorance of these universal and natural motivating laws. You and I have been saying this for years; we intrinsically know this to be true. Every human being does, unless they have been so badly damaged to date that all their feelings and sensitivities have been eroded away. Let's face it, we know some pretty damaged characters, but even those people will admit there is something else around us that makes us tick, apart from ourselves. Lesson 1 is all about explaining what that is."

"You must enlighten me. What does lesson 1 say?" Paul asked.

"I'm sorry, Paul, you are not ready for lesson 1, yet. As my guide said to me, 'Before you can truly learn, you must unlearn first.'"

"What?!" Paul exclaimed. "We've got to unlearn first? I don't understand: help me out on this one, Maya, please."

"OK," Maya replied, "but this is all we will have time for tonight. Have you got another hour or so for me this evening to explain some of this further?"

"Does the Pope pray!" Paul replied.

Chapter Three

Maya leaned over and handed Paul a sealed envelope. "Now, before you open this, I need you to make me a promise."

"Y–yes, go on, what is it?" Paul asked, a little hesitantly.

"I want you to promise me that, if you really want to understand and use these universal laws, so that you can have anything you desire in life without limit, you will go through every one of the lessons I bring to you, and complete every exercise and instruction without exception. Please do not start on this journey without promising that you will see it through to the end. OK? Promise?" Maya was very earnest.

"But I don't know what they are and whether I will be able to master them", replied Paul.

"Paul, let me assure you that every principle and practice in every lesson is well within the grasp of every human being. You don't need any academic qualifications or special physical attributes to make these universal laws work for you in any area of your life you choose. It is a good idea to find some time when you will not be interrupted, so that you can give the studies your full attention. In fact, I suspect that the biggest barriers you will face on this journey will be, not in the difficulty of what you will be asked to do, but in the total simplicity of it all". Maya went on, "Many people think that the principles and practices they are asked to understand and master are so simple they must have little or no value and can not be life changing. Believe me, nothing could be further from the truth, so be warned! Now, are you going to promise?"

"Of course I am," Paul replied, "I would be mad not to, when I can see such a difference in you. Let's face it, Maya, if you can do it, so can I."

"Exactly!" Maya replied. "Hasn't it always been that way for us both?"

"So, what's in this envelope then, the arc of the covenant or something?" asked Paul. "No, not quite," said Maya, "but what you've got in your hands is something that will start the process of dramatically and positively changing your life for the better. But let me ask you a question before you open it and read what's inside. Do you want your life to change dramatically and positively for the better? Really? Honestly? Madly? Truly?" Maya looked at Paul intensely. Without losing eye contact, Paul replied, "Of course I do, haven't we been searching for that since we were little?"

"Yes," Maya said, "but don't you think there is a big difference between saying you want something that you don't really believe you'll ever have, and saying you want something you know is well within your grasp?" Paul replied, "Maybe, but not for something as big as this! Who wouldn't want to find the secret to unlimited wealth, health, happiness and success!"

"Surprisingly, lots of people don't", Maya said, "because, as the principles and practices are mastered, there can be no more excuses for not achieving anything. That terrifies a lot of people. They don't want the responsibility or accountability.

"You're going to be guided to understand deep and significant truths, and I caution you not to open that envelope unless you are willing to accept the 10 most important words strung together in the English language as a sentence, and these are '**if it is to be … it is up to me**'. Once you are guided through the lessons, it will become crystal clear that every success and failure we enjoy or endure is created by ourselves. So there is no more blaming others, the government, the economy, the market, the weather, your upbringing. I've got to tell you now, Paul, that the mere thought of that frightens the living daylights out of most people. They love to blame the reasons for their circumstances on a whole list of things; and their own names are never on the list! So what about you? Are you up for that level of personal responsibility?"

"Oh, yes," Paul replied, "I've always been willing to accept personal responsibility. In fact, I am probably too far the other way; I blame myself for everything! But I think you are telling me, here, that there is a big difference between blaming myself and accepting personal responsibility for creating a life that works. Is that right?"

"You bet that's right! It sounds like you're ready to open the envelope", Maya replied, eagerly. "It does, doesn't it?" Paul remarked. "So, what am I going to find, did you say?" Maya repeated her earlier words, "You will find on the piece of paper a sentence, a very profound sentence, that will, from the reading of it, start the process of dramatically and positively changing your life for the better!" "Wow," said Paul, "it must be some hugely significant and philosophical truism. Is it?" Maya fixed her gaze on Paul and, with a twinkle in her eye and a smile, said, "Just open the envelope and read the sentence, and be prepared for a lovely and wonderful realisation and feeling of wellbeing to shudder through your entire body. Apparently, it happens like that sometimes."

Paul ripped open the envelope; before opening the piece of paper inside, for some reason, he looked around furtively to make sure no one was trying to get a sneak preview. As he opened the folded piece of paper the sentence revealed itself. It said:

FINISHED FILES ARE THE RE-
SULTS OF YEARS OF SCIEN-
TIFIC STUDY COMBINED WITH
THE EXPERIENCE OF YEARS

As Paul read the words, he felt nothing. They didn't make any sense. He read the sentence again, very slowly, and it still didn't make sense; a frown furrowed his brow. "What do you think?" Maya asked.

"Well, after your big build up to this and its meaning, I am ashamed to admit that I don't know what to think," said Paul. "In fact, I feel frustrated and let down!"

"Paul," said Maya, "have I ever let you down in the whole time we've known each other?" Paul replied, "No, I must admit you never have. Whatever you have ever said will happen, *always* happens, I'll give you that." "Well," Maya responded, "I am not letting you down here, either, and I am *deadly* serious when I say that this sentence will start the process of changing your life dramatically for the better. Now, read it one more time, please!"

FINISHED FILES ARE THE RE-
SULTS OF YEARS OF SCIEN-
TIFIC STUDY COMBINED WITH
THE EXPERIENCE OF YEARS

Paul was getting really frustrated. "I'm sorry Maya, I must be really stupid or something, but this sentence is doing nothing for me at all; it makes no sense to me!" "OK," said Maya, "let's try a slightly different approach. This time, I want you to read the sentence through again but, instead of trying to get the whole meaning out of it, just do something really simple. Just read the sentence through one more time and this time count the number of 'Fs' it contains. OK?" Maya's new instructions were clear and Paul nodded in agreement. "When you have counted the number of 'Fs', turn the piece of paper over and leave it on the table between us, face down."

Paul read the sentence through again, counted the number of 'Fs', and then confidently put the paper upside down between himself and Maya. "Well, that was easy enough", he said. "OK, how many did you count?" asked Maya. "Three", said Paul in a confident tone. "That's fine," said Maya, "but I'd like you to double check before I give you the correct answer." Even though his frown had now turned into a bit of a scowl, Paul turned over the paper again, reread it, counted the number of 'Fs' and once more confidently slapped the paper face down between them. In a slightly raised voice, he said, "Three! Definitely three." Maya looked kindly at Paul and commented, "Mmm, I thought so. You *are* sure, aren't you?" "Totally and utterly!!" replied Paul.

"OK Paul, I'm going to tell you something now, but let me also tell you that, in the lessons to follow on how to create a life for yourself that works, you will not be told many things because you will discover them for yourself. But now I *am* going to tell you that there are actually *six* 'Fs' in that sentence." "Six!" Paul exclaimed, "never!" Maya remained calm and politely asked Paul to read through the sentence again, with the knowledge now that there were six 'Fs' just 18 inches from his nose. Paul grabbed the paper and read it through slowly, this time using his finger to identify the 'Fs': "There are definitely only three 'Fs' on this piece of paper. *Definitely!*"

"Paul," said Maya, "trust me: there are six. I'll stop prolonging the agony, here's a tip to help you see what is really in front of your eyes. Read it again and, this time, count the 'Fs' in the word 'of'."

Paul's face was a revelation as the realisation dawned on him. "My goodness!" he blurted out. "How on earth could I have missed them? I feel so completely stupid!" Maya jumped on Paul's criticism of himself and said, "Whoa, don't beat yourself up over this. It's nothing to do with you, or how clever or stupid you are. This is not a test of intelligence or anything like that." "Yeh," said Paul, "but how could I have missed the three 'Fs' in the three 'ofs'; it's so blindingly obvious!" Maya went on, "Yes, it is *now*! Now that it has been pointed out to you, but you would have been here all night if I hadn't helped you." Paul agreed, "Yes, you're probably right, but how could I have missed them?"

"Well, let's talk about that in some detail," said Maya, "Why would you, or anyone else, miss something as blindingly obvious as this? What do you think the reasons might be? 85–90% of people who have never seen this before only see two or three 'Fs' first time around and, yes, before you ask, even when they have been told that there are six!" "That's astonishing!" exclaimed Paul. "Yes, it is," Maya replied, "but it is a fact. So why do you think that might be? What are the reasons?"

"Well," said Paul, "it could be, because you gave this such a big build up by saying it was a profound sentence that would change my life, that, therefore, it kind of forced me to look at the big words." Maya was impressed, "Yes, that's one good reason. But it's not the main reason that 85–90% of people miss the 'Fs'." Paul pondered further, "Well, could it be that we just skim read and therefore miss the insignificant words, the joining words. Oh, what did Miss Tinsley call them in our English lessons? I remember! Prepositions!" Maya was doubly impressed, "Mmm, that could be a reason, but it's not the main reason."

Maya moved closer to emphasise what was going to be a significant part of this first lesson. "OK, let me explain. The reason that most people miss most 'Fs' is this: we are all conditioned, or brainwashed, if you like. We are all conditioned, we are all brainwashed, in many ways, and we are all conditioned and brainwashed in this instance by the way we are taught to read the English language. You see, we are all taught to read it phonetically, based on how the letters sound, not how they look. So the letter 'F' in the word 'of' sounds like a …" "'Vuh'," Paul volunteered, "and not 'fuh'." Maya continued, "Yes, you've got it. So we tend to pick up the 'F' in the word 'finished' and the word 'files' and in the word 'scientific', although many people miss the last one because it's buried in the middle of the word. But, all the 'Fs' here make the sharp 'fuh' sound when we say the word, so we latch onto them. However, the 'Fs' in the word 'of' make the flat 'vuh' sound, so we skip over them and miss them. Do you follow?"

"Yes," said Paul, "I've got that, but I don't understand what all this has got to do with finding the secret behind having an abundance of wealth, health, happiness and success in my life." "I know what you mean," said Maya. "It wasn't clear to me at first but, strap yourself in for this one, because it is mind-blowing: you see, the sentence itself is a nonsense sentence. It doesn't mean a thing."

Paul interrupted, "But you said it was a profound sentence that would dramatically change my life for the better." "What I actually said," replied Maya, excitedly, "was that it was a profound sentence, which would start the process of changing your life dramatically and positively for the better. And believe me, it will! Not the sentence itself, because it is a nonsense sentence. What will start the process is understanding the profound universal principle that lies behind the reason that most people miss most of the 'Fs' in that sentence.

"You see, we, as human beings, do not act or behave in this world according to what is real; we all act and behave according to our **perception** of what is real. This sentence is a really crystal-clear example of demonstrating how awful our perceptions can be! Let's face it, if our perception can be so far removed from reality on something as simple as this sentence, where we miss half of what is actually there right in front of our eyes, what else might we be missing in life? And where else might we be making really important decisions on how to act or behave in all aspects of our lives, not based upon what is real, but upon our **perceptions** of what is real?! We could be missing half the 'Fs' out all the time, and wondering why, if the world is our playground, we aren't playing."

"So, what you're saying to me," Paul summarised, "is that everything we need in life to allow us to have an abundance of health, wealth, happiness and success, could be all around us, all the time, but we have been conditioned and brainwashed not to see it?"

Maya smiled, "You've got it in one, Paul, and your journey has just begun! And let me reassure you that all human beings are the same; we've all been conditioned and brainwashed, not by some evil government agency, or anything like that; it's just the way civilisation has developed. Being brainwashed is OK on one condition, that we all realise we are! One of the biggest problems everyone faces today, and it was certainly true in my case until recently, is that they think that only they see what is real or what is the truth, and it's everyone else who gets it wrong!! This is where most conflict and strife in the world comes from.

"Change this," Maya said calmly, with total confidence, "and you can change your world. Now, can you stay for another half hour, so you can get an idea of the full picture?"

"Yes," said Paul in eager anticipation, "but I need a sandwich and a cup of tea. This is all a bit much for me on an empty stomach. Do you fancy something?"

A waiter appeared, as if from nowhere, and enquired, "Would you like something from the bar menu?" Paul appeared surprised by this seemingly sheer coincidence, while Maya smiled knowingly. "Yes please", they said together.

Chapter Four

"You knew that the waiter was going to come over then and ask if we would like something to eat, didn't you?" asked Paul, slightly amused. "Well, kind of", said Maya. Paul went on, "It's as if he was reading our minds or was summoned over to us, without a word being said!" Maya replied, "Let's not go into that just now. I've got some other important foundations to lay with you tonight, before I leave in half an hour. Once you've got this next bit mastered, you will be ready to begin the lessons proper." "Oh," said Paul, "I can hardly wait! But, and this is a big but, is what you are about to share with me some kind of new religion, or are we about to dabble in the supernatural, or something?"

"Paul, let me assure you that this is not a religion of any kind, and it is anything but supernatural. In fact, it is so natural and so big and so all round us that most of us have missed it!" Paul, in a flash, interjected, "So, it's a bit like the 'Fs' in that stupid sentence, then? So blindingly obvious, we can't see it!" Maya responded with an enthusiastic, "Precisely! When you have been guided through all the lessons, you will find that all spiritual traditions have some of the key elements at their very core. After all, what is, is!"

Maya continued, "Let me just explain something about the learning process I will guide you through. To fully appreciate the fact that, if there is any lack whatsoever in your life, be it health, success, happiness, wealth, relationships, etc., it is because you are not following or using the universal laws that govern and control everyone's behaviour, lives and destinies, a particular style of learning is recommended that is called R^2A^2."

"It's called what?"

Maya said it again: "R^2A^2. It's really simple. The first R stands for **recognise** and, as your guide, it is important that I get you to recognise all the principles upon which this great and universal power is based. The good thing is that the principles we are going to explore together are really simple, 'in your face', principles of human behaviour. That means you don't need any academic qualifications to be able to recognise each and every one of them. In fact, the only qualification anyone needs is to have been on planet Earth observing what people say and do to and for each other for about a week or so; they will then be more than qualified to recognise all the principles. OK?"

Paul replied with a hesitant, "I think so." Maya stressed, "No, no, Paul. This is really important. Everyone on the planet is able to recognise the principles. Unless, of course, they only landed from the planet Mars yesterday. But within a week or so, even they would be qualified!" Paul confidently replied, "OK, OK, I get it."

Maya continued, "For instance, we've just covered the first principle; about human beings not acting or behaving in this world according to what is real, but according to their **perception** of what is real. Yes? Well, you can't miss that can you! It's so simple and easy to recognise. All the principles are the same.

"And the second R is this: once you have recognised a principle, you will then be urged to **relate** it to your own particular set of circumstances as much as you can. What I mean by this is, take the principles back into your own particular set of circumstances as much as you can, and really let your mind wrap itself around the principles and how they have impacted on you, and on the people you know or have heard about. I'll give you a good example in a minute.

"The first A is connected with recognising the principles and relating them to your own experiences and set of circumstances.

The more you can do for the first two Rs, the more you will be **assimilating** the principles. When I say assimilating, I mean the principles need to become embedded really deeply. This is not merely about imparting a bit of knowledge and a few techniques. The principles need to be assimilated into the very fibre of your being, into your DNA or subatomic structure. The secrets you are going to learn are tools for life. The deeper the learning goes, the longer the principles and practices will stay with you for you to use. The deeper the roots, the richer the harvest we can expect."

"So, what is the second A, then?" enquired Paul. Maya smiled, fixed his gaze, and responded very seriously, "The second A is the most important element of this life-long learning process. It represents **action**: actually putting the principles and practices into action, once they have been recognised, related to and assimilated by you. The principles and practices then need to be put into action in your daily life. There are some simple daily disciplines that are required; simple actions that, when followed, make the unchanging, great and universal power, that governs success, health and wealth, work for you and through you, so that you can have anything your heart desires, without limit!"

Maya went on enthusiastically, "You must take action. Understanding the principles and thinking about them is not enough. My role as a guide is to encourage and motivate you into action. I love you like a brother, you know that, which is why you are one of the first people I'm sharing these secrets with. But part of my role as a guide is not only to impart the principles and the practices, but also to inspire you into action: to get you to want to do what needs to be done, the simple daily disciplines. If you do what you've always done, you'll get what you've always got: unhappiness, ill health, poverty and failure."

Paul interrupted and said, "Well, you know one of my favourite phrases, about the best definition of insanity." Maya chipped in, "Of course, I'd nearly forgotten that one, but isn't it so apt here?

What was it again? Oh yes: insanity is simply doing the same things over and over again, expecting a different result! Good one, Paul! So my message to you here is clear: as you go through the learning and awakening, you must precisely and consistently follow the techniques and actions required. If you go away from our meetings and do nothing with the principles and practices you learn, let me tell you what will happen: *nothing*! *Absolutely nothing*! Nothing will change in the slightest, which is why I asked you to promise me that you will go through all the lessons and complete all the instructions to the letter, because, if you don't, it won't work for you the way it has worked for me and thousands of others."

"OK, Maya," said Paul, "you've made your point, and I accept it wholeheartedly. What you are going to show me is not an academic exercise to be contemplated, it's a daily doing, to be actioned. Right?"

Maya expanded, "Yes. Although, it's a bit more than that, actually. It's a minute by minute, second by second doing, but you're on the right lines. Let me give you a simple example of how R^2A^2 works. Let's use it in conjunction with the sentence I showed you with the 'Fs', OK?"

"That's OK with me", Paul replied happily.

"Let's go back to Christopher Columbus's day." Paul leaned forward to listen intently. "Imagine you are Christopher Columbus's bank manager and he comes to you with the plans for three ships tucked under his arm, and a request for some money in the form of a loan so he can get them built. Christopher Columbus is a good customer of yours, and has never missed a single payment on any of his previous loans with you. So he now asks for the biggest loan he has ever had, and you, being the professional bank manager you are, follow the proper process. You are as encouraging as always, and enquire whether you can see his plans for the ships. He hands over the plans and you open them out and study them, even though you know next to nothing about ships and shipbuilding. One thing does strike you about all three ships, however, which causes you to make a comment: 'These are mighty big ships, Chris, what on earth are you going to do with them?' And he replies, quite calmly, that this is his biggest adventure to date and he is going to sail around the world!"

Maya continued, "You, Mr Bank Manager, then continue to be encouraging, and are not in the slightest bit fazed by his ambitious plans, nor concerned about granting him the loan. The main reason for this is that, at this point in time, almost everyone thought the shape of the world was ..."

"Flat!" Paul replied immediately. "Everyone thought it was flat, didn't they? In fact, they didn't just think it was flat: they *knew* it was!"

"Exactly," said Maya, "so sailing around the world is, to you the bank manager, like sailing around the edge of a plate! So no problem there! But when Christopher Columbus comes along, and believes the world is shaped like an orange, and tells you he's effectively going to sail straight over the edge of your plate-like world, what's your decision likely to be then in relation to giving him the money to build three ships?"

Paul quickly replied, "Well, you'd have to be mad to agree to that!"

Maya pressed home the point: "So, what would your decision be, Mr Bank Manager?"

Paul emphatically replied, "A very firm 'No'!"

"That is the very principle I want you to relate to here," Maya said. "Do you see how, in the past, what was real was not what we know to be real today? Today the reality is that the world is almost spherical, like an orange or a football, hanging in space. However, people's perceptions in the past were that it was flat and, therefore, decisions that people would make about lending Christopher Columbus money, or joining his crew, would not be based upon what is real, but on their **perception** of what is real. See? And also, remember that, once a decision has been made, all subsequent actions and behaviours will reflect the perception of reality, not what is real. Even with the sailors at that time, their behaviour reflected the perception that the world was flat. Every day they would be sailing out from ports on the coast, and they would go out only so far, but not too far, just in case they slipped over the edge, and then they'd come back again. And then the next day they'd sail out in a different direction and again, they would go out so far, but not too far; so they lived their lives in a very limited way.

"So, tell me, have you been living your life in a limited way? Not based upon what is real, but based upon your **perception** of what is real? Could it be possible that you might have made, and continue to make, decisions on what you are going to do, or not do, and that you have missed loads of 'Fs' out in your understanding of the situation? Can you relate to that?"

Paul looked visibly shaken, as his mind raced through examples from his own life. "Are you kidding? Can I relate to it! Do you remember the move I got offered for a 2-year secondment to the Australian operation at work? We discussed it, and I told you that the general belief was that it was a 'wilderness job', i.e. you do that for 2 years and then come back and get stuck in the back office for the rest of your life."

Maya nodded, "I remember it well. Didn't the guy who took your place in Australia on that secondment just get promoted to Chief Executive of your company? Didn't I read that somewhere?"

Paul nodded, "Yes, he did. Maybe he didn't listen to the gossip and rumour, and saw the secondment as it really was, a fantastic opportunity, rather than perceive it as a passage into a 'wilderness job'." Maya added, "He saw six 'Fs' while you looked at the same thing and were convinced there were only three … And…"

"Flipping heck, Maya, what have I been missing in my life because of my conditioning? It's frightening!" Paul's words were strong and sincere. He knew the lesson here, and he knew it applied not only to him but everyone else too.

"Paul, let's just take this to another level, and then I'll leave you to think about it some more. Imagine now that you are Christopher Columbus and you've just found someone who will give you the money to build the ships. Somebody did, in fact. It was Isabella, King Ferdinand's wife. A woman! Just think of the conditioning we've all had over the years about women and what they can and can't do, eh? And here was a woman whose vision and foresight allowed the discovery of the New World and all its riches!

"Anyway," Maya continued, "imagine, once you've got the money and a launch date for the new ships, what your next big problem will be?"

"I guess I will need a crew, or rather three crews, because the ships can't sail themselves."

"So, imagine how successful your recruitment campaign will be for the various positions on the ships, the captains, bow swains, riggers, navigators, etc., when you tell them which way round the world they are going to sail! Because, think about it, no matter how good the pay might be, or the conditions on board, or the bonuses, or whatever, when they realise that, as a potential member of the crew, they are going to sail *that* way around, their enthusiasm will just evaporate. Who would volunteer to go on a journey like that, with the mindset and belief that the world is flat?!"

Paul added, "You would be volunteering to go to a certain death by sailing over the edge of the world into the void!"

Maya exclaimed, "Exactly!", completely oblivious to the other customers in the pub, who were beginning to look at them. "But let me ask you something else: would this have anything to do with your ability to be a brilliant captain, navigator or chief cook and bottle washer on this journey?"

Paul responded, "Well no, of course not. It would have nothing, whatsoever, to do with my ability to be brilliant."

Maya fired another question at him, "So, what gets in the way?"

Paul had an 'ah, ha' moment: a dawning, a realisation. "Well, it's the conditioning that these people have been subjected to that would get in the way! So they would never get the opportunity to use their talents, skills and gifts and show the world what they are really capable of. They would get buried, and remain buried, yes? And with this going on all the time all around us, is it any wonder most people never come close to realising their full potential, and don't live life to the full and can't create a life that works for them?!"

Paul was fired-up now: "This has hit a bull's-eye with me, Maya. I have got to be one of the most negatively conditioned people in the world! Whenever anything new is suggested, the first thing that comes into my mind is the 'going over the edge of the world into the void' scenario."

"You are not the most negatively conditioned person in the world, I can assure you of that," said Maya. "You are just 'normal', I'm afraid!"

"So, what have I got to do, then?" Paul enquired.

Maya replied, "Well, you've got to do a bit of **un**learning before we can get to the learning proper. You are at the stage I was at just 6 months ago. You've been putting your foot on the accelerator, trying to get your life to work out properly, but, unbeknown to you, you've had your foot on the brake at the same time. The harder you have pushed the accelerator, the harder you have unconsciously pushed on the brake at the same time. You have ended up wearing out the engine and all the vital parts and you've got nowhere."

Maya continued, "Between now and when I see you next, all I want you to do is listen to what is going on around you and tune into the conditioning that goes on. Start asking yourself some questions about where the beliefs you currently have about yourself, about other people and the world in general, have come from and whether or not they are real, true and absolutely irrefutable. Perhaps these things have become real for you because you've missed half the 'Fs' out?! I have to go now, but I'll call you when you are ready for the next lesson. *Don't call me*. Study this subject well. Observe, listen, think."

Paul asked, "But how will you know when I will be ready?"

"*I'll know*," said Maya, "but, most importantly, so will you." And they stood up and left the pub together.

Chapter Five

The phone rang in Paul's office a week after his meeting with Maya. In half a ring he had answered it: "Paul Adams speaking. How may I help you?"

Maya's voice was a welcome sound: "Hi, Paul, it's Maya. You sound different. You sound like you're ready for our next meeting to complete the first lesson. I knew you would be."

"Maya! I've been ready for days! And, believe me, I don't just sound different, I *am* different."

Maya's sincerity was tangible, "Why? What have you learned from your observations?"

"Well, I've learned nothing more than you taught me when we met last week, but I've discovered loads and loads. I was trying to explain it to someone in my office yesterday, and she said that I had had my eyes opened. I disagreed with her, and said that I hadn't, I'd had my eyes open all the time. Instead, I told her, what I had discovered was how to see; how to really see what is going on, and not let my years of conditioning get in the way! What I've also discovered is that by working hard to see more 'Fs', as it were, you can make better decisions about life, work, health, relationships, wealth … everything really."

"Just give me one practical example, Paul." Paul spluttered with enthusiasm, "I could give you a hundred examples, but here is a very relevant one. Just let me close my office door so I can't be overheard … OK, about a year ago, I got a new boss. He had been transferred from another division and, before he had even arrived, all the talk in 'the tribe', as we call the jungle drums and gossip that goes around the place, was about what a ruthless individual he was. Rumour was that he'd laid people off as a cost-cutting measure in his last job, just to make a name for himself. We all believed he'd been sent here to do the same.

"We had also heard he was the chairman's 'blue-eyed boy' because he was a distant relative, and was destined for the top job one day, and would do anything to get there. So, when we eventually met him, we were all highly suspicious. He began talking about expanding the department, about us being the 'battering ram' that would break down the doors and reverse the condition that had caused the company to decline steadily over the years. He also said we needed a significant restructure to get us 'battle ready'. So, our attitude was 'eh-up, this guy is just softening us up', and our opinions were reinforced when some of the senior members of the team, who were vociferously against any changes, were offered early retirement or transferred out of the department. That got everybody feeling really twitchy and nervous about the future, falling into the 'is it going to be me next? ' mindset.

"About 6 months ago, I was so worried about what was going on, I was off work with stress for weeks, and so were a good few others. No-one was really concentrating on getting the work done, so productivity and performance slumped, and, after 3 months, 'the tribe' was laughing: 'the guy with the golden touch has dropped a real clanger'.

"What is really interesting is that he has just kept banging out the same message, and everything he says is positive and supportive about each member of the newly structured team. The trouble is, none of us have believed him. Since you and I met last week, I've tried to re-assess everything this guy has ever said to the team or to me personally and, do you know what? Nothing he ever says or does matches the preconceived ideas we have about him, and I've realised that I've been blocking him. In my performance reviews, he has been telling me what a talented and gifted person I am, how I am a vital member of the team with a bright future ahead, and that he loves my ideas and wants to put them into practice. Because of my conditioning, I've been thinking, 'you just want all my ideas and then you'll bin me'. He has been telling me and showing me there are six 'Fs', and I've been hearing and seeing only three! What an idiot I've been; I don't know how the company has put up with me for so long with my attitude!"

"Don't beat yourself up about it," Maya said. "It's not your fault; it's this 'tribal thinking' nonsense, and we can all get sucked into that. But tell me something, when you discovered this, what did you *do* about it?"

Seizing on the question, Paul responded enthusiastically, "Well, that's the best bit. I discovered it in the car driving back from our meeting last week and, the very next day, I changed my attitude towards my boss, the company, the challenge ahead and our new direction, and *wow*! And I mean *wow*! Ideas came flooding to me. I had a meeting with my boss in the afternoon and left my resistance behind, and the 'bond' we developed was awesome. Everything he said made sense. We totally agreed with each other. We've now agreed a plan to follow, and it looks like it will involve the creation of a subdivision within our department, and he wants me to head it up and run it for him.

"This is the big promotion I've wanted for so long, and I've just realised that what was holding me back was: *me*! Maya, you know as well as anybody, that I've blamed everybody and everything for that promotion not coming my way. Who was it that said, 'I've seen the enemy, and he is me'? Anyway, I changed my attitude and, within a week, a result; a positive result!"

"I'm thrilled for you," said Maya. "You're discovering the power that lies within the reach of every human being, and we've hardly started yet. You are definitely ready for the next lesson. When do you want to meet?"

Paul was enthusiastic: "Can you make tonight?"

"OK," said Maya, "I'll see you at 7.30. Same place, same table."

"That's fine, providing the table is free. If not, I'll be at the nearest available one."

"The table will be free," replied Maya, calmly, "I guarantee it."

Now that Paul had chosen and adopted his new attitude, the time flew by between putting the phone down and making his way to The Old Fox. He had got the whole team at work buzzing with excitement about some of his projects, which allowed him to go home slightly earlier than normal, to spend time with his wife, Jackie, and children before going to meet Maya. The change at home was as dramatic as the one at work. He realised that his conditioning had taught him to focus on what was lacking at home rather than on what he had. He told a neighbour, who had noticed the difference: 'Most people would be twice as happy in life if they had half as much and fully appreciated it'. Paul's neighbour nodded politely, but didn't understand. Paul did.

Paul and Maya arrived at the pub at the same time. Maya was driving a brand-new, top of the range car, but one that suited her new, quietly understated but obviously successful self.

"Nice car," Paul remarked. "Is it yours, or a company car?"

"It's mine", replied Maya.

"I thought you'd always said your ultimate car status symbol was an Aston Martin, and that as soon as you could afford one you'd get one."

Maya smiled, "That was then, and this is now. Maybe I'll treat myself to an Aston Martin one day, but I doubt it. One of the underlying principles, which we'll discuss later, is that people of stature don't need status. It's what's on the inside that matters, not the outside. But most of our conditioning teaches us to judge people based upon what is on the outside. Big house, big car, big spender, means big person. Nothing could be further from the truth, as you will discover when you are ready. Shall we?" she asked, gesturing towards the door of the pub.

As they walked towards the door, Paul glanced through the window and noticed that the table they had sat at last week, and which Maya had guaranteed would be free, was occupied. Paul erred on the side of caution and didn't say anything. Which was a good job, because the moment Paul and Maya walked in, the people at their table started saying their goodbyes and left. Paul's face was a picture, 'How remarkable!', he thought.

A waiter appeared and they ordered some drinks. Paul commented to Maya how surly the waiter was, before launching into their conversation with great excitement. "I've got so many things to tell you since our last time together. Our perceptions are awful because of our conditioning, and I'm not sure anything in reality is the way we see it. Did you know that planet Earth is spinning at around 1000 miles an hour and hurtling through space at 67,000 miles an hour? I can't perceive that! I think it is standing still! And my perceptions tell me that I am solid, but you and I, and everybody, is made up of cells that are made up of atoms, which are the smallest items of matter. But an atom, when studied under a microscope, is mainly space filled with energy, with a nucleus and electrons and protons whizzing around it, so we are 99.999999% empty space! And …"

Maya interrupted, "Whoa, there, Paul, easy! You've got the idea on conditioning, but there is more that you need to know about how it affects every aspect of our lives. And I've only got an hour, because I have a meeting with someone else later tonight."

"Oh, OK," said Paul, a little embarrassed, "sorry to rabbit on."

Maya replied, "There is no need to be sorry! Your enthusiasm tells me that you have assimilated the first principle, and your story on the phone tells me you are taking action. That's all you've got to do, every step of the way, to access the true, true treasures this universe has to offer us. Anyway, are you ready for the next part?"

"Yes I am," responded Paul emphatically.

Maya began, "Let me explain to you explicitly what you have discovered implicitly within a week of starting this journey. Probably unbeknown to you, you have discovered what makes people 'tick' and what makes people behave in certain ways."

Paul was slightly bemused by this. "I don't think I understand what you mean, but this thing," he said, pulling out the piece of paper with the 'Fs' on and waving it at Maya, "was one of the biggest revelations I've ever had in my life!"

"Well, *that* wasn't," corrected Maya, gesturing towards the paper in Paul's hand, "but what was behind it was. Missing the blindingly obvious the whole time was the revelation, because of the way we are conditioned."

"Well, that's what I meant."

"OK," said Maya, "but let me explain further. May I borrow your piece of paper?"

"Yes, but only if you let me have it back."

Maya smiled knowingly. "I'm going to write something on the back and, when I'm finished, you'll want it back more than ever. Here, let me show you something." Having turned the paper over to show the blank side, Maya drew a smallish triangle in the middle of the paper at the top. "Tell me, on a day-to-day basis, what do we, as human beings, manage?"

Paul thought for a moment and, slightly confused, answered, "Well, at work I manage a team of people, at home I manage a family and … and I manage me."

"You're right, you manage people and yourself, or rather you manage other people's and your own behaviour."

Maya wrote 'Behaviour' inside the triangle. "And let me explain what I mean by behaviour: behaviour is just words and actions or, put another way, it's what you do and say every second of the day. If you are responsible for other people at work or at home, it's what they do and what they say every second of every day. Right? Have you got that?" Paul nodded. "That's what behaviour is," said Maya, now writing 'Words and Actions' below 'Behaviour' in the triangle. "At work, our behaviour may get *measured* in a whole variety of different ways, a profit and loss account, a production report, a project management chart, or something else, but what you're managing is people's behaviour. What they say and what they do, every second of every day. In an ideal world, what kind of behaviour would you love for yourself and everyone else around you to exhibit every second of every day? Give me some words that describe that sort of behaviour." As Paul answered, Maya wrote each word on the outside of the triangle on the right-hand side.

"Hmmm. What about 'positive' to start with?"

"Great! What else?"

"What about 'enthusiastic'?"

"Brilliant! You've got the idea; go on."

"Well, 'happy', 'content', 'cheerful', 'friendly', 'honest', 'professional', 'loyal', 'co-operative', 'proactive', 'creative', 'flexible', 'innovative'," Paul gushed.

"Terrific! What else?"

He continued, "'reliable', 'energetic', 'understanding', 'stress-free', 'healthy', 'confident' …"

Maya stopped him, "OK. That will do for starters. Quite a list, eh? Let's just call all this 'Best' behaviour for now." Maya wrote the word 'Best' at the top of the list. "Imagine what it would be like if you could get yourself, and everyone around you, to exhibit that kind of behaviour every second of every day for the next 12 months or so. What impact would it have on your life at work and at home?"

Paul's jaw dropped open, "Well, I'd, I'd, and we'd … be unstoppable! There would be nothing we couldn't achieve, at home or at work."

Maya nodded in agreement, "Precisely. I wish you could've seen your face for that nanosecond that you were there, actually imagining it. Your face lit up. It had a radiance I haven't seen in you since you were about 6 years old. Although it did only last for a nanosecond, before all the negatives came flooding back to wash the picture away, and the radiance in your face turned to a frown. But don't worry about that; I wouldn't expect anything else at this stage of your journey.

"However, do you know something else? I could read what was going on in your mind. As you reeled off the words it was like, 'wow', just for a nanosecond, and then, 'what a load of pie-in-the-sky wishful-thinking nonsense, you can't get people to behave like that all the time'. But that's what I'm here to show you, because I've discovered that you can; *everyone* can. You first need to understand something about what really drives behaviour in human beings, because this bit," Maya pointed to the triangle, "the behaviour bit, is just the bit on top of a larger triangle. This is the bit that sticks out of the top, the bit that most people see most of the time, the bit that most people, including you, think is you. The real you, however, lies much deeper inside, and that's what you've got to see and understand. Then you need to learn how to connect with the real unlimited, mightily gifted and talented you, and direct the real unlimited you towards achieving anything you desire: success, happiness, wealth, health, anything. And, providing that they are truly what you desire, and right and proper, they will be yours!"

"Wow! I know you said what you had to tell me was big, but this is bigger than a big 'un isn't it?" 'Big 'un' was one of Paul and Maya's old phrases that described something monumental in life.

"I think you'll agree that finding the key to what life is all about, and how to master it, is an awesome discovery!"

"I think you're probably right," Paul replied, slightly tongue in cheek. "So, tell me what lies underneath and drives our behaviour? Where does our behaviour come from, then?"

Maya drew an extension to the triangle underneath the 'Behaviour' section and, before writing in any words, asked, "As human beings, what do you think immediately drives our behaviour?"

Paul was a little unsure, "Err, is it our experiences?"

Maya's response was keen and reassuring, "It undoubtedly is our experiences or, rather, our perception of our experiences that affects our behaviour, but our experiences are not the immediate drivers. We are not robots or androids; we are human beings, and, therefore, the immediate drivers of our behaviour are feelings and emotions. It's one of the things that differentiates us from the rest of the animal world. We are emotional creatures. We make decisions emotionally. Don't be so naive as to think anything else; we may justify those decisions rationally, but we actually make them emotionally. So our feelings and emotions are the immediate drivers of our behaviour."

Maya wrote 'Feelings and emotions' in the extended empty section of the triangle. Paul looked a little puzzled. Maya continued, "Let me give you a practical example rather than talking theoretically. When you feel good about something… madly, deeply, passionately good, how do you behave towards it?" Maya wrote the word 'Good' on the outside of the section of the triangle marked 'Feelings and emotions', on the right-hand side:

"Well, that's easy," said Paul, "I behave enthusiastically, positively, creatively, energetically and…"

Maya interrupted him, "Or, in other words, all the things you told me here, right?" She pointed to the list of words she had written on the outside of the 'Behaviour' section of the triangle. Paul nodded. Maya went on, "But let me ask you another question. Do you have to press a button to get that behaviour?"

"No," said Paul, "I'd say that kind of behaviour just gushes out automatically. Doesn't it?"

"Of course it does. But is it the same for everyone?" Maya asked.

"Yes!" Paul said emphatically, "It's exactly the same."

"So what is the trigger that makes all this wonderful behaviour come flying out of people?"

"Feeling good!" replied Paul, immediately. Then he reconsidered for a moment, "But then, you can't feel good all the time, can you?"

"Paul, you need to make up your own mind on that one when we've finished this first lesson but, before you do, let me explain a little more about the role that feelings and emotions play regarding our behaviour.

"We, as people," Maya continued, "have not come to terms with our humanity in this sense and, in fact, our conditioning often tells us not to trust, or even to ignore, our feelings and emotions. This is especially true in the workplace. How many times have you heard bosses say, 'Oh, there's no room for any feelings and emotions in this place, we are running a business.' So try to leave your feelings and emotions outside the door as you come into work!"

Paul replied, "I must hear something like that every day!"

Maya continued, "In fact it's ridiculous for bosses to talk like that. If you have had a big fall out with your partner and you've been sleeping in the bath for 3 nights, do you come bouncing into work full of the joys of spring? Of course you don't. Equally, if you are having a horrid time at work, you take it home with you, and some unsuspecting, innocent person suffers from your resulting anger."

Paul nodded enthusiastically, "You're not kidding. I do that all the time, or rather I did it all the time before this week. And lo and behold, I've had one of the best weeks I've had in my life, at work and at home."

"Just a coincidence, eh?" said Maya wryly.

"Mmm" was all Paul could manage in response.

"It does show you how instantaneous the results of some of these lessons can be, though, Paul, doesn't it? Anyway, there's a bit more to this. People who deny the importance of feelings and emotions in driving behaviour are often focused on key metrics and performance indicators, and the old adage of 'if you can measure it, you can manage it'. These people are ignorant of the 'behavioural triangle' and, therefore, in the dark when it comes to understanding what really makes people tick. They think that you can't measure feelings and emotions and, because of this, you can't manage them. The reality is that you can measure them, or at least the effects they have on our bodies. Ask any doctor what happens to you physically when you feel good, and they will tell you that your brain transmits a signal to your body to release trillions of chemicals, called endorphins or endo-morphins, that actually cause you to feel good and so exhibit your best behaviour, automatically!"

Paul was excited, "You're so right; this is dynamite!"

"Yes, it is, but listen! Do you know what the principal component of endorphins or endo-*morphins* is? It's morphine! It's the purest form of morphine known to humans, and we produce it naturally when we feel good. Morphine is actually known as the 'feel good' drug. In fact, it's not just morphine that gets produced; there's dopamine, serotonin, a whole 'feel good' cocktail! The important thing to remember is that the process is one of cause and effect, not hit and miss. Feeling good drives our best behaviour, full stop! The cause will always produce the same effect. By controlling our feelings, we control our behaviour. How good is that?"

"Now," Maya continued, "what's really interesting is what happens to our behaviour when we feel bad." Maya wrote the word 'Bad' on the left-hand side of the triangle, by the section marked 'Feelings and emotions'. "Any thoughts?"

"Well," Paul replied, "I would hazard a guess that it is the opposite of all those positive behaviours you get when you feel good! So it's all the negative behaviours … reluctance, unfriendliness, lack of enthusiasm, apathy, and the like."

"Spot on! And again, Paul, do we have to press a button to get at this behaviour? No! It's just as automatic as the positive stuff, just as much cause and effect. This time the chemicals released are called oxytoxins and they prevent all the good behaviours emerging. The behaviours exhibited by people who feel bad fall into two major categories. The first category is the ultimate in negative behaviour: *no* behaviour at all! Someone gave me a great phrase for this that describes the effect perfectly: 'Creative avoidance'." She wrote this on the left-hand side of the triangle. "Just how creative do you think people can be when it comes to avoiding something they feel bad about?"

Paul laughed, "Well, if they're anything like me, they can be exceptionally creative; genius, in fact, if it's required." He described some examples, "Like the number of people who feel bad about working Fridays and call in sick, 'Friday-itis' they call it at work. And that boring neighbour who invited me to his Christmas party last year; I didn't quite tell him I was 'washing my hair' but I told him a white lie, that I had a prior engagement, and then volunteered to visit my mother-in-law rather than go!"

Maya continued for him, "And, if we can't get out of such things completely, we revert to the second category of behaviour, which is procrastination. We take an age to do things or slow things down, or we keep putting things off by using all kinds of excuses in the hope that whatever needs doing eventually gets forgotten about."

Paul blushed, "Like those shelves I've been promising to put up for the last 3 years! Oh, blimey, I'm so embarrassed …"

"Don't be, Paul. Again, you are just normal. Most people do this most of the time! They think they're being, oh, so clever and, oh, so original. But don't get me wrong, these are not bad people; they are just people who feel bad. They may feel bad about themselves: 'I'm no good at DIY and whatever I do always ends up in a worst state than when I started'. They may feel bad about the person who has asked them to do something: 'Why should I do that 10-page report for you! You only steal my ideas and never give me any credit'. They may feel bad about what they are being asked to do: they may have had the figures on the boss's desk at 10 a.m. every Wednesday morning for the past 3 years, as requested, and no comment has ever been made about them, good, bad or indifferent! They begin to wonder whether anybody ever looks at the figures, even though they take ages to compile.

"The important thing to remember is that, for whatever reason, they simply feel bad about themselves, some other person or something they've been asked to do, and that is all that is needed to kill their enthusiasm and creativity for making positive things happen. These bad feelings and emotions mask the magnificent array of positive behaviours that are available to anyone; the good behaviours lie dormant and unused."

Paul responded in a resigned fashion, "That's me. That has been me for most of my adult life. I didn't realise how much choice and control I've actually got. I just put it down to which side of the bed

I get out of in the morning. Ye gods! Is it any wonder life has been such a struggle for me!

Maya interjected, "Oh it's worse than that! Let me explain one more thing, and then you'll have to excuse me for 5 minutes while I say hello to someone I know at the bar."

Paul smiled, "New boyfriend?"

Maya smiled back, "No, another person I'm helping guide on his journey who needs some clarification.

"Getting back to what we have just been saying, most people don't realise how much choice and control they have over their behaviour and performance in life. They don't understand how the choices they make regarding attitudes and associated feelings and emotions drive their behaviour. It's down to our conditioning. What does our conditioning encourage us to do with feelings and emotions?"

"To suppress them, of course," said Paul, "to hide them."

Maya nodded, "Here we are again, denying what being human is all about! We are, as human beings, emotional creatures. Our feelings and emotions make us human and motivate us to behave in certain ways. It is impossible, a word I rarely use these days, for human beings to hide or suppress their feelings and emotions for long. These drivers of our behaviour have got to have an outlet! Once we understand and accept this, there is only one thing we can hope to do with our feelings and emotions. What do you think that might be?"

Paul looked puzzled, "Erm … you've got me on that one."

Maya elaborated, "The only thing we can do with them is channel and direct them. Think of our feelings and emotions as the cream in the middle of a cake. If you squeeze the top and bottom layers together what happens? Does the cream turn into anti-matter and disappear out of the universe? Of course not! It simply gets squeezed out of the sides. Feelings and emotions are just the same; they come out on one side or the other."

At this juncture, Maya pointed to the 'bad feelings' side of the triangle. "In other words, you can't suppress or hide them in the hope that they will go away. As life puts the pressure on, and it will, our feelings and emotions come oozing out on one side or the other. So, knowing this, what is the very best we can hope to do with feelings and emotions?"

Paul responded positively, "Well, channel and direct them towards the good side, of course."

Maya confirmed, "You're absolutely right. Unless you are really perverse, of course, enjoying misery, failure and suffering in your life, or inflicting these things into other people's lives."

Paul replied, "Well, that makes no sense at all! Channelling and directing our feelings and emotions onto the good side is the only thing to do, because look at the positive, dynamic, creative and energetic behaviour that comes flying out of us when we do!"

Maya sat back in her chair. "But how many people do you know who constantly make people feel bad, at work and at home, about themselves, about what they do and how they do it … and about the world in general … instilling feelings of fear, inadequacy and uselessness, in the belief that this is somehow motivational? Somehow, they feel that this is the way to get people to do what they want them to do! Then they wonder why it doesn't work!"

Paul took a minute to digest Maya's last revelation. "Is this positive channelling and directing of your feelings and emotions behind the transformation of your life? Is this the secret of your success, happiness and vitality, or have you developed some new powers or something?"

Maya replied sincerely, "We haven't even got to our powers yet. We are just talking about how the unlimited force that is available to us is expressed each day as positive or negative behaviour. And let me stress that I don't possess anymore powers than you or anyone else on Earth. All I have done is learn to control, channel and focus those powers. Most people scatter and dissipate theirs. There is no secret to success: it's just about following some simple, universal laws. And if the laws are universal, which they are, it means they are everywhere. If they are everywhere, it means there is nowhere they are not! So, if they apply and work for one person, they apply and work for every person, including you!" Maya looked around the crowded room, "And her, and him, and her, and them … need I go on? Now, I must go and speak to my friend for 5 minutes. He's come a long way to see me. OK?"

"Yeah, fine," said Paul.

"Just try a little experiment for me while I'm gone. You know the waiter you commented about earlier, who looks like he has the weight of the world on his shoulders? The one you said was really surly? Order us something to eat from him, and make an effort to make him feel really important and valued and good about himself. Don't go over the top, but be sincere and see how he responds to you. We'll talk when I come back." Maya then excused herself.

Ten seconds later, that particular waiter passed their table. "Will you be dining with us tonight?" he asked. Paul nodded.

Chapter Six

Exactly 5 minutes later, Maya returned to the table with a big smile on her face.

"You look happy with yourself", commented Paul.

"Do I? I'm not happy for myself, I'm happy for Jurgen, the guy I've just seen. He flew in from Germany today to see me. Well, to see me and to do some business in Manchester tomorrow. I'll tell you about it later, but he is a very happy bunny! How did you get on with the waiter?"

"Quite remarkable! Rather than just ask him for a menu and give him the order, I asked him a few questions about how busy it was here and how he seemed to be on his own and how, under the circumstances, he'd coped admirably. Well, that was it! He told me his life story in 2 minutes! He told me how he'd been working since 10 o'clock this morning, and his relief hadn't turned up, so he had to work right through, and how his boss doesn't appreciate him. I told him that we appreciate his courtesy and attention and hard work. He smiled. We talked about a couple of items on the menu. He told me what to have, and what not to have … I'm looking forward to what he's recommended."

"It will be the best they have to offer here, I guarantee that", said Maya, confidently.

"Do you know, I'm quite convinced of that, as well", responded Paul.

"The most important thing here is not the food we get, but the fact that you channelled and directed not just your own feelings and emotions, but also those of another human being, towards the 'good' side and created some positive behaviour. Such a result will be doubly enjoyable because you know what caused it! The power of influence we have makes me quite dizzy sometimes!", said Maya, in a tongue-in-cheek kind of way. "Anyway, back to our piece of paper. So we have got 'Behaviour' at the top of this triangle, and we now know that 'Feelings and emotions' are the immediate drivers of that behaviour. We also know that there are two sides to both of these. Now, what do you think it is that drives our feelings and emotions?"

Paul looked stumped. "OK, let me tell you", said Maya, as she drew in another section of the triangle and wrote the word 'Attitude'. "It's attitude. Now, let me ask you something: do you know people with negative attitudes?" Maya put a big minus sign outside the 'Attitude' section on the left-hand side of the triangle.

"You're kidding?!" exclaimed Paul, "I know loads of negative people, absolutely loads."

"OK, and what are these people with negative attitudes like to be around?"

Paul jumped on this question, "They're just horrible, they really drag you down. In fact, they are a complete pain!"

"Why?"

"Well, because of the way they make you feel when they are around you. They make you feel really bad; you get totally de-motivated by their very presence." Paul was getting quite agitated talking about them.

"The main reason for this, Paul, is that these people tend to steal your energy, so you're not just de-motivated, you're de-energised!"

Paul laughed, "There is this one guy at work who is so negative that, according to 'the tribe', when he walks in a room, the lights dim!"

Maya laughed too, and then went on, "On a serious note, I've got to tell you, human beings give up their energy very easily to people with negative attitudes. We all have an energy that flows within us and through us, and people with negative attitudes feast on it, at our expense! That's why no one wants to be around people with negative attitudes. Now, do you know people with positive attitudes?" She drew a plus sign on the paper, while Paul replied quickly, "You bet I do."

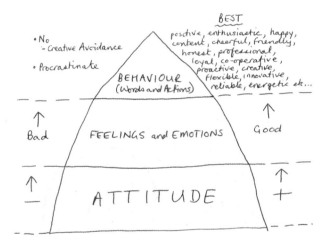

"And, what are these people like to be around?"

"They are fabulous! Quite often, just being in their presence for a relatively short period of time gives everyone a buzz."

"And so, what do you think that buzz might be?"

Paul had another 'ah, ha' moment: "It must be the energy they're giving out freely to other people."

"Of course it is! These are people who radiate positive energy. They can affect other people for weeks and months in the most positive and dramatic manner. You only need to be in their presence for a short period of time. It's like being plugged into the electricity mains and being 'supercharged'."

"It's better than that sometimes!" Paul responded.

Maya continued, "Nowadays, there is a lot of nonsense talked about attitudes, especially by people who pretend, on the surface, to be positive. They think that if they say they're positive enough times, it will convince others that they actually are. Yet, deep down inside, they know they are actually negative people, and they wonder why their lives are full of abject failure after failure. They think that hoping that everything will work out fine is part of being positive, but clearly they don't understand the part they must play in the process. Do you know what I mean?"

"I think so", replied Paul, a little hesitantly.

Maya went on, "A good place to start appreciating the importance attitude plays in the process of living a successful life, is to understand what attitude actually is. The best definition I've ever heard is: '**Our attitude is simply our chosen response to a given set of circumstances**'. Accepting this definition of attitude is one of the most empowering realisations in anyone's life. Think about it: 'a chosen response to a given set of circumstances'. We can't always choose our circumstances; life does deal us some awful cards sometimes. However, no matter what life throws at us, we can *always* choose our response to it. This means that we are always in control; not in control of what happens, but in control of our response to what happens. Life goes on in much the same way it always has. There will always be times of trouble and strife, when people let you down, lie or cheat, times when tyrants, bullies and dictators rule the world stage or the street corner. These things are never going to change, so to keep in control and win through, we need to use the only tool we've got, our attitude. Do you follow?"

"Yes. What you're saying is that, whilst we can't gain control over life by choosing what happens to us, we can gain control by choosing our response to what happens", replied Paul, enthusiastically.

"Exactly! Let me give you an example: a group of climbers has made three unsuccessful attempts to climb Mount Everest. One chosen response would be to say 'Enough is enough, it's obviously not meant to be for us. Everything that could go wrong with our previous assaults on the summit, has gone wrong, etc., etc.' Another chosen response would be to say 'This mountain can't get any bigger, *but we can*, so let's try again'. And it's that difference in attitude, or chosen responses to circumstances and situations, that separates the winners from the losers."

Paul's mind was turning over example after example where he had chosen responses to circumstances wisely, and not so wisely, in his life to date.

Maya continued, "Think about this: 'Attitudes are contagious. Is yours worth catching?' Is it worth catching every second of every day? Because attitudes rub off on people, positive and negative, just like pollen rubs off on bees. The lives we live, the highs, the lows, the good stuff and the not-so-good stuff, are merely an accumulation of our attitudes over a period of time. Most people's approach to life is to spend it waiting for their circumstances to change for the better: the government, the tax system, prices, the economy, neighbours, their partners, etc. What these people have failed to realise is that they themselves can be in control of building the kind of life they want, by choosing the right responses to the cards they have been dealt. In fact, the whole study and understanding of human behaviour and performance revolves around the 'Attitude' section of the behavioural triangle. The reason for this is that this is one of the very few areas in life where we take control, complete control. We can't necessarily take control of our situations and circumstances, but we can always take control of our responses to those situations and circumstances, *always*, no matter how awful they may appear."

Paul wasn't convinced. "Surely not *all* situations and circumstances, not if they are really awful?"

Maya smiled, "I said exactly the same thing to my guide. I wasn't convinced until I met Matt, another guide. He'd had a terrible accident at work. In fact, he had nearly died. He told me that when the accident happened, he was in so much pain it would have been easier to die; but he chose not to. And, even though he ended up losing an arm and a leg, his chosen response was that this was going to be the best thing that had ever happened to him in his life. Now that's one heck of an attitude! He fought his way back to health and, always having been active and now realising what it was like to be disabled, he decided to lead by example, showing what disabled people can do. He runs marathons, manages his own business, raises millions of pounds for charities, appears on national television; the list goes on. In short, he has worked a miracle for himself in the most desperate of circumstances, because his attitude, or chosen response to his circumstances, was so completely positive. As we travel down this road, we should learn that there is no force, power or set of circumstances outside us, greater than the force, power and set of resources available inside us, if we choose the right attitude. The right attitude for any set of circumstances is always a positive attitude. That doesn't mean the choices we have to make are easy choices, but what we need to understand at this point is how much control we have. It's really empowering isn't it?"

"It's mind-blowing! I can barely get my head around it all but, deep inside, I know you're right; it just takes a while for things to sink in for me sometimes. Carry on though: this stuff is just brilliant! I can see already how and why your life has been transformed in such a short time by understanding and applying these principles. I can't wait to have a go myself and get started."

"Before you do get started, there are a few things you'll need to know to make it work for you effectively, especially this attitude thing; there are four important areas in our lives where attitudes have the biggest impact. The first area is that of the past. What's your attitude towards the things that have happened to you in the past?"

Paul thought for a moment but, before he could get the words out, Maya continued, "Do you let the past overwhelm you, or instruct you? Do you allow the past to be a burden, or a school? You see, many people blame where they are in their lives today on the past, and say things like, 'Oh, I never did very well at school and didn't get any qualifications to speak of, so I've never really come to much'. Other people may say, 'Oh, I never did very well at school and didn't get any qualifications to speak of, but now I can learn new skills vocationally and on the job, and I can more than make up for lost time!' Both sets of people have the same set of circumstances to deal with, i.e. not doing very well at school, but one attitude is negative, 'Oh, well, the die is cast; I'll never really make anything of my life as a result', and the other attitude is positive, 'Now I'm out of the learning environment that I didn't like, I can get on with learning new skills and building a life that works!'"

Paul thought about the situations and people he knew that fitted these descriptions. He sighed deeply, as he remembered one life in particular that had been ruined by a negative attitude towards the past. In the street where Paul grew up, there had been two brothers. One brother, Richard, had a model life: lovely wife, two gorgeous kids, a nice steady job; and he was well respected in the community because of the work he did with the scouts and youth club. The other brother, Stuart, turned out to be a tearaway: he left his wife, abandoning three kids in the process. He became an alcoholic and a petty criminal and, as a result, couldn't hold down a job. Because most of his crimes were committed within his local area, he wasn't well respected in the community. Paul remembered how fascinated he had been about how these two boys turned out to be *so* different, with totally different characters and lifestyles.

In fact, most people in the community mused over how two children brought up in the same circumstances could be so different. The brothers had the same parents, lived in the same house, had the same friends, went to the same school, had the same teachers! Paul remembered that he had actually asked each brother, on separate occasions, how they had turned out the way they were. Both had replied, 'how could I turn out any other way when you consider the father I have?' Their father had been an alcoholic who couldn't hold down a job and was involved in criminal activities, and the brothers both attributed their current life style to the family circumstances they experienced when younger.

Paul reminded Maya of these two brothers they had known as children, and commented "It's all so clear now: Stuart's attitude, or chosen response, to the past was 'Oh, I must be a chip off the old block and just like my Dad; this alcoholism thing must be in my genes'.

Maya briefly interrupted with, "Which it isn't, by the way."

Paul continued, "Whereas Richard's attitude was one of 'Hold on a minute! I'm better than this. I'm going to build a better life for me and my family within my community'. They turned out differently because of their different attitudes towards the same set of circumstances they'd experienced in their past."

Maya smiled at Paul, as he sat lost in thought, remembering more and more incidents where he had always wondered why things had turned out how they did. With his new insight, so many things he hadn't been able to figure out before now seemed crystal clear.

Paul smiled back, "I guess I'd better get used to these shocks of enlightenment?!"

Maya continued, "The next area in our lives where attitude is important is the future. I now want you to think about your chosen response to the future. Do you look forward to the future with excitement and anticipation? Or do you look forward to it with dread and trepidation? Because, come what may, the future *will* happen. And, probably more than anything else, our attitude towards the future is determined by the price : promise ratio."

Paul looked puzzled, so Maya elaborated, "Have you got a clear picture of what your life will be like in, say, 3 years time? The house you will be living in, the job you'll have, the salary you'll be earning and the responsibilities you'll have? How much money there'll be in your bank account? What kind of relationship you will have with your wife, your children and your friends? Have you got a crystal-clear picture or, as I prefer to call it, a promise?"

Paul mumbled an answer, "Er, well, not really, I've only got a kind of vague idea."

"But, Paul, if you don't have that crystal-clear picture, or a promise of what you are working so hard to achieve, how can you be certain that the price you are being asked to pay on a day-to-day basis is the right price? Is it too much or too little? You see, if the promise is weak or non-existent, very vague or very small, almost any price you have to pay can seem too much. To some people, even getting out of bed, never mind doing a worthwhile job, is too much of a price to pay! Let me give you an example: say I could promise you 3 million pounds in your bank account in 3 years time, that would be yours with no strings attached, and you would not have to do anything illegal, immoral or unethical to get it. How would you feel about having those 3 million pounds, to do with as you liked?"

"It would be fabulous."

"OK, now let me ask you this: what price would you pay to get it? To turn the promise into a reality? I don't want you to negotiate with me and say you'd give me half a million pounds for it; what I mean is what price would you pay in terms of how much learning would you be willing to do? How many sacrifices would you make?

How much midnight oil would you burn? How much discipline would you show? You see, if the promise is big enough, I think most people would willingly pay the price, don't you?"

Paul nodded, "I know I would certainly be willing to pay the price, for something like that anyway. Something that would give my family the security and lifestyle they deserve."

"So, what promises or goals have you made for yourself and your family?"

Paul was embarrassed with his reply, "Well, none really. Not proper ones. I've promised to take them to Disneyland in Florida one day, but it'll probably never happen."

"Paul! With a resigned attitude like that, can you see why sometimes every day can be such a struggle? There's no direction, no certainty, no commitment from you to do whatever it takes to make it happen for your family. It sounds like a life of drudgery and disappointment to me."

"I guess it is", said Paul, in a resigned tone.

Maya continued encouragingly, "These promises or goals are the foundation of the motivational magic you are going to discover. They will help pull you through life's low points. When you understand the great and universal force that is available to us, and how to tap into its power, how to set proper goals and promises for yourself in every aspect of your life, you will be able to achieve every right and proper desire you have."

Paul jumped in, "What? Even 3 million pounds in the bank?" Maya replied, "Yes, of course, providing that is what you really, really want."

She continued, "Another area in life where our attitude is vitally important, is our attitude towards other people. What is your chosen response towards other people? Is it mainly one of frustration? Do you tend to dismiss other people relatively quickly if they disagree with what you say or act in ways that are different to the way you would? If you do that, you'll tend to steer clear of those people and never really get to understand their point of view."

Paul interrupted, "You mean like the 'space cadets', as we call them, in our marketing department, the 'geeks' in IT and the 'credit prevention specialists' in our credit management department?"

Maya smiled, but replied earnestly, "Yes, those are exactly the attitudes I'm talking about. How close do you ever get to these people, to try and see certain situations from their viewpoint?"

"Never! Nobody does! They are totally isolated in their respective departments, because everybody steers clear of them; they are regarded as a necessary evil!"

"You are all on the same side, aren't you? All part of the same team? I wonder if these attitudes towards your colleagues have got anything to do with your company's poor performance over recent years?"

Paul did not have an adequate response.

"You see," Maya continued, "if your attitude towards other people is one of fascination rather than frustration, you can learn about what makes them tick, climb inside their heads if you like, and see situations from their point of view. Armed with that knowledge you can make them see your ideas as their ideas also, and vice versa, and of mutual interest, not just your own. And this is one of the keys to success, because, let me tell you, you can't succeed on your own! You need other people and, if you have a refined and sophisticated understanding of what makes different people tick, and the right attitude, people will always help you out. It's about treating people with respect and empathy and making sure that it is also in their interest to carry out a project or help you out. You may be a well-meaning guy and a kind boss but, in order to get the most out of your relationships with friends or the best out of your staff, it must be in their interest as well to do something for you."

Paul volunteered, "There was a good example of that recently at work. Iain, who was the lynch-pin in a big project we were involved with, came up to retirement before the project was finished. We begged him to stay on a little longer to see it through, but he would hear none of it. We used everything we could think of, but looking at it now, they were all geared around our point of view, not his. Anyway, at his retirement party, I met his daughter, who was just about to set up her own business and was struggling to raise the necessary finance. Iain had helped as much as he could, but they were still a few thousand pounds short of what they needed to get the business up and running, and no bank would advance them the money. I had a word with my boss and we put a proposal together for Iain to see the project through, though on a part-time basis while, in return, we would advance him the money to get his daughter's business off the ground. Iain agreed right away, and now I can see why."

"That's an excellent example! Well done! Now, there is one final area in our lives where attitude is important, and this is the biggest. What is your attitude towards yourself? Do you feel valuable enough in and of yourself, as a fully functioning, wonderfully gifted human being, to really go to work on yourself and become all you were designed to be? And just think for a nanosecond what the **all** you were designed to be might look like; I bet it's pretty spectacular! Do you want to be all you were destined to be? Or do you just want to be part of what you were destined to be? Because, believe it or not, that's a choice we all make. Our lives are shaped by our attitude towards ourselves. Let me illustrate what I mean. If I took a 10 cm sapling of a tree and planted it in metres of the most gorgeous, nutritional, loamy soil imaginable, and if the ideal amount of rain fell on it and sun shone on it, how tall would that tree grow? It would grow all it could! Every single year of its life, that tree would push its roots down as deep as it could, grow its trunk as thick and wide as it could, throw out every single branch and pop out every single leaf it could. It would grow the maximum it could. Have you ever heard of a tree only putting in half the effort it could? Of course not! Now if, by some miracle, we could go back in time and take the same 10 cm sapling of a tree and plant it in 8 or 9 cm of pretty poor soil, and it got plenty rain and sun, how much would that tree grow?"

Paul blurted out the answer, "It would be the same! It would grow all it could."

Maya continued, "It wouldn't be a patch on the first tree in terms of its actual size, but every year of its life it would still push its roots down as deep as it could, grow its trunk as thick and wide as it could, throw out every single branch and pop out every single leaf it could! So, what's the difference between a tree and a human being in this sense?"

Paul couldn't find the words to explain, so Maya helped him out. "The difference is that a tree doesn't have two things that we do have. First, we have the power of choice. A tree can't choose, it just grows all it can all the time. Human beings can choose, to 'grow' all they can or only 'grow' part of the way. Most people choose to be only part of their full potential. There are many reasons for this, although one of the main ones is that most people don't understand the great and universal forces available to us that can help us achieve anything. The laws that govern the degree to which we master our attitudes also govern the degree to which we master our lives. The attitudes we've chosen and accumulated throughout our lives impact on the lives we are leading today.

"Second, a tree can't move. If a tree finds itself in a less than perfect place to grow, it can't uproot itself and find a better place. Humans, on the other hand can move. If we are in a 'place' that doesn't allow us to be all we were designed to be, we can move and find the right place. Most people don't realise that.

"The right attitude for any set of circumstances is a positive attitude, and it is through a positive attitude that we become aware of, and connected to, the unlimited power that flows within and through us and the universe. By using this intelligently, any right and proper desire is within our grasp. The power is awesome, and connecting to it is simple. You'll be amazed."

Paul was absorbed with what, on reflection, seemed to be such blindingly obvious pearls of wisdom. He knew he was on the path towards revolutionising his life and fulfilling his heart's desires. He was beginning to realise just who and what he was, and he had seen a glimpse of his true potential and the resources available inside and around himself. What excited him most, however, was the realisation that this potential was not just available to him, but to every human being. There was a force, a power, governed by a series of universal laws that, when understood and applied intelligently, would deliver whatever was necessary for his complete happiness. He could sense it; he knew it intrinsically; and he now knew he had always known it: the force, the power, the universal laws and himself were undisputedly linked. He was very, very excited.

Maya could tell Paul's mind was buzzing and that he would need time for the revelations of the past hour to soak in completely. "Tell you what, let's have a coffee while we finish this lesson on the behavioural triangle. And wasn't that meal the very best you've ever had in a pub?"

Paul nodded enthusiastically, "You bet it was, and served with such joy and happiness as well! It's powerful stuff this, Maya Baxter!"

Chapter Seven

Maya took the piece of paper and drew in two more sections at the base of the triangle beneath 'Attitude'. She then asked, "So, what do you think it is that controls and drives our attitudes?"

Paul thought, and replied, "Well, surely it must be our own individual experiences in life: *everything* that happens to us."

"That's true, but that tends to be in the bottom section. There is something else in between. Our attitudes are driven and controlled by our beliefs. What are your beliefs, Paul? Don't answer out loud. Just think about them for now: what are your most firmly held and deep-seated beliefs? If you begin to feel confused, or uneasy, at this point, don't worry because that is why I am here to guide you." She wrote 'Beliefs' in the section below 'Attitude'.

Paul had never analysed his beliefs before, and was silent.

Maya continued, "What's your philosophy towards work? Is your philosophy '5 days work, 2 days off, 9 till 5, never a second more?' I'm not being judgmental and saying whether it's right or wrong; I'm just asking the question to help you work out what your philosophy is: you've probably never really thought about it before, but you do have one, everyone does. Maybe your philosophy towards work is '6 days work, 1 day off, 8 till 8, take 3 hours-worth of work home to do on Sunday, and lie awake every night worrying yourself sick'. And what are your values, your principles, your expectations?" she asked as she wrote these words in the 'Beliefs' section. "What are your prejudices, even? You will see soon how important it is to identify clearly what your beliefs are. But you then also have to ask yourself 'where did I get these beliefs from?' Because, understand this, you weren't born with any."

Paul was looking increasingly confused, so Maya went on, "Most people will eventually admit that they didn't choose their beliefs, their beliefs about themselves, other people, the world they live in. My own journey made me realise that I've probably never had an original thought in my life about anything, let alone an original belief! You see, most of our thoughts and beliefs have been conditioned into us by other people. Other people are constantly telling us who we are and who we are not, who we will never be, the way our relationships are, the way they are not, the way they will never be. Do you see what I'm getting at here?"

Paul nodded as Maya wrote the word 'Conditioning' in the bottom section of the triangle. She then asked, "So, who's been conditioning us all our lives? What categories of people?"

Paul had many suggestions for this, "Well, everybody, parents, teachers, friends, relatives, bosses past and present, colleagues; even the media!"

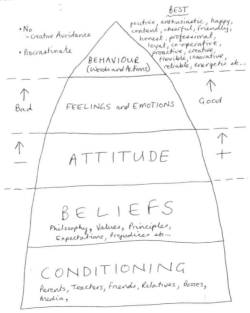

Maya wrote down all these categories under the word 'Conditioning' and said, "All these people are influential figures in our lives. They are authority figures, and what they've been doing is giving us their opinion of the way we are, the way other people are and the way the world is. Because they are authority figures, we accept much of what they say as the absolute gospel truth! Let me try and illustrate this with an example. Did you ever have a teacher at school who told you you weren't very good at something?"

"You know I did! Mr Entwhistle, the history teacher. He made my life hell."

"Yes, I remember! Now, because Mr Entwhistle told you you were no good at history, frequently and with feeling, you had little option other than to believe him. I'm willing to bet you've still got problems with that subject today. Am I right?" Paul agreed wholeheartedly; Maya went on, "And I bet it crops up all the time, even when you're playing a board game like Trivial Pursuit! Trivial Pursuit is a brilliant game, isn't it?! When you're trying to win the last segment to win the game, who picks the subject?"

"The people on the opposing team!"

"So, let's say Jackie is on the opposing team and, for the 15 years you've known her, all you've ever said about history is how bad you are at it."

Paul laughed, "That's so true! I can't deny it."

Maya went on to clarify the point, "So, what subject would she choose to try and stop you winning the game?"

Paul sighed, "History!"

"And, as soon as you hear that the topic is going to be history, what happens in here?" Maya pointed both index fingers to her temples.

"Oh," Paul exclaimed, "the shutters come down and I begin cursing under my breath about how terrible I am at history and how I never get any of the questions right. And, do you know," he continued, "I could then be asked the easiest history question imaginable, and I still wouldn't get it right!"

Maya smiled at Paul's honesty and candidness, "You are absolutely right, and do you know why that is? I must make sure you understand this before we go any further: if you think you are no good at history on the inside," Maya tapped her temples again, "you'll never be any good at it on the outside! Or, in other words," she pointed to the 'Behaviour' section at the top of the triangle, "human beings become on the outside what they think about on the inside." Now she tapped the 'Beliefs' section of the triangle, "Let me give you a couple of simple examples. See if you can relate to these. OK, what do accident-prone people think about all day long?"

Paul smiled, "Having accidents, I guess!"

"And what do hypochondriacs think about all day long?"

Paul laughed out loud as the point sank in, "Being ill!"

"There are always people at work who claim 'Oh, if there is anything going around, I get it first' And how do they know? Because they're always right, aren't they?! People who say, 'I get two colds a year, regular as clockwork, every March and October, it always happens', will get them. The reason for this is that, whatever we believe with feeling, becomes a self-fulfilling prophesy. Human beings become what they think about. Is that clear?"

Somewhat stunned by the clarity and simplicity of the lesson, Paul replied, "Yes, crystal clear!"

Maya continued earnestly, "I can't over-emphasise this enough, because it is the underlying principle of the laws that control the universal force that governs the degree of success, health, wealth, happiness and abundance in our lives. Here is one last question. What do depressed people think about all day long?"

There was no need for Paul to answer; he and Maya looked at each other knowingly.

Maya said, "You see, it is *impossible*, and, as I said earlier, you will rarely hear me use that word these days, it is impossible for a human being to behave in a depressed way without having depressing thoughts first. Impossible!"

Paul couldn't get over how he had missed these obvious truths all his life. "So, what you're saying to me is that, before we can hope to change our circumstances on the outside," he tapped the 'Behaviour' section of the triangle, "we need to change our thinking and our beliefs on the inside."

Maya rocked back in her chair and smiled lovingly at Paul, "If you've got that, your guidance is well and truly underway! Congratulations, and welcome to the world of abundance! All meaningful and lasting change starts on the inside, with our thoughts and beliefs, and eventually works its way to the outside. I must emphasise the word eventually, because it doesn't happen instantly; but it always happens eventually.

"As I mentioned before, you must remember that, when we are born, we are born with no beliefs. This 'Beliefs' section of the behavioural triangle is blank to start with but, over a period of time, beliefs get built, or conditioned, into us. The conditioning process is carried out by our interaction with parents, teachers, friends, colleagues, bosses, relatives, the television, the radio, the church, etc. From this conditioning we decide what to believe and what not to believe about ourselves, whether we are good or bad, shy or outgoing, and what other people are like and what the world is like. The problem is that, as people are telling us, and as we sort out what to believe, what we don't realise is that all these people are missing out loads of 'Fs' along the way! We get carried along, accepting what most of these authority figures are telling us about ourselves, other people, the world, as the incontrovertible truth! And, as a result of being conditioned by the opinions of these other people, what do you think most of our beliefs end up being about? Our gifts? Our talents? Our resourcefulness? Our unlimited potential? Our worthiness to receive unlimited love, friendship, success, health, happiness, wealth and joy? I very much doubt it! Most people's beliefs centre around their inadequacies, their shortfalls, pitfalls, how unworthy they are, how life is such a struggle, how other people are horrible and not to be trusted, how relationships never work, etc. And guess what, if that's what most people believe, that's the way it will show up in their lives!"

"Well, that has certainly been the case with me," Paul interrupted, "but don't be too disparaging about the instantaneousness of this process. I changed my belief about my boss and within 24 hours the whole thing on the outside had changed. This process is just so uplifting and empowering!"

Once again, Paul became lost in thought as he considered the principles Maya had just explained to him and assimilated the poignancy of his recollections. He thought about his sister, who had been teased continually for years by the whole family for being shy. It all began one Easter Monday when she was 4 years old, because she didn't want to come out and play with the other kids. She confessed to Paul, years later, that the reason she hadn't wanted to come out to play had had nothing to do with shyness; she was feeling sick from eating too many Easter eggs the previous day. That's all. More 'Fs' missed, resulting, after years of the constant haranguing that made up her conditioning, in his sister being a chronically shy person. Paul was embarrassed at his part in this process; he had been the chief teaser for much of the time.

He then thought back to when he had been about 5 years old, sitting in the bath and dreamily playing with the bubbles. A large spider had crawled out of the overflow pipe, perhaps to have a look at what was going on. Paul had looked back at it, calmly and with curiosity. But then his mother had seen it and leapt to her feet, screaming and shouting and running around. Her hysterical behaviour affected him so deeply that, from that moment onwards, he too was terrified of spiders.

The conditioning was only momentary in terms of time, but hugely intense and permanent in relation to the impact on his beliefs. Paul had tried to overcome his fear of spiders, by telling himself there was no rational or logical basis for this fear; in Britain, at least, there are no poisonous spiders and only a few that can even give you a nip you can feel. Maya's words now gave him new insight, 'Whatever you believe with feeling becomes a self-fulfilling prophecy'.

As if reading his mind, Maya interjected, "Our beliefs are not only learned but also acted out automatically. People who believe they are shy don't have to practise being shy for 2 hours in front of a mirror before they go out to a party; they just show up and they are shy! Here's another example: you believe you've got a bad memory, don't you?"

"Yes," answered Paul, a little sheepishly.

"I bet you never forget that, do you?"

Paul laughed out loud again. He was learning major truths about life and what makes people tick, but he was enjoying the process at the same time. It was as if he had known about all this all his life; now he could see it, feel it, touch it, and absorb and understand its significance. He knew that his life would never be the same again. Never. He knew that, if beliefs could be learnt, they could also be unlearnt. He knew he could now get rid of the baggage he'd been given by others, baggage that had held him back in life.

Maya continued, "Some of your conditioning will have given you wonderful beliefs about yourself, about other people and about the world you live in. Those beliefs will be in line with what you are trying to achieve in life, and, in those areas, your life will be working out just fine. But you'll have some really inappropriate beliefs, and some areas of your life where things aren't working out so well. Now you know why. Let's just check on what you've learnt so far. What do winners think about all day long?" No answer was necessary, so she went on, "And what do losers think about? More importantly, what do *you* think about all day long? But don't answer me! Well, not yet anyway. You see, people need to learn to control the thoughts that build their beliefs in the most positive and constructive way imaginable. When they do, incredibly positive and constructive things happen, things that before now they only dared dream about."

"Here's one last example," Maya said, "and then we can both go home inspired, happy, and full of wonder at what we will be able to do with our lives once we have really, truly, learnt to master all the principles and practices behind the universal power at our disposal."

"But, aren't you a master already? Your life has changed beyond all recognition, you're …"

Maya stopped him mid-flow, "No, I'm still a novice at this. True, my life has improved dramatically for the better, but I have barely started on my journey towards true mastery. I *am* in control, but not yet a master. I am working on it though!" She winked at him, and he smiled in return. "Anyway, back to my example. In 1954, something wonderful was achieved in the world of athletics that had never been done before. Roger Bannister did it. Do you know what it was?"

"It was the first time anyone had run a mile in under 4 minutes. Roger Bannister broke the 4 minute barrier, the first person to do so, and so he set the new world record. He did it at Iffley Road in Oxford, as I recall", Paul replied confidently.

"OK, stop showing off! I know sport is one of your strong points; you're right. But, what is really interesting is that, in 1900, the world record for running a mile was over 4 minutes and 15 seconds. By 1933 the record was just over 4 minutes and 7 seconds. By 1945 the record stood at 4 minutes 1.4 seconds. But, despite many other attempts, it wasn't until 6th May 1954, that Roger Bannister took to the track and ran the mile in 3 minutes and 59.4 seconds. Have I got my facts right there, Mr Sports Mastermind?"

"Oh yes, spot on!"

"Nothing had changed in the world of athletics from a technical point of view between 1900 and 1954. It wasn't until 1964 that 'tartan' running tracks were introduced at the Tokyo Olympics. Prior to 1964, all races were run on cinder tracks, and all runners wore old-fashioned spikes. You know: the ones that look like bedroom slippers with panel pins knocked through the bottom. There were no high-tech running shoes made with super viscosity stuff or some such. The only thing that had changed between 1900 and 1954 was belief.

"Before 6th May 1954, the belief was that running a mile in less than 4 minutes was impossible; it simply could not be done! This belief was supported and reinforced by many experts of the time, including medical experts, who were convinced that anyone running the mile in less than 4 minutes would cause terrible physical damage to themselves. One group of experts said an athlete would end up 'brain dead' because the body would require too much oxygen to perform such a feat and would starve the brain of its essential supply. Other experts predicted that a runner's heart would explode in the rib cage or the lungs would collapse."

Paul interjected, "So the prognosis was not particularly good for any athlete who was hell bent on trying to break through the 4 minute barrier."

"Exactly, which is why Roger Bannister is such a hero, attempting to break the 4 minute mile against that backdrop. Yet, on the 6th May 1954, the 4 minute barrier is broken, a new world record is set and, more importantly, Roger Bannister lives to tell the tale! No ill-effects at all. He didn't end up brain-damaged for the rest of his life, or a physical wreck. So, what was the one thing that changed on that day? The belief: the belief that this feat could not be achieved. And what is amazing is, once the belief had changed, it only took 46 days before someone ran an even faster mile and set another new world record. Over the next few years, the 4 minute barrier was broken umpteen times, and the only thing that had changed was the belief.

"This is the power of what we are learning, the real power. When we learn to change beliefs for ourselves, and for other people, things that were previously regarded as impossible start to be achieved, and, and this is an important word, consistently. We are not talking about flash-in-the pan improvements that last a short time and then things go back to the way they were. We are talking about consistent improvements in any and every aspect of your life, wealth, health and vitality, happiness, success, relationships, any area, with virtually no limits. What do you think of that?"

"It's all great, but what do I need to do to become the master of my own destiny, to be in control?"

"Only one thing for now: simply repeat to yourself, when you are at your most relaxed, '**I believe in the power within my grasp**', as many times as you can. Don't chant it like a mantra; say the words slowly and deliberately. Believe them wholeheartedly. This begins the process of absorbing them into the very fabric of your being. I'll explain, when we meet again, how and why this begins the process. I also want you to have a really good think about what you want in life. Don't limit yourself; there is nothing that you can desire, providing the desire is right and proper, and intense and sincere enough, that is outside your reach. The great universal power governs it, and you're beginning the process of letting it work for you. You need to be sure that you get lots of the things you want and none of the things you don't want. Is that clear?"

"Oh, yes, very clear."

"OK, I must go now. I'll be in touch when you are ready for your next lesson. It will only be a week or two, but I'll know when you're ready, and it will reflect how much of a good student you are at practising your first affirmation."

"My first what?"

"Affirmation! 'I believe in the power within my grasp': repeat it as often as you can, when you are completely relaxed. Let it soak into your subatomic structure; believe in it deeply. You *will* notice a difference. I'll be in touch. Take care."

And with that Maya left Paul, but the wisdom, the simple yet profound instructions, did not. He sat for what seemed like hours, although it was only a few minutes, with the warm glow of an awakening, and with the now completed triangle on the piece of paper on the table in front of him. Picking up the piece of paper, Paul floated out of The Old Fox and all the way home, or at least that's what it felt like to him.

Chapter Eight

The next week of Paul's life was an emotional rollercoaster, as he recognised example after example of the principles Maya had revealed to him. He was amused, entertained, amazed, shocked, horrified, frustrated and disgusted at what he saw; but he was never ambivalent. In fact, he found he was talking out loud to himself with outbursts like, 'This has been going on around me all the time, and I've never really noticed how many people force their perception of the way they see things onto others, and in so many different ways'. In that week he realised he had been half asleep for most of his life, as indeed most people were. He was now awake, wide awake, to it all; he missed nothing; he was on full alert. He felt alive, truly alive, for the first time in his life, and it felt wonderful.

Things improved significantly when he decided to initially suspend judgement on everything he saw and heard. He decided to look for all 6 'Fs' in every situation that presented itself, to begin to see events as they really were. He felt his life was becoming multi-dimensional; gone were the days of one-dimensional tunnel vision, he was now beginning to see colours and shades to life and people that he had previously been conditioned to miss. John, his work colleague, constantly went on about never being able to rise to the top of the organisation because he didn't have a university degree. Because of this perceived inadequacy, he never really applied himself to any project. 'What's the use?' he would say. What John and Paul, up until now, had been overlooking was the fact that only two of the nine-member board of directors had university degrees, and one of the well-publicised values of the company was to be promoted on merit, not background or qualification. How could he and John have missed that? 'Tribal thinking', or conditioning, *again*.

Everywhere Paul looked, the evidence of conditioning was overwhelming. If people had any limitation in their lives, it was, to a large extent, self-imposed. He was beginning to see that this limitation was because of the way people were conditioned, and the negative beliefs they had picked up along the way. As he saw things as they really were for the first time, he began to feel total compassion for the human race. He saw that people are mostly imprisoned by their beliefs, not liberated, inspired and empowered by them. He saw people struggling through an existence that was little more than a self-imposed hell. He saw that this was nothing to do with what the world was really like, but was merely a reflection of what they had been conditioned to believe the world had to offer.

Paul noticed example after example supporting the fact that human beings really do become what they think about. He saw that most people are paranoid, believing that the whole universe is conspiring against them. However, Paul saw the universe as it really is, positively responsive and abundant. Indeed, if someone believes that the human race is, on the whole, conspiring against them, the universe responds positively by delivering on that belief in abundance. By the same token, if someone believes the human race is behind them, working for them, ready, willing and able to help make right and proper desires come true, the universe responds positively by delivering on that belief in abundance. Paul realised that the power in the universe is positive and responsive to our beliefs, but it is not judgmental. Whatever we believe with feeling, whatever it is, it becomes a self-fulfilling prophesy. Paul had seen his first glimpses of the power and control he possessed.

This revelation shook him to the very core of his being. He felt he had known this intrinsically all his life, as almost everyone has, but he had needed Maya, his guide, to point it out explicitly so that he could discover the full extent of it for himself. He decided to become an inverse paranoid for the rest of his life: to be someone who believes that the universe is actually conspiring to bring him all the good things life has to offer. He realised there could be small setbacks sometimes, but that there would always be reasons for them and lessons to be learned from them. First and foremost, from his recent observations, he now knew that the universe always delivers. 'Maybe that is one of the fundamental beliefs that needs to be locked in our hearts and minds, in order to co-operate with and control the great and universal power Maya keeps referring to', he thought to himself.

Paul was elated, on cloud nine, for some time, but then a shadow appeared on his horizon. To some extent he now knew the process, but he still didn't know why it worked and how to take full control of it. He was musing over these questions, staring out of his kitchen window, when he was startled by the sound of his mobile phone ringing. He picked up the phone and was answered by Maya's soothing voice at the end of the line.

"I've got the feeling that you're ready for your next lesson. Just answer me one question: what is the one overriding thing you've discovered for yourself since we last met?"

"The universe is positively responsive and abundant," he replied instantly, "the universe always delivers."

Maya beamed down the phone, "I thought as much. I knew you'd have no difficulty understanding the essentials. You're ready to begin the next part of our journey. Are you OK to meet tonight, usual place, usual table, at 7 p.m.?"

"I'll be there!"

"Great!"

As he swung into the car park of The Old Fox, Paul experienced a feeling of serenity and incredible power all at the same time. It was odd but nice. He arrived 5 minutes early, hoping to be there before Maya and waiting at their table when she arrived. But Maya was already there, along with five other people, at their table; they were in deep discussion. There was something about the six of them that Paul couldn't quite put his finger on. As he walked towards them, Paul could feel a buzz in the atmosphere and sensed that everyone's attention in the pub was drawn towards them. All six people around the table looked fabulous, but without any signs of ostentation. He realised there was a powerful simplicity about them all.

Maya looked up and smiled at Paul, "Be with you in 3 minutes."

"OK, there's no rush." Paul replied, but then he chided himself as he walked towards the bar to order a drink. 'What the heck did I say that for?' he thought. 'No rush!' He smirked to himself, 'I'm just about to find out more about how to take control of the great, universal forces that govern our health, wealth, happiness and success, and I just said there was no rush. Who am I kidding?' His thoughts raced. 'I do worry about myself sometimes,' he mused, 'Why do I always say the opposite of what I mean? Why didn't I just say "OK, that's fine"?' He had another epiphany: 'Conditioning again,' he swore under his breath, 'we've all been conditioned to do that for most of our lives.'

He glanced up to see the barman looking at him quizzically, "What can I get for you sir, the usual, sparkling water and ice?" Paul nodded with a "Yes please".

The people at Maya's table stood up, said their goodbyes and left. The eyes of everyone in the pub followed them with a look of awe and admiration. When they had gone, the lights in the pub appeared a little dimmer.

The hug of greeting Maya gave Paul made him tingle, but the tingling went beyond physical; he was tingling at another level altogether. He didn't comment to Maya about it, he didn't need to.

"Well," Maya said, "you have obviously seen some revelations since we were together last, and I thought the way you put it was exquisite: 'The universe always delivers'."

For the next 15 minutes Paul talked non-stop about all the different examples he had uncovered that proved the point. He drew them from every facet of his, and other people's, experiences. He had not only recognised the principle and related to it; he had assimilated it; it was in his DNA; he was ready for the next step.

Paul pulled himself up short when he realised that he was doing all the talking. "Oh, I'm sorry, Maya. I came here to hear what you had to say. What's the old adage? 'You ain't learning when you're talking'. I'll shut up now."

Maya smiled kindly, "It's fine, really. But before we start, have you anything you'd like to ask me?"

She'd done it again. Even though he had been in full flow for a long time, Paul had a burning question he wanted to ask her, but how did she know? Paul's voice was sincere and inquisitive, "Who were those people you were with? The whole place was spellbound with your collective presence."

"They are fellow guides. We're all committed to helping as many people as possible to understand and master the great universal power at our disposal. They're a few stops ahead of you on the journey at the moment, but you are coming along so well you could be miles ahead of us all soon. You could easily end up being the guide to any one of us!"

"But I thought you and they would always be guides to novices like me?"

77

"It doesn't necessarily work like that. We are your guides for now. People take the journey at their own pace. As the principles and practices are revealed, we develop our powers and master them differently as individuals. As you know, the power and forces that drive it are universal; they are within the grasp of us all to use as we see fit. Some learn to master them more quickly than others, which is why sometimes the teacher becomes the student and the student becomes the teacher."

"But I thought you were the …"

Maya cut him off mid-flow, "Paul, if you thought I was some kind of guru all of a sudden, or a reincarnation of a mysterious being with mystic and supernatural powers, forget it. I am still me, the girl you went to school with. I've just learned to master some aspects of the great and universal power in order to take control of the circumstances and situations in my life. Before we go on, you have to take me, Maya Baxter, the individual, the personality, out of this equation. I am no more special than you, I have no more special powers than you; I am not superior to you in any way. I'm still as human as I ever was, and still just as human as you are. I have not made the discoveries on my own. I am guiding you to master the principles and practices in much the same way as I was guided. The power, and the control, is available to everyone. As you have discovered already, even at this early stage, you will have no difficulty putting these principles into practice in your everyday life. No one will, if they really want to."

"OK," said Paul, "I get the picture."

"Have you been doing your affirmation?" asked Maya.

Paul responded with an enthusiastic, "Yes." Maya then asked, "And?" Paul responded with, "You would not believe the power I've felt and used to good effect this week."

Maya answered, "Yes, I would believe it, I really would, but just remember that you're still at the beginning of this journey, you've hardly even started yet. One of the first things we need to get you to see is the full extent of your potential. And, before you can hope to see that, there's one big barrier we need to make sure is down. That barrier is made up of the word 'it'!"

"It?" Paul echoed, "What do you mean, 'it'?"

Maya went on, "Have you ever heard yourself say that 'some people are born with it, and some are born without it', whatever the magic 'it' might be?"

"I say that all the time! Let's see: at work, at the badminton club, at the golf club, everywhere!"

"And, throughout your life, you've probably been put through assessments, and interviews, and a battery of examinations to determine whether you've got this mysterious 'it' or not, right?"

Paul nodded.

"Now, if you are one of the few people who, after your results are analysed, are told at regular intervals that you have definitely been born with 'it', you're probably OK, quite happy and successful. However, if you are anything like the majority of people, who have been told distinctly that they have definitely been born without 'it', you'll probably be struggling in certain important areas of your life. My own view on this is that these assessments and examinations are some of the worst injustices ever perpetrated on humankind! Because the results are used to try and predict what we are capable of doing, not simply as a measure of what you can remember, or what your current level of capability is.

"You see, all the research suggests that human beings have a virtually unending potential for growth and development. You must have heard the phrase 'you can do anything when you put your mind to it'." Paul acknowledged this. She continued, "Of course you have, but do you believe it? I mean really believe it? Most people do. The problem is that they are never shown how to put their minds to it, not properly. Oh yes, they get shown how to put their backs into it, and their hearts and souls, but not their minds. They never get shown why and how the mind works so effectively and powerfully, and how to control it in order to marshal the unlimited forces in the universe to deliver every right and proper desire they may have.

"Now you've got the basics, your guidance will be focused completely on this. What do you think?"

"Let's get started!" A memory had surfaced that struck a particular chord with Paul. He was remembering his brother-in-law's experience at school. Phil was a bright lad at primary school yet, when he came to take his 11-plus examinations to determine whether he would go to secondary or grammar school, he flopped and failed. He was then destined to a secondary school education for the next 5 years but got a lucky break at the age of 13 when he was put into a class taking O-levels. Six months before taking his O-levels and leaving the secondary school, he had his big interview with the local careers advisory officer. When asked what he wanted to do when he left school, Phil had replied proudly, 'I want to be a teacher'. The careers officer had looked at him with derision and said, 'Look sonny, lads from this school don't end up being teachers. What do you really want to do?'

Phil had later told Paul how he had burst into tears at this point and protested that this was all he'd ever wanted to do for as long as he could remember. The careers officer reminded him that he had failed his 11-plus and was in a secondary school, so his exam results wouldn't be good enough for him to study as a teacher and that he needed to be more realistic. The careers officer then arranged an interview for him at a local company as a factory worker.

Paul remembered Phil saying that, from that moment on, he'd made up his mind that he was going to show this so-called expert on careers just what he was capable of. Paul remembered being impressed that this pupil of seemingly 'limited ability, with ideas well above his station' was, after brilliant O-level results, subsequently transferred to the grammar school. There he got great A-level grades, went to university, and ended up teaching not in a school but in a university. One of the highest academic establishments in the land! With all the odds supposedly stacked against him, he simply made his mind up, dug in deep, worked hard and achieved his goal. It was a dream come true.

'That's what winners do,' Paul thought. 'They don't accept other people's limited beliefs about them. They make their own minds up about what they'll do. They work harder, go further, sacrifice more, and keep going until they get there. It's that simple! Simple, but not necessarily easy.'

He redirected his attention to Maya, but was already acutely aware that he was being exposed to powerful life-changing principles and practices with no limits!

Maya emphasised, "There are virtually no limits to what we, as human beings, can achieve; we are all gifted, talented, resourceful and adaptable creatures. Our potential is infinite. For instance, have you ever run a marathon, a full marathon, 26 miles 385 yards?"

Paul's face dropped, as he answered, "No."

"No, but do you have the potential to run one?"

"Of course I do!"

"You see, we have to separate potential from motivation, in order to deepen our understanding of this principle. You've got the potential, we all have, but maybe it's the motivation that is lacking. And what I'm trying to do here is separate the two for you. For instance, if one of your children became chronically ill, heaven forbid, and needed an operation and 6 months' convalescence, and the only place you could get the operation done was the United

States, and it would cost you £100,000, and the only way to raise £100,000 was by running five marathons, sponsored to the tune of £20,000 for each one, you'd run the five marathons, right?"

"You bet I would", agreed Paul.

"There are lessons all around us that demonstrate the unlimited potential of human beings," Maya continued. "Did you see the London marathon on television the other week? The whole event is quite a humbling experience if you think about it, and I don't mean because of the performances of the elite runners or most of the fun runners. What's humbling is watching the achievements of disabled people and older people. One guy, for the last 2 years, has run, if that is the correct term, his marathon on crutches. The reason being that he has only got one leg! Yet he completed the marathons in fantastic times. Now, let me ask you something, does someone with a leg missing have more or less potential to run a marathon than you do?"

"Well, he's got a lot less potential, because he's got a significant bit of equipment missing: a leg!"

"Precisely! So, how can someone, with supposedly considerably less potential, outperform you and me, who have got the full complement of arms and legs? I've never run a marathon, either. Here we are, two able-bodied people with two of everything we should have, and our performance in comparison to the disabled marathon runner is pathetic! We just sit at home and watch the marathon on television! What is going on here, Paul? We've got so much more potential, in this example, and yet we manage to do so much less with it."

"I see what you're getting at now." Paul remembered another conversation with his brother-in-law, the university lecturer. Phil had told him of the achievements of some students who had Downs Syndrome and managed to get good honours degrees. He had read somewhere that people with Downs Syndrome don't necessarily have problems assimilating information; their problem is disseminating it. They don't have the free and easy recall that the majority of their fellow students would enjoy, but they can manage to outperform them. Paul was again overwhelmed, thinking of example after example.

Maya broke his train of thought, "Have you ever heard of a lady called Helen Keller?"

Paul nodded, "Yes, she was, er, deaf, blind and dumb wasn't she?"

"Well, not quite. She was deaf and blind from an early age but she wasn't dumb. That's the point in question: if someone, as a result of contracting a chronic illness at a very early age, is left deaf and blind, how can he or she ever learn to speak and communicate effectively? Imagine being trapped in a dark, silent world from, say, the age of 19 months."

Paul thought for a moment and said, "Well, I don't think you could teach anyone in that situation how to speak or communicate. Could you?"

Maya went on, "That's what the medical experts who were around at the time said, too. But Helen's parents refused to accept their advice and got some very gifted, inspirational teachers involved, and gradually, over time, they taught Helen how to communicate and even speak. Do you know how they did it?"

Paul shook his head.

"They did it by using vibrations! Two of her major senses were not working, sight and hearing, but she could still feel. Imagine a large balloon pressed up against your face and your throat and chest, with your arms wrapped around it, and you make sounds against it. The vibrations would be different for the different sounds: ber, ber, ber; der, der, der; mm, mm, mm; zz, zz, zz; yes? So, over a period of time, they taught Helen to string the sounds together to make words, and then the words together to make sentences, and then her learning really took off! She learned to read Braille and understand the finger alphabet. She graduated from Radcliffe College in the USA in 1904, and Radcliffe is one of the toughest colleges in the US to get in to. In fact, at first, the college didn't want her! And, as Helen once said later, 'Because they didn't want me, and being stubborn, I chose to override their objection'. She then went on to head the Helen Keller Foundation, an organisation dedicated to helping people with hearing, sight or speech difficulties to communicate. Imagine that! A lady who was effectively born deaf and blind being the head of a company helping people communicate! Are human beings adaptable, resourceful, limitless and brilliant, or what?"

Paul was very excited by all this, "I think, for the first time in my life, I've had a glimpse of what we've all got locked away inside, and it is awesome!"

Maya smiled and said cheekily, "You ain't seen nothing yet, kiddo!"

Paul's mind went into overdrive, as he thought of yet more and more examples of the triumph of human spirit over adversity. He didn't really need any more help to appreciate the sheer scale of the largely untapped potential all human beings possess. Now he understood something that he had read years before: that human beings only use about 1.5–2% of their potential in their lifetime. He could see that clearly now.

Maya now handed him a piece of paper. It summed up this part of the lesson perfectly and it moved him deeply. It read:

Cripple him and you have a Sir Walter Scott. Lock him in a prison for 27 years and you have a Nelson Mandela. Raise him in abject poverty and you have an Abraham Lincoln. Strike him down with infantile paralysis and you have a Franklin Roosevelt. Burn him so severely that doctors say he'll never walk again and you have a Glen Cunningham. Deafen him and you have a Ludwig van Beethoven. Have him or her born black in a society filled with racial discrimination and you have a Martin Luther King or a Marion Anderson. Call him a slow learner, 'retarded', write him off as uneducatable, and you have an Albert Einstein.

Maya then said, almost in a whisper, although her message was louder than anything Paul had ever heard before, "No living soul has ever completely grasped the intensity or vastness of the ocean of power and resourcefulness lying within the reach of everyone, but a few have come close. These people are the first ones to say that, even though the rest of the human race may look upon them as gifted or special, they are just the same as everyone else. The same force, power and resourcefulness that they have used is available to every person on Earth. We're all given the same. It's just that some choose greatness and some choose mediocrity."

Maya continued, "Once a person has had a glimpse of their limitless potential and learned how to connect with it and channel it, no right desire can be denied them. So, knowing that, what are you going to choose, greatness or mediocrity? But don't misunderstand me, greatness appears in all kinds of roles, not just world class writers, composers or statesman. What about being the greatest father or mother, brother or sister, wife, husband or partner, friend and confidante, bedtime story teller or member of the family? Greatness comes in all shades and colours. With Mother Teresa it was compassion, with my mother it was always being there for her children. This force and power within, and the great unlimited universal force and power without, are waiting to be used. You can accept them or refuse them, but they are still there, waiting. If you refuse to use them, the only one that suffers is you. So, are you going to accept your greatness, your limitless potential, and design and build a life that works for you?"

"Of course I am!" said Paul, "who wouldn't?"

"Lots of people. Those who can't or don't want to see. And you'll be amazed how many of those there are around! I call them 'Hypnos'!"

Without even speaking, Paul's face expressed the question, 'Why?'!

"Have you ever seen anyone hypnotised live on a stage?" Paul nodded. "Good," said Maya, "tell me about it and what the hypnotist had people doing."

"It was on holiday last year," described Paul. "We went to a show and the hypnotist was brilliant and got about 10 people up on stage. They were doing amazing things. One guy had his head on a chair seat and his feet on another as he lay flat, straddled in between. They sat on him and everything but he didn't bend in the middle or collapse. Another lady was convinced that every time a certain word was said, her chair caught fire, and one guy was eating an onion believing that it was the tastiest apple he'd ever had in his life! We were four rows from the front and the onion that the bloke was eating was so strong it made our eyes water, yet there he was, devouring it in big bites and salivating because it was so delicious!"

Maya commented, "It's amazing what these hypnotists can get people doing. But do you know what hypnotists actually do? I don't mean their techniques, and I'm not going to turn you into a hypnotist. I mean, do you know what they do to people up here?" She pressed her temple.

Paul's expression was blank.

"Well, let me tell you. All they do is take one belief you currently have, and get you to change that belief to a new one, by using their power of influence with very specific words, phrases and gestures. For instance: this is not an onion, it's an apple and it's the tastiest apple you'll have ever eaten. Once that new belief takes root in your mind, the new behaviour associated with it is acted out automatically. You've already learned this, but we are now looking at it from a slightly different angle.

"So, once a belief is locked in place, the behaviour appropriate to the belief is acted out automatically. My point here is that I don't think hypnotists actually hypnotise us; I think they *un*-hypnotise us. *They* don't hypnotise us because we are *already* hopelessly hypnotised! And who's been hypnotising us? Yes, parents, teachers, friends, colleagues, relatives, the media; remember? And, more importantly, what have these people been hypnotising us to believe? All the good stuff about ourselves; all the limitless potential; our gifts and talents; how abundant this world is for caring, sharing, compassion? No! No! No! Is it any wonder that most people's lives are such a struggle and they're so unhappy?

"The beliefs that we have built up over the years tend to be about our limitations, our inadequacies, the lack in the world, the differences, and a look-after-yourself mentality. There is a fundamental truth that is being repeatedly discovered and proved over the millennia that, no matter how many times it gets said, very few people seem to either understand or believe in until they are ready, and that is that human thoughts have a tendency to turn themselves into their physical equivalent. Concentrated thoughts, whether consciously chosen or not, seem to have a long standing and direct relationship with all the forces in the universe. This direct relationship can be summed up very simply: thoughts are things! Our thoughts seem to marshal all the forces in the universe to turn the world we have created in the thought realm into its equivalent in the physical realm."

The power of what Maya was saying hit Paul hard. He had always believed in positive thinking, but had never understood its full significance at this level. His mind was flooded with instances where he had waited for circumstances on the outside to change so that his life could improve; new government, new tax system, lower prices, new company pay structure, a new boss, etc. There he was, 42 years old, and he'd spent all his life waiting for it to change on the outside, and now he realised how he'd got it the wrong way round. Before things could change and improve on the outside, he would have to change and improve on the inside first.

His mind kept whirring, as he remembered the times he had changed his thinking and, providing he had changed his thinking permanently, how this had always been reflected in the physical realm. His change of mind towards his boss was the most recent and obvious example. He then thought about all the times he'd changed his mind about various things and, after a few days, changed his mind back again because it wasn't working out the way he thought. He hadn't given any of those seeds of thought time to germinate, let alone take root and flourish. He realised that, in this instant world, we are sold on the idea of instant results but that the world doesn't work like that. If it takes 6 months for a corn seed to produce a crop, it takes 6 months. If it takes 50 years for a cactus to flower, it takes 50 years. Providing you leave the seed planted, the world will always deliver the desired crop when it's time.

Even the quote from the Bible made sense now: 'You reap what you sow'. If you want to change the crop, you need to change the seed first. This works with thought seeds as much as corn and wheat seeds. What he was currently reaping in his life on the outside, Paul concluded, was only a function of what he had sown in the past in his mind, on the inside.

Without Maya saying another word, he had already resolved to apply himself properly to this fundamental principle. Rather than waiting for everything and everyone else to change, he himself was going to change. He was going to take charge of his thinking and take control of his thoughts from this moment on, and develop a constancy to purpose so clear and focused that it would marshal all the forces in the universe to deliver on the 'thinking equals reality' principle. And he was going to do this in new directions of his own choosing. He was elated.

Paul came to the conclusion that all his life he'd convinced himself that the problems he'd faced were all on the outside. He'd blamed everyone and everything for the way things were, and now realised that the problems were not outside, but the challenges and opportunities were actually internal. At this moment of awakening, Paul became a human 'being' and ceased to be a human 'doing'. He was, for the first time in his life, at peace with himself and the world; his resolve was unshakeable, his faith and belief in himself unfathomable. He was alive. It felt wonderful.

Maya sat quietly whilst Paul digested these life-changing revelations. Through her own guided journey she'd experienced the same seismic shifts in her consciousness and knew how important it was to let others, under her guidance, do the same. 'You can't rush it', she thought to herself, 'It takes as long as it takes, and when it hits, it hits!'

She then spoke, "There's a lovely story that illustrates how personal this taking control is. A hard-working female executive needed some time to write a report and decided to work from home. The big problem was that, at 3.30 p.m., her 9-year-old son came home from school and he insisted that she play with him. She said she would, but that she just needed another hour to finish off her work. There was no chance of that happening. After several interruptions within a 20-minute period, and with eyes raised looking for inspiration on how to keep her son entertained, she had a stroke of genius. One of the magazines she had been reading contained an article about 'The New World Order' and in its contents was a map of the world. This map was a 2002 version, so there was no USSR or Yugoslavia; it contained the newly independent states of Russia, Latvia, Estonia, Lithuania, Bosnia, Kosovo and Montenegro. 'Ah, ha', she thought as she cut the map up into 100 different pieces and put them into an envelope. She handed the envelope to her son and announced a game for them to play. This was a challenge against the clock, and he had been picked to go first. The challenge was to go into the dining room to start the game and then reassemble the cut-up map in the shortest time possible. The time was now 3.59 in the afternoon. He had no time to waste, and was to report back the second the task was complete.

"Off he ran in eager anticipation. His mother, rather smugly, restarted her work, thinking it would take him a considerable amount of time. Most people, let alone a 9-year-old, have never even heard of Latvia and Lithuania, let alone know where they are on a map. She was completely confident she would have at least an hour to finish her work project.

"After exactly 9 minutes and 42 seconds, her son appeared with triumphant cries of, 'Stop the clock! I've done it!' Her amazement was tinged with a little pride that her son was quite clearly a geographical genius. How else could he have managed to complete the task in such a short time? She escorted her son, or rather her son escorted her, into the dining room to examine his work. Sure enough, there was the map of the world, the new world order, reassembled in the middle of the table on top of a large place mat.

"'Wow,' the mother exclaimed, 'that is perfect, and it must be a world record time'. However, just after she'd said that she noticed that one of the other place mats had been moved and was now sitting on the table upside down. Suspecting that a particular technique might have been used, she asked how, exactly, he had managed to complete such a difficult task in double-quick time.

"'Well,' her son replied, 'I've got to tell you, Mum, at first it was really tough because I don't know where Latvia is. Then I noticed that on the back of the map you'd cut up there was a picture of a man, so I concentrated on getting the man right first. Then, I put another place mat on top and turned it over very carefully and lifted off the top one. I figured that if the man underneath was right, the world on top would have to be right as well!'"

Paul loved the simple and profound message of this story.

Maya continued, "Most people are waiting for the world to sort itself out first, and it's not going to do that. It's been the way it is for thousands of years, since the dawn of civilisation, and will probably be the same for thousands more. If people concentrated on getting themselves right first, they would soon see that that is the first step to unlimited health, wealth, happiness and success. Accepting total responsibility for oneself as a powerful and resourceful human being, making a difference through your own thinking and efforts and not merely waiting for things to be different, is the foundation of achieving anything.

"Things don't change. People change! When people willingly accept the responsibility to become all they were designed to be, the changes in their lives are always dramatic and positive. These are the people who want for nothing, ever! We all too easily get sucked in to wrong thinking and end up blaming everybody and everything for where we are in our lives. How sad is that?

"You play a little golf, don't you?" Maya knew he had taken up the sport and didn't wait for an answer. "Have you ever known any golfer complete their best round ever and walk off a golf course saying things like 'the greens were awful' or 'the fairways were terrible'? When they're right, the world is right; even in the world of golf!

"To continue on your journey, these new lessons must become part of your very being. Number 1, our resources are unlimited. There is no force, power or set of circumstances on the outside of us that is greater than the force, power or set of resources available to us on the inside. Number 2, we have to willingly accept total and personal responsibility to make a difference through our own thinking and actions. We need to commit to nurturing our minds with great thoughts, about ourselves, about other people and about the world we live in, because we can never go any higher than we think.

"I need to go now, but think about what we've said tonight, and I will get in touch with you when you are ready for the next stage of the journey. If, for whatever reason, you can't absorb the fundamental truths I've given you tonight into your very being, your journey will end here and you will not be able to proceed any further, no matter how much you want, wish or hope to.

"I'll know when you are ready to proceed, and, more importantly, my fellow traveller, so will you! It will be obvious. You will know; I will know; the world will know. Take care." With those words, Maya kissed him on the cheek and left.

Paul's thoughts went deep, into his very core, consciously and subconsciously. He drove home safely. These insights meant his world had changed. But then it hit him: of course his world hadn't changed. He'd changed! It wouldn't be long before he was ready for the next step.

Chapter Nine

During the next few days, Paul was struck time and again with the awareness that human beings really do have a virtually unending capacity for growth and development. Someone had told him of a book on Thomas Edison that revealed what a remarkable individual Edison was. Edison was thrown out of school for being 'uneducatable' but he had refused to be discouraged by anything or anyone; his belief and optimism had a positive effect on all around him.

Edison's belief that an incandescent light bulb fuelled by electricity could be invented was absolute, motivating him to conduct more than 10,000 different experiments in order to discover how to do it. A visiting friend advised Edison to be realistic and come to terms with the fact that the world was meant to be lit with kerosene. As Edison had at that stage tried more than 5000 different ways to have light without flame, the friend pointed out that he had failed more than 5000 times. Edison refused to see it that way and informed his friend that, quite to the contrary, he had in fact succeeded in finding more than 5000 ways that would not work and, therefore, he was more than 5000 steps closer to finding one way that would work!

'What a terrific attitude,' Paul thought. 'Isn't it amazing how people can look at the same thing and see something completely different!' Edison's belief was such that he *knew* a solution existed: it was just waiting for him to discover it. Many people regard Edison as a genius but, when asked about how he'd discovered the incandescent light bulb, Edison's answer was simplicity itself: 'I had just run out of trying things that wouldn't work!'

Paul then realised that, as well as being the world's greatest inventor, with more than 1000 patents registered, including some that were the basis of the microphone, phonograph, storage battery and talking movies, Edison was probably the world's greatest failure at the same time! Edison was always curious about what any particular experiment *could* be used for, even if 9 out of 10 of his experiments were of no practical application at all. Paul remembered reading somewhere that definiteness of purpose and desire are the top two criteria for success. Trying, trying and trying again until you succeed. 'Winners never quit,' he thought, 'and quitters never win!' How very true that was of Edison!

Paul could see and feel the limitless potential that he and all other human beings possess once fuelled by a vision and belief and faith in themselves and what they are trying to achieve. He found that the one affirmation he had been driving into the very fabric of his being had changed into two: '**I believe in the power within my grasp**' and '**I am finding, feeling and using the power within my grasp**'.

Paul believed firmly in these two affirmations because of what he had been guided to see and feel. The more he believed, the more alert he was. He now had bagfuls of energy and creativity, and any task he tackled, no matter how difficult, seemed to have a myriad of viable options on how it could be completed. Paul felt he was becoming a conduit or vessel for achievement, and not, as he had been most of his life, a barrier or blockage to achievement. Something serious was going on and, while he didn't understand what it was, he liked it. He liked it a lot.

Maya's timing, as usual, was impeccable. Paul answered the phone just as he was having his biggest wallow yet, being overwhelmed with the enormity of the power within the grasp of human beings.

Startled by its ring, though not by who was on the other end, Paul answered calmly when Maya asked the question, "Paul, I get the feeling you are ready to continue your journey. Tell me, what do you know?"

"I know," said Paul, "that I no longer just believe in the power within my grasp. I am actually finding it, feeling it and using it now. I know that the feeling is getting stronger every day, and it is totally gorgeous! I have never known a feeling like it in my life. I feel like I'm unstoppable, but not in a Superman, 'I can do anything, including fly', kind of way. I feel like I'm unstoppable because I know, with the right things going on inside my head, creating a 'can do' attitude, I have access to all the resources in the universe to help me achieve every right and proper desire I could wish for. The only barriers to achieving anything are in our minds. It's a very strange realisation, isn't it?"

Maya replied, "It's normal at this stage of the journey, and it shows you have learned. It also shows that you're ready for the next stage. When do you want to meet up?"

Paul could barely contain his excitement, "Well as soon as we can of course, I need to understand what is going on inside me. In fact, it's more than what is going on inside me; it's understanding what's flowing through me. This feeling is too strong and too powerful for it to be generated solely by me. I think I have started it, I've ignited it, but there is something much bigger than me involved here. I don't feel fully in control of it yet, it's too intermittent, too hit and miss. However, I am not concerned or frightened by it, I'm more curious and intrigued about it. The one thing I do know is that, whatever is in me and flowing through me, it is benevolent, it's here to do me good: I *know* that."

Paul and Maya agreed to meet the following evening at the usual time, place and table. Paul was aching with anticipation for the next 24 hours. However, he learned even more in that 24 hour period than he had since he'd met the 'new' Maya. He concluded that, with the vastness and intensity of what lies inside each and every human being, the principal cause of us not having everything we desire in life is the false belief that there is a force, power or set of circumstances *outside* of us greater than the force, power or resources available *within* and flowing through us. It was a startlingly obvious discovery to him now, because he was well on his journey. 'How could I have not seen and felt this before?' he thought. 'Conditioning again', he concluded.

When Paul arrived at The Old Fox, Maya was already sitting at their table. Health and vitality shone from her and her whole demeanour radiated a calm control, an assuredness, that made Paul feel the same way instantly. On greeting her, Paul felt no urge to rabbit on at Maya about his latest experiences and discoveries. They both just knew.

Maya began by saying that tonight Paul was going to discover how he had the life he had been living up to now. He looked bemused as she explained that, from such understanding, he could learn how to take complete control in the future and live the life he had always wanted: a life of unlimited abundance in health and vitality, happiness, wealth and success of any kind; a life where any worthy purpose could be achieved quickly and simply by learning to master the guiding principles and practices that make the world a better place for everyone in it.

"Tell me, what is running through your mind now?" Maya asked, knowing very well that something significant was about to emerge.

"I know at least three things," Paul said. "Firstly, that you are very good at letting me discover certain aspects of how the guiding principles work for me. You could easily *tell* me, but you are wonderfully patient and wait for me to have those 'ah, ha' moments on my own. I'm sure it is part of the journey of discovery, of guided self-discovery, through which you are navigating me.

"Secondly, I also know that the more I understand what is going on and how to take control, the simpler it is becoming. In fact, it strikes me that the whole thing is so simple and, as you've said to me before, its simplicity causes it to be overlooked. So many people continue pushing and shoving, stressing and straining, striving and coercing, scattering and diffusing their precious life forces and awesome powers, it ends up with their lives being filled with disappointment, discouragement, disillusionment and dissatisfaction. However, they are driven by an intrinsic knowledge that there is a way; they just can't find it and end up as failures, or hopeless and helpless victims.

"The third thing I know is to reveal nothing of how this works to other people, unless they want to know, and are willing to pay the price. I've tried to explain it to three people, because I've been so excited and enthusiastic about it myself, and I wish I hadn't bothered. The whole exercise totally drained me. So, I've discovered that the guiding principles and practices are strictly a matter for those people who are genuinely seeking to find the truths about life. Only then will individuals discover them. Only then will the awesome and unlimited powers available to us in the universe make themselves available for us to achieve every right and proper desire. It's the personal quest of discovery that opens up our access to the great and universal powers."

"Paul," Maya said with feeling, "you really are a first class student. Your eagerness, sincerity and insight make you a pleasure to travel with. At this rate you will be guiding me soon!"

Paul blushed slightly and said, "So, what have you got for me tonight then?"

Maya began by explaining the basic tenant of the guiding principles: that human beings become what they think about. Paul therefore needed to have a fundamental understanding of what goes on within the mind when a person is thinking.

"What actually goes on under the 'thatched roof' is really important, if we are to appreciate and ultimately control the connection between the world of thought and the world of the physical. Let me explain how the mind works. And I'm talking about mind here, not brain. The brain, the left brain, right brain, cerebral cortex, etc. that is the hardware. I am talking, here, about the software: the driver, the mind, of which there are three elements."

Maya drew three ovals on a piece of paper and handed it to Paul. In the top oval, Maya wrote 'Outer conscious' and in the bottom left oval 'Inner subconscious':

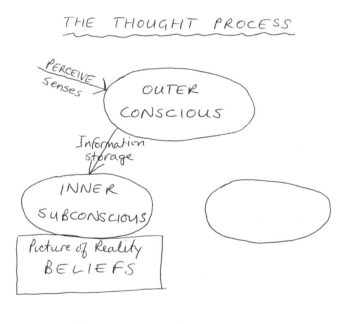

Maya continued speaking, "The outer conscious is the part of our mind that is in touch with the outside world, where we perceive what is going on via our senses. In other words it is our conscious mind. It may be simpler for you to consider your outer conscious as a computer screen and QWERTY keyboard; your inner subconscious is your database. Instead of the information being stored on a silicon chip, as in a computer, in your brain this information is stored in your neurones, or brain cells."

She then drew in an arrow and wrote the words 'Perceive' above the arrow and 'Senses' below it. "Now, what we perceive, via our conscious minds, is simply stored in our inner subconscious mind as thoughts. But remember, we are not storing what is real; we are only storing our perceptions of what is real, so we could be missing out loads and loads of 'Fs', if you remember. Over time, if we store enough of the same thoughts, we begin to build a picture of reality in our inner subconscious mind, based on our beliefs, about what we are like, what the world is like and what other people are like."

Maya drew a box below and connected to the 'Inner subconscious' oval, and wrote in 'Picture of reality' and 'Beliefs'. "The first part of the thought process is simply storing all the outer conscious information we have received since the day we were born. Anything we have consciously experienced, or rather our perception of that experience, be it good, bad or indifferent, gets stored at the inner subconscious level. Every opinion anyone has ever given us, and our perception of that, gets stored. Everything we've ever read, heard, seen on the television, etc., gets stored. Our perceptions of all these things get stored via our thoughts. Over time, based on the intensity and frequency of our thoughts, this stored information becomes the basis of our beliefs. As our beliefs become established, we might even refer to them as the truth: the ways things are; the way the world is; the way other people are; and, more importantly, the way *we* are.

"In other words, our beliefs about ourselves, other people and the world we live in are no more than a hotchpotch of our own and other people's perceptions piled on top of each other, built up in our thoughts. These beliefs then become the foundation upon, and around which, our whole thought process operates. This is because the second stage of the thought process involves a degree of association with the stored information or beliefs. When we are faced with a certain situation, our thinking automatically carries out a kind of database interrogation. We ask ourselves the question, 'Have I seen anything like this before?' We interrogate the stored information in our inner subconscious database for any similar situations or matches.

"For instance, if you had to attend a training course as part of your skills development at work, as soon as the joining instructions landed on your desk you would ask yourself, 'Have I seen anything like this before?' You may have plenty of training course experiences stored in your inner subconscious memory banks, supplying you with lots of feedback. You may also have stored experiences other people have related to you about courses they had attended."

Paul was nodding vigorously, "That is so true. I've got lots of my own experiences of training courses I could tell you about. I've also got lots of experiences that other people have told me about. Most of them are horror stories, though!"

"You can tell me the details later, but let's just understand that the thought process now looks like this." Maya added to her drawing on the paper.

"The process of association automatically triggers the next stage of the thought process: the evaluation stage. It's an extension to the 'Have I seen anything like this before?' question, raising new questions, based upon the feedback from the association stage. 'Where is this likely to be leading me? Is it something good, or is it something not so good?' Depending on the answers, a decision is then made regarding the most appropriate behaviour for that certain situation. This decision making is the fourth stage of the thought process." Maya completed the diagram she was drawing, detailing the process:

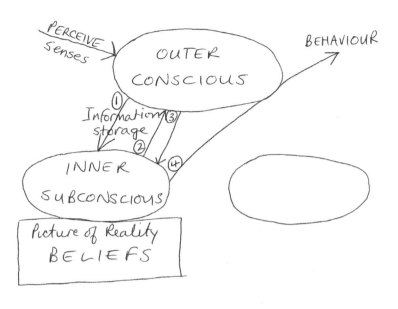

Stage ① : Information storage
Stage ② : Association – "Have I seen anything like this before?"
Stage ③ : Evaluation – "Where is this likely to be leading me?"
Stage ④ : Decision making.

"In other words," Maya continued, "our present day-to-day behaviour is guided and shaped by our perceptions of what's happened to us in the past. Based upon our perceptions and evaluations of what has happened in the past, our behaviour will probably repeat itself, and it will bear no relation to what could happen in the future! This type of thinking kills most people's potential, because they've already made their minds up, that the training course is going to be rubbish before they've set foot in the room or met the trainer!

"Imagine," Maya said, "that in the past you have only attended what you perceived to be at best mediocre, at worst painfully embarrassing, training courses, where the trainer was little better than a psychopath, hell-bent on humiliating you and everyone on the course with puerile role-play exercises, followed by vicious and negative feedback. You have nothing but negative perceptions stored in your subconscious about training courses. The memo arrives informing you that you are to attend a course next week. How will the thought process work? Stage 1, information has been stored. Onto stage 2, you have strong associations with previous courses. At stage 3, alarm bells start to sound because on previous courses you found the whole experience humiliating and painfully embarrassing. At stage 4, you will probably send an e-mail saying a client has requested an urgent meeting that happens to be on the day of the course; you can't let the client down, therefore you will have to miss the course. If you get an e-mail back saying the course is mandatory, what do you think your behaviour will be like when you turn up?"

"I'd be pretty anxious and unco-operative, I guess", answered Paul.

"You bet," replied Maya. "So, if this is the way we think, and, as human beings, we *all* think this way, what is most of our present-day behaviour based upon?"

Paul mused for a while before he answered Maya's question, "Well, I guess it's based upon things that have happened to us in the past?"

Maya added, "It's certainly based upon our **perceptions** of the things that have happened in the past, that's for sure. Now, let me ask you, what are some of the pitfalls that may emerge in that kind of thought and decision-making process?

"It's as clear as night and day," Paul said, "if we only live in the present and constantly dwell in the past, well, we are bound to miss the future. If I was about to go on a course with the best content and the best trainer in the world, because of what I've got stored in my subconscious, and the subsequent thought process, the trainer doesn't stand a chance! I've already decided the course will be rubbish and have switched off; I will probably miss some real pearls of wisdom that, if I'd listened, would have made a huge difference to my job performance. How limiting our thought process can be!"

Paul remembered all the occasions when he had done similar things in the past. He began to reprimand himself for the wasted opportunities over the years.

As if she could read his mind, Maya said reassuringly, "Don't beat yourself up over missed opportunities you might be thinking about and remembering; just learn from them and move on."

"That's easier said than done, Maya, because most of the stuff I've dumped into my subconscious has been negative and destructive, when the actual experience was probably nothing like as bad as I've stored and recalled. And, isn't everybody the same? For instance, I was talking to Samik the other day. Remember he was in our class at school? Well, he was telling me that a couple of years ago, he'd nearly quit his job at the college where he teaches, because his boss had asked him to give a talk at a big conference that would be attended by 500 fellow lecturers. He knew it was a terrific opportunity to impress, and a good career move and all the rational stuff, but he was terrified and refused to do it. His boss got really frustrated, and no matter how much he reassured him that he could do it, and that he would help him write his presentation, practise it and the like, the more Samik dug his heels in and protested.

"What makes this example even more amazing, is that he was a college lecturer used to giving talks, but only to 15 or 20 in a class. It was the thought of 500 that terrified him. And yet, he is one of the most eloquent, charismatic and, on the surface, cool and confident people I know. But here he was, a 42-year old, falling apart at the thought of giving this talk. When I asked him about it in detail, about why he was so resistant to it, he took me through the process his boss had taken him through to get to the root of the problem.

"His boss is a great guy, according to Samik, and could see that Samik had the talent and ability to give the talk, and that there must be something in his mind getting in the way of him doing it. His boss asked him directly, 'Samik, if you've never done anything like this before, how do you know you can't do it?' Now, that's a really good question, don't you think? And Samik told me he had had great difficulty answering it, until his boss had nailed him for an answer.

"Samik was shocked with where the blockage and barrier to his doing this talk actually came from. Guess where, Maya? It came from school. It came from 30 years before! Do you remember when Samik did his 'Show and Tell'?" Paul asked.

Maya laughed, "You bet I do! How could any one of the 28 of us in the class forget it!"

Paul continued, "Oh God, weren't those "Show and Tells" the worst experience of your school career? Fancy having to bring in a hobby or an interest and talk to the class about it for 30 minutes! And then, to make it worse, answer any questions anyone had for another 15 minutes. Arrgghh! Excruciating or what? I think Samik's talk was about the pet rabbits he was keeping, but do you remember him dashing back to the classroom after paying a visit to the little boy's room just before his talk? Remember him leaving his flies undone and having his shirt flap sticking out? He hadn't realised his wardrobe malfunction as he started his talk. Nobody could take him, or what he was saying, seriously! And, do you remember him getting really flustered and upset when everyone was giggling uncontrollably, to the point where he was so humiliated and embarrassed, he ran out of the class, still not knowing what everyone was giggling at?"

Maya nodded, as she remembered. Paul continued, "He had just presumed everyone was laughing at his first attempt at public speaking, and it had nothing to do with that! He told me that he was in the changing rooms at school for a full hour sobbing his heart out over this. Eventually a couple of teachers found him, and Samik told them that he had made his mind up that he would *never* do another public speech as long as he lived. He'd managed to keep that promise, up until the point where his boss had asked him to do this conference speech. Poor old Samik didn't seem to have an escape route to get him out of the situation and, as a result, seriously considered moving jobs rather than having to do the speech! Crazy, or what?

"I now understand what was going on with Samik. His thought process was working overtime, in a really negative and destructive way. So, not only had he associated this with the 'have I seen anything like this before' stage of the thinking process, but also the 'where is this likely to be leading me?' stage. The answers went way beyond the 'something good' or 'something not so good' evaluation; it was approaching the 'something disastrous will definitely happen'. So much so, that he was willing to quit his job rather than do the talk! So, his talent, his ability to do the talk and do it well, was completely buried by his thought process."

"Yes," said Maya, "those things are called black holes, or restrictive zones, because they massively restrict people's unlimited talents and abilities from being expressed in their behaviour or performance. How many black holes do you think you have? And what about other people?"

Paul just shook his head in despair; it took him no time at all to count many of his own.

"People have them in all kinds of areas, even with simple things like names," continued Maya, "When my son Thomas was born, Andy and I had a big fall out over what to call him. We had had many discussions about suitable names for both boys and girls, because we didn't know the sex of our child until he was born.

"When he turned out to be a boy, we decided to throw the girls' names away, thinking that calling a boy Gladys wouldn't be brilliant for his development!" She had a cheeky grin on her face, which reflected her sense of humour, compassion and humanity that, in essence, summed up the new Maya.

"Anyway, when it came to decision time between Thomas and Lawrence, which were the two names we had chosen for a boy, Andy asked me which name I preferred. He muttered something about my having done the hard work actually giving birth, and it was the least he could do to give me the final say in the name. Well, I was exhausted; I thought for a moment, looked at my new born baby and announced that he looked like a Lawrence to me. Andy's reaction was amazing. He completely blew his stack! 'I'm not having a child of mine called Lawrence', he exclaimed with pent-up anger. 'What!' I shot back, 'I thought that we'd already decided we liked those two names.' 'Well, we might have done, but now it is a *fait accompli*, I realise it's not going to happen. No child of mine will *ever* be called Lawrence!'

"His behaviour was outrageous, totally illogical, emotional and irrational. When I asked why he felt so strongly about this, having assured him that as he felt so strongly the name Thomas was fine by me, he offered the following explanation. When he had been at school, when he was about 10 years old, he had been made to sit next to a boy called Lawrence Atherton. Lawrence was the scruffiest, smelliest child in the school. Andy explained that, even though he'd only just realised it, when he held his new-born son and heir in his arms, the very mention of the name Lawrence automatically brought a picture into his head of this poor neglected 10-year-old, smelling to high heaven and looking like an unmade bed!

"Guess the number of people I've told that story to, who get really agitated and tell me that they had exactly the same experiences naming their children! Immediately discounting names because of miserable misanthropic aunts, uncles and next-door neighbours, etc., who had probably been dead for more than 30 years!"

Paul replied, "I guess lots and lots. But how do we put all this right? I can relate to everything you are telling me."

"Well," Maya said, "there are a few more basics about the thought process you need to understand, before you will be able to appreciate the answer and learn how to begin the process of taking control.

"The first of these basics is that we are all masters of our own destinies and we can make our lives anything we wish them to be via our thought patterns. In fact, it's not that we *can* make our lives anything we wish them to be, it's that we *do* make our lives what we wish them to be via our thought patterns. Let me ask you something. What kinds of thoughts race through your mind all the time? Positive ones? Constructive ones? Are you constantly emphasising and reinforcing the gifts, skills and talents that you possess, your unlimited nature and the incredible abilities you have to overcome any challenges? Or, are most of your thoughts about the pitfalls you and other people have to face, your inadequacies, shortfalls, doubts and fears? If you are anything like me, as I was a few months ago, I bet you've got thought patterns that constantly rake over, recycle and reaffirm the negative stuff. Am I right?"

Paul answered, "Well, until a few weeks ago, I would say I probably had the most negative thoughts of anyone that I know! But I'm no-where near as bad now, since you got back in touch with me."

Maya added, "And you've only just started the process of change. As it continues, you'll be able to learn and understand how to channel and direct the universal power available to you. You will be awesome. You see, we *all* have access to this power. All people use this power. There is, in the universe, only one power or source of energy, and it is everywhere at all times. People who don't understand its existence, and how to use it properly, unknowingly allow it to produce misery, disease, poverty and mediocrity in their lives. When it is understood, it can be used to produce abundance and greatness in any area of our lives. What I've been guided towards is how to control this power by understanding and applying the simple laws that unerringly determine all outcomes in life. And now I'm guiding you, the end results will be different, but the laws and power driving them are the same. It is like electricity; it can be wired to flow through a refrigerator to chill everything down, or an oven to heat everything up. And, just like electricity, this power or force has always been there in the universe, just waiting for us to discover it and develop ways of how to harness it. By understanding and applying some simple laws and knowing how and why they work, you, and everyone else on Earth, can learn to control, channel and direct this universal power that flows from and through us, in order to achieve any right and proper desire, without limit!

"One of the laws concerns planting the right seeds, in terms of thoughts, in fertile ground, which is our mind. Without the right seeds, we can wish, hope, pray and work as hard as we like, but we'll never get the harvest of abundance we truly want. Think of your mind as a computer, which effectively is what it is, a huge electro-bio-chemical computer with a virtually unlimited capacity. If you programme that computer with all the wrong information for all its working life, what are the chances of it ever giving you the right answers, approximately?"

Paul looked puzzled, even though the answer seemed obvious, "Well, er, none, I suppose."

Maya smiled and she responded, "Exactly! Have you heard the saying 'GI equals GO'?"

Paul shook his head.

"'Garbage In equals Garbage Out'," Maya elaborated. "If you have been programming into your mind all the negatives about yourself, about other people, about the world you live in, all your life, what's the only thing that is in there to come out? Our thought patterns, our most frequent and habitual thought patterns, have a tendency to weave themselves into the very fabric of our being and manifest themselves in the physical realm. Our thoughts, in other words, create our physical reality, not instantly, but eventually. Where we channel our thinking, tends to be reflected back into our lives and our world; it is part of the laws. It demonstrates that this universal force, or power, is not just omnipotent; it's intelligent. It responds to our thoughts.

"Before you start thinking about all the things that you can't control, like negative relatives, or negative bosses, or the economy, or taxes, or prices, or the government, understand that an essential element of taking control of this great and universal power lies in accepting a sense of personal responsibility for *everything* that happens in our lives. This is a real toughie, because it is *so* easy to blame everyone and everything for the circumstances we find ourselves in. When we do this we are, by default, believing that there are greater forces on the outside of us than there are resources on the inside of us. We've cut ourselves off from the great and universal power.

"So what can you actually do about the negativity of your boss? Or the weather? Nothing, absolutely nothing, apart from maybe keeping your distance, changing jobs or buying a brolly. And what can you do about the economy, taxes, prices and the government? Well, the first 3 you can probably do nothing about, and for the last one we do at least get a vote every 4 years or so. But if you think all the problems are out there," Maya pointed in 4 different directions, "you've got no chance of accepting the great and universal power, and directing it towards creating the kind of life you really want and desire. The problems aren't out there: the challenge is in here," she said, tapping her temples.

"And, of course, once you accept the great and universal power that permeates everything, including us, and begin to learn how to work with it, develop it, channel it and intensify its power, why wouldn't you believe and accept that the challenge is in here?" She tapped her head again. "The problems are not out there. Not with the government, the market nor other people. In fact," she continued in a mischievous voice, "if you want to wait here, I'll happily go and guide the rest of the world on how to use these principles and practices, and tell them, in particular, to treat you properly; that way, your life is bound to work out the way you've always wanted it to, isn't it? Although, please don't hold your breath because it could take me a little while, there being 6.2 billion other people on the planet. It may take me a little while to get around to them all! Do you understand where I'm going with this?" Paul nodded, and Maya went on, "So, are you ready to really accept the 10 most important words strung together in the English Language as a sentence? I mentioned them to you before you opened the envelope with the 'Fs' in, but you'll understand them at a much deeper level now."

Paul sat bolt upright, nodding and giving Maya his full attention, "You know me, Maya, always open-minded, keen and enthusiastic to be guided! Go on, hit me with those words again."

Maya calmly recited, "'**If it is to be, it is up to me**'. You see, you make the difference, you are in control, and you have the power. Accept the meaning of those 10 words into the very fabric of your being, and you will become omnipotent, invincible and unstoppable. The reason for this is that, when you drive any beliefs into the very fabric of your being, good or bad, the great and universal power that is the source of all creation takes hold of them and makes them manifest. So, the brilliant news is that you don't need to be the way you are now, unless you choose to be! Because you weren't born that way! We've been conditioned to think in certain ways and to build certain limiting beliefs. When we learn to recondition our thinking and build brand new, unlimiting beliefs, we can change our world. I did. My guide did. You can. Everyone can. And there is a part of your mind that is responsible for making all this happen."

Chapter Ten

"Before I describe the deeper and more mysterious parts of the mind," Maya continued, "You'll need a deeper appreciation of the sheer size and capacity of our capabilities and potential. The reason for this is that, coming back to our computer analogy, many people believe that they are somehow lacking the hardware to achieve everything they could want in life, and nothing could be further from the truth. As I've mentioned before, think of your inner subconscious as your database, and one that has had its memory stored on neurone cells rather than hard disks or silicon chips. In fact, imagine that, from the day you were born, everything that you have ever read, seen, heard and experienced has been stored in that database. It's a database of more than 100 billion neurone cells, 100 billion!

"Now you know how I like making sure that you've got a crystal-clear picture of every principle and practice that we need to master, in order to make the great universal power work for us?" Paul nodded, and Maya went on, "Well, this is no exception, do you know just how big a billion is?" Paul shook his head this time. "It's a thousand million. Can you conceive the sheer scale of it?"

Paul shook his head again and confessed, "Well no, not really. I just know that it *is* big." Maya continued, "To understand the sheer scale, capacity and vastness of the potential we have available to us, can you hazard a guess at how long a billion seconds is? A thousand million seconds? That's 60 seconds every minute, 60 minutes every hour, 24 hours every day. How long is it?" At his puzzled look, Maya volunteered the answer: "31.7 years. Not only have we all got 100 billion neurone cells, but each and every one of them can store between 1 and 2 million pieces of information. Because of our brain's electro-bio-chemical nature, each and every piece of information stored can almost instantaneously communicate with any other piece of information stored on any other neurone cell. This means that the combinations and permutations are enormous. When you consider the scale of this capacity, it's easy to understand why we only use 1.5–2% of our potential in our lives. In fact, it is one of the great mysteries in life. If we use so little of our brain capacity, why the heck is it so big? Why build a motor car capable of a top speed of 1000 m.p.h. and only allow it to run at 15 or 20 m.p.h.?

"In the supposed advance of our civilisation, some people believe we have lost the knowledge of how to access and use our full capacity. We've just simply forgotten some of the techniques that allow us to turn our power full on. We have also unwittingly cut ourselves off from the universal field of energy and power that has been with us since the moment of creation. This unseen creative force connects every cell of every living thing, and every atom of every non-living thing. When this power is communed with, directed and channelled properly, it controls and supplies health and vitality, success and wealth, happiness and peace of mind, and the unerring ability to achieve any desired goal or objective in life. Modern science is only now beginning to accept and understand the existence of this universal creative force. This isn't new knowledge; it's ancient knowledge and wisdom being newly discovered.

"The basic message of all this, is that people do not lack capacity; they lack understanding, belief and connectedness. They also lack the guides who can show them how to reconnect with the great unseen universal creative power, and build their belief in their own unlimited potential and develop their understanding of how

113

to use the principles and practices we're learning here in order to achieve anything.

"Most people are 98.5% dead and don't realise it. Their full power and glory is there. It's within their grasp, they have just never been shown it. They know it's there instinctively or intuitively, which is why so many people have been searching for these answers for so long; and here they are, all around us, and we just can't see them. It reminds me of a great story about the gods: they were having an emergency meeting to decide where to hide the secrets of success because humans were getting ever closer to finding them and, of course, once humans did find them, they, the gods, would not be needed anymore. There followed a ferocious argument about where to hide the secrets of success. One god suggested hiding them in the far reaches of outer space because the chances of humans finding them in such vastness would be very slim. Another god argued against this idea because humans are both builders and explorers, and one day they would build a machine capable of going into outer space; their inquisitiveness would drive them to explore and map every cubic centimetre, and, therefore, they would be bound to find the secrets eventually.

"Another god suggested putting the secrets of success in the deepest ocean trench underneath miles of mud; others suggested hiding them in the molten centre of the Earth, a place so inhospitable and inaccessible that the secrets of success would surely be hidden forever. Again, these ideas were dismissed, because humans are not just builders but, in order to build, they have to excavate as well and, if they excavated a lot, which they would do, they would eventually unearth the secrets of success. No agreement could be found until the oldest, wisest god of them all, who had dozed off during part of the earlier debate, called the meeting to order and said, 'Just remind me what we are trying to do, here?' Impatiently, he was told, 'We are still trying to decide where to hide the secrets of success, so that humans will never find them, and we seem to have ruled out just about everywhere in the universe. Have you got any suggestions?' He replied with, 'Oh, that's an easy one to resolve'. The other gods were startled by the complete certainty in his voice, 'Why don't you just hide the secrets of success deep inside each and every person on the planet because, let me tell you, that is the last place that they will think of looking! They'll go to the ends of the universe, the bottom of the sea and the centre of the Earth and all points in between, but they won't look inside and discover what they already know. Put the secrets of success there, and let me assure you, my friends, they will be there, undiscovered, for a very long time!'

Paul was almost shaking with excitement as he blurted out, "I knew it, I knew it all along! In fact, we knew it and, if you stop and think about it, we all know it."

Maya added calmly, "That's the problem, people don't stop and think about it, not properly and not for long. Or rather, their thinking is all over the place, in all the areas they don't want it to be, about fears, regrets, shortfalls, pitfalls, inadequacies, hurts, being let down, and so on. You see, we are all influenced initially, and our thinking is shaped by external events, the opinions of other people, and the like, especially the authority figures that show up in our lives. With these influences being mainly negative, our own thinking takes over and replays the same negative messages and attaches the same negative outcomes to almost everything. With all this noise going on inside our minds, it's never usually quiet enough to listen to and discover our true selves, so that we can connect our personal power with the one, creative power within the universe. Our disconnectedness makes it impossible for us to channel, and then learn to direct, this great universal creative power, to deliver for us every right and proper desire we have.

"In many ways it's like owning a satellite or cable television with hundreds of channels, and only tuning it in to receive certain ones. From then on, the only channels you see on the screen are the ones you have chosen to tune in to. No others will appear, although they are available in the airwaves. This is especially important to remember in order to understand what the principles and practices of how all this works tell us; the sounds and pictures don't reside in the television set, they flow through it and are determined by what it has been tuned into or programmed to receive. So, what have you tuned yourself in to receive, Paul? The poverty channel, the misery channel, the struggle channel, the stress channel and the failure channel?"

Paul responded by saying, "Well, all of those, before you showed up again in my life, as well you know. And, if I recall, you were just as bad as I was."

"No, no," Maya said, "I was much worse than you were. Much, much worse! But do you know something? I think the worse you've been, the more impact this new-found knowledge has on you. My guide told me that he, and other guides he knew, had pulled themselves back from all kinds of pain and suffering, from alcoholism, drug abuse, child abuse, violence and even clinical depression where it had reached the point of contemplating and attempting suicide. Really bad stuff. Now, by using the principles and practices that you are learning, they are in control, happy, successful, healthy, and every aspect of their lives is terrific. You see, in extreme cases you can be tuning into all the bad channels at once. Life can then resemble living in the crisis channel or the horror channel 24-7-52!

"One last illustration, and then we can begin to understand what processes drive all this in and through our minds and bodies. Tell me, what is an orange full of?"

Paul looked confused, "Well, er, juice." Maya smiled and said, "Good, yes, orange juice; and?" Paul volunteered, somewhat awkwardly, "Well, er, segments and pips, and things." Maya nodded and continued with, "Absolutely right! An orange is full of orange juice, orange segments, orange pips, orange pith, orange zest: an orange is full of orangeness, yes? So when you squeeze an orange, what comes out?" Paul replied, "Orange juice, orange flesh and orange pips and …" Maya interrupted with, "Yes, it's full of orange stuff, an orange is full of orangeness, so when it gets squeezed what's the only thing that can come out? Orange stuff, in all its forms: juice, flesh, pips, zest, etc." Paul looked bewildered, and Maya continued, "People are exactly the same; if you fill a person with thoughts of hate and anger and jealousy and regret and envy and hurt and evil, when they get squeezed, what are the only things that can come out? If there is nothing else in there? Do you see?"

Paul's bewilderment turned to excitement, as the power and simplicity of what Maya had said hit home. Maya then asked, "What have you been full of, all your life, up until now?"

His immediate thought was that he'd been full of s**t, but he kept the phrase to himself. "No need to answer that one," he said, "but it's going to change from here on in."

Maya went on, "You see, there is another element of our subconscious mind, the deeper subconscious, that operates unerringly to ensure that, whatever pictures of reality or beliefs we have chosen to plant on the inside in the inner subconscious, eventually get projected onto the outside in the real world. In other words, whatever beliefs we have built up on the inside in our inner subconscious minds, or in our thought realm, invariably gets delivered to the outside, in the physical realm. These are the beliefs about what we are like, about what other people are like and about what the world is like. One of the fundamental principles of what we're learning is that thoughts are things. Thoughts invariably become things! The element of our mind that takes care of this is, as I've said, our deeper subconscious."

Maya then referred to her earlier diagram and filled in the remaining oval. "The principal role that the deeper subconscious fulfils is to serve as a check and balance system, to maintain something that we call sanity. In this instance, sanity is making sure we always behave on the outside, on a long-term, automatic and consistent basis, in a way that matches the person we have come to perceive or believe ourselves to be on the inside. You see we, as human beings, can not behave on a long-term, automatic and free-flowing basis on the outside any differently from the person we have come to perceive or believe ourselves to be on the inside. It is, to all intents and purposes, impossible, because of our deeper subconscious. Acting as the check and balance system, or the servomechanism, if you prefer, the deeper subconscious maintains the direct link between the internal beliefs we've built about who and what we are in our minds, and the external reality that is our behaviour. That is why people who believe themselves to be shy are automatically shy, and why people who believe themselves, or perceive themselves, to be outgoing, automatically are outgoing:

THE THOUGHT PROCESS

PERCEIVE
Senses
OUTER CONSCIOUS
BEHAVIOUR

Information storage ① ② ③

INNER SUBCONSCIOUS
④
DEEPER SUBCONSCIOUS
) Maintains SANITY

Picture of Reality
BELIEFS

Stage ①: Information storage
Stage ②: Association - "Have I seen anything like this before?"
Stage ③: Evaluation - "Where is this likely to be leading me?"
Stage ④: Decision making.

"One of the keys to understanding how all this works, is the fact that our inner subconscious does not have a valve or filter on it that only allows the good stuff in. Our inner subconscious will accept, as the truth, any thoughts that we deposit in there often enough. And, be ready for this one, the thoughts we deposit don't need to be true; we just need to **believe** them to be true, for our deeper subconscious to latch onto them and begin the process of delivering them into our behaviour and real world. Remember the Christopher Columbus story? How did everyone behave? Not in accordance with the truth, but in accordance with the truth as they perceived it to be and believed it to be. Their behaviour, and what they experienced in their real world, became a reflection of their thoughts.

"So, depending on what you've been programming into your inner subconscious all your life, your deeper subconscious becomes one of two things: either your very best friend, or your worst enemy. One thing is for sure, your deeper subconscious is always your most loyal and obedient servant. It will never let you down. It will always deliver into your physical realm whatever you've been programming into the inner subconscious via your thoughts; good or bad, health or illness, wealth or poverty, happiness or misery, success or failure. Your deeper subconscious is by far and away your most loyal and obedient servant, so the question is, what beliefs, qualities and expectations have you been asking of it, given its access to the awesome and unlimited universal force that can and does transform those thoughts into a reality? All the things you want? Or all the things you don't want but think about all the time? Your deeper subconscious does not differentiate between what you want and what you don't want. It is servile. It simply finds the resources and circumstances to deliver into your world what you think about and believe in most. Therefore, it delivers dreams and nightmares into your real world with equal efficiency and effectiveness.

"You see, it's the deeper subconscious that directly communes with the great universal force that is the field of creation. It is within this field that all possibilities already exist; all the health, abundance, happiness, as well as all the illness, lack and misery. It is our deeper subconscious that claims the future that we create with our own thoughts and beliefs. We create our own destiny."

Paul's mind started racing again, as he thought of example after example in his own life, and other people's lives, that illustrated and proved this major point. "So, human beings really do become on the outside what they think about on the inside", he said with an ever deepening understanding and certainty about what he had just learned. He continued, "It explains so many things in my life." Maya added, "It explains so many things in everybody's life!"

"Yeh, I see that," Paul said, as he absorbed the sheer simplicity and power of the message that had been revealed to him. "It's all so clear to me now. When I was going through a bad time with my health, I was consumed with negative thoughts about my health, and it just got worse as I was hit by one thing after another! And, it's just dawned on me, I was inviting those ailments into my life, with my thinking! In fact, I remember telling Jackie that if things continued like they were going, I'd end up with shingles or something, and be off work for months, and guess what! But what you are saying here is, there was nothing wrong with me as such, there was just something wrong with my thinking."

Maya responded sympathetically, "Well, that isn't strictly speaking true, but the two realms are so closely connected that it's more a matter of consequences. People rarely fully appreciate how close imagination is to reality. As with your shingles, the thoughts came first, the physical reality second."

Paul was nodding in agreement as he replied, "It explains so many things in my life: when I was having a really bad time at work, a period of self-doubt and uncertainty was sparked off by a couple of my friends being made redundant. They convinced me that all companies were the same and it was a waste of time going the extra mile because, when it was time for the chop, they would just chop. And do you know what happened? I actually stopped trying, because I thought 'What's the point?' Which, when you think about it, is totally crazy, because those types of belief, attitude and feeling only create the kind of behaviour that makes it more likely that you will get chopped if redundancies are on the agenda! I did realise the error of my ways, however, just in time; but, good grief, I only escaped redundancy by the skin of my teeth, and I now realise that it was my thinking that nearly led to it."

Maya went on to say, "If you hadn't changed your thinking, you would have created that situation. Something must have altered your thinking process. Do you remember what it was?"

Without hesitation, Paul replied, "I certainly do! It was the fact that Jackie became pregnant with our first child and we decided she would give up work, so I needed a job. All my thinking then was focused on keeping my job, not losing it! This thinking 'stuff' is quite subtle and sublime isn't it?"

Maya nodded and said, "It can be at times. It can be." Paul then laughed self-consciously, as another realisation hit him. "What is it now?" Maya asked. Paul elaborated, "It's all so crazy, because once I'd got the job thing sorted, by avoiding redundancy, all my conscious waking thoughts were about my being the breadwinner, and how on earth were we going to make ends meet with an extra mouth to feed? And guess what, for the next 10 years we lurched from one money crisis to another!"

"You must understand what is happening here," Maya said. "Whatever we believe, with feeling, becomes a self-fulfilling prophecy in our lives. Beliefs are built on the repetition and intensity of our thoughts, not just by single ones, or occasional, superficial ones. You also need to appreciate fully just how obedient our deeper subconscious is at delivering into the physical realm that which we dwell and focus on most in the thought realm. Let me give you an example of what I mean: do you take part in the National Lottery or do the football pools at all?" Paul nodded and said, "Well yes, I am in a syndicate at work on the football pools and do the lottery myself most weeks."

"OK," Maya said, "and so do millions of others, right? Now, what do you think, for the most part, people who do the lottery or the football pools believe about their current financial status? What do you think they keep telling themselves about their current financial status?" Paul looked slightly unsure of himself, and replied, "Well, I think they'll be thinking 'I'm doing OK, I'm comfortable, but an extra injection of money would be very much appreciated and welcomed'." Maya continued, "So, in a whole variety of different ways, what they're actually telling themselves is that they're of modest financial means. Not poor, not rich, but could do with a little bit more." Paul agreed, and Maya went on, "Their belief is that 'I am of modest financial means' and they probably reinforce that a thousand times a day with all kinds of other supporting thoughts to that belief, yes? Paul was nodding vigorously by now. "So, let's imagine, in that case, that the miraculous happened and the numbers just happened to drop in the right order, and you won a considerable amount of money; I'm not talking about £10, I mean a 5 or 6 figure sum. Now, let me ask you this. With most people that this happens to, after the initial 'Yippee!', what do you think the first thing they say is, particularly to their friends?" The realisation hit Paul hard, "Well, I know what I would say, I'd say, 'It won't change me!'"

Maya continued, "Knowing the way that we're wired, and how what we think builds our beliefs, and how our heart-felt beliefs work to create our physical reality; in this instance, what is the worst thing anyone in this situation could say? Yes: 'It won't change me'! And why? Because they're merely reinforcing their existing belief, so their most loyal and obedient servant, their deeper subconscious, simply delivers no change into their world. And, guess what? In 2 or 3 years, almost irrespective of the amount of money they have won, they will be back to being of modest financial means. I've got a friend who works in a bank with high-value customers, and many of them have won the lottery or the football pools, and he tells me that up to 90% of people who win more than £50,000, which is not an inconsiderable amount of money, after 3 years have got virtually nothing left in their bank accounts; they are back where they believe they belong! This is really powerful stuff, because, even though some good fortune happens to us on the outside, if we don't change our thinking and beliefs on the inside, we just go back to the way things were."

"It's as if we've got an auto-pilot inside our minds that is governed by our beliefs, and it is this that controls, directs and determines who we are and what shows up in our lives," said Paul. "That is exactly what we've got," Maya agreed enthusiastically, "That's a really good analogy." Paul continued this time, "And I guess it is like any auto-pilot system: it can be manually overridden." Maya clarified, "Well, yes, the only problem is that we have to think consciously and continuously about any behaviour that is not in line with our beliefs, in order to override it, and we, as human beings, can't do that very effectively. You have to consciously remember all the time that you no longer smoke or that you're not shy, and that's beyond most people!"

"So, how do we change it, then?" asked Paul. Maya replied, "We can't rush into that one yet. You need to understand first, at a deeper level, how the subconscious elements of our minds work, and especially how we come to believe certain things about ourselves, about other people and about the world we live in. Before we do that, however, let me just remind you of how obedient our deeper subconscious is. Have you ever heard of a lady called Viv Nicholson?" Paul nodded and said, "Yes, she won the football pools in the 1960s, didn't she?"

Maya replied, "Yes, she did. She actually won £152,319, which is equivalent today to more than 3.5 million pounds. And, rather than say, 'it won't change me', do you know what she said she was going to do?" Paul nodded, "I think most people know this one. She said she was going to 'spend, spend, spend!'" Maya continued, "Yes she did. So, she gave her deeper subconscious a very clear instruction to fulfil, and it obeyed her to the letter, and even though it is almost inconceivable how someone could use up all that money, that's what she did; I think it was within 4 years that she was declared bankrupt.

"Irrespective of what is happening on the outside, our physical world, which we experience all around us, is merely a multi-dimensional, multi-sensory reflection of our inner thought world. It's as simple as that! All the events and people in our lives are there because we've drawn them towards us with our thoughts and heart-felt feelings and beliefs. And, as a result, trying to change things on the outside, by consciously changing our behaviour, will only lead to temporary and short-lived results. People who smoke have a very clear subconscious belief that they are smokers and they love cigarettes. Their belief is total: 'I am a smoker, I love it and can't live without my cigarettes'. Now, let's say they decide to make a New Year's resolution to quit. How do most people go about doing it? What do they change? Most people would try and change their behaviour first. They would throw away the cigarettes, but then go through hell, as the continuing belief they are a smoker finds ways of forcing itself out. The reason for this is that the real driver of behaviour, their beliefs, begin to go to work via their deeper subconscious to find and recreate the environment in which the smokers believe themselves to belong. The deeper subconscious will provide them with cravings, grumpiness and a whole batch of reasons why they should have a cigarette and, eventually, the internal picture, the belief 'I am a smoker', will win its way through back into their behaviour, and they are smokers again. Does this sound familiar?"

Paul nodded and laughed, "It certainly explains why I tried to give up smoking so many times and failed! And, it also explains why I succeeded when I did. One day, I just made my mind up, just like that! I just decided! And, lo and behold, everything else just seemed to fall into place. No withdrawal symptoms, no cravings or putting on weight, or anything like that."

Maya interjected, "That's exactly what it is like. Your beliefs about yourself, other people and the world you live in, your deepest beliefs, steadily and surely get projected into the world around you. So, as we have said, people who believe they are shy automatically act shyly, because that is the primary role of their deeper subconscious, to find the resources and circumstances that makes behaving shyly automatic and inevitable! Your deeper subconscious never lets you down, ever! It always delivers. As we have already touched on, you can consciously act differently than the person you have come to know yourself to be. So, shy people can act in an outgoing way, but they will feel very uncomfortable and eventually go back to the way they perceive they should be, to the way they believe themselves to be, namely shy. It's as certain as night following day. It's a precise, unerring, universal law that is being followed.

"When we come to the conscious realisation that we are doing something, or something is happening, on the outside that doesn't match the picture of the way it should be on the inside, via our inner subconscious beliefs, then our deeper subconscious kicks in and balances things up, so that the internal picture and external reality match.

"Here's a perfect example: what is your golf handicap these days?" Paul told her that it was 16. "OK, 16 is pretty good. Now, if you were to come to my golf course, the par for the course is 72. So, if you played this course, a par round for you would be 72 plus 16, which is 88. Our course is pretty well balanced, and the front 9 holes are just as difficult as the back 9 holes. So, if you were playing par golf for you, you would shoot a 44 on the front 9 and 44 on the back 9, making an 88 in total, right?" Paul nodded and Maya went on.

"Golf, in my view, is a really good analogy for life, for a number of reasons. One is that you keep your score as you play each hole and, half way round, your playing partner will add up your score and confirm how well you're doing by telling you how many shots you've taken. Have you ever gone round the first 9 holes of any golf course with a truly outstanding score, like 38 shots, or something?" Paul nodded vigorously, "A good few times, in fact." Maya continued, "And your partner announces, with some incredulity, 'Good grief Paul, you're playing unbelievably well! Do you realise you've just shot a 38!' Whilst you had realised you were doing well, you hadn't realised you were doing that well. The conscious realisation now hits you that you are doing way too well for you. This is because your golf handicap, your official golf handicap, is telling the world the standard to which you play golf. So your belief is, 'I'm supposed to shoot a 44, and I've just shot a 38!' So you come to the conclusion that the way you are playing doesn't match the expectation you are carrying in your inner subconscious self-image. Now, what happens to your game and score on the back 9?"

Paul chuckled as he said, "Well, your game just falls apart doesn't it? But isn't that just pressure?" Maya replied, "Well it may be, but where does the pressure come from? It comes from the fact that the score you actually achieved doesn't match the picture of what it should be in your mind. So, your deeper subconscious kicks in and takes control, and basically says, 'I'll sort this out'. Because you know in your heart of hearts that a 38 on the front 9 holes, if it was matched by a 38 on the back 9 holes, equals a round of 76, which is 12 under par for one round of golf, and not even Tiger Woods can do that! So, your deeper subconscious does what it is meant to do, in order to maintain sanity, and in order for you to finish the round close to your handicap, you now shoot a 49 or 50 on the back 9 holes, to come in with around 88, which is 'the way it should be'! You see, within certain boundaries and over the right timescales, our deeper subconscious, as a check and balance system, always delivers and will never let us down. It hasn't, up to now, in our lives, and it won't in the future. The key to getting everything we want in life is understanding this, and working intelligently with it."

Paul was nonplussed yet ecstatic, because Maya's description of the process that goes on within people's minds explained so many things in his life. So, so many things. Paul reflected on this simple, yet not simplistic, truth, and many different examples flashed through his mind. His reverie was interrupted as Maya pushed a piece of paper in front of him and said, "I think these words sum up the process beautifully, and also explain the relationship between the three basic parts of the mind, namely the outer conscious and the two elements of the subconscious. Someone gave me this 15 years ago, but I never understood what it was describing until I began to understand and master the principles and practices of how to take control of life."

Paul read the words and was completely mesmerised:

I am very accommodating

I ask no questions.

I accept whatever you give me.

I do whatever I am told.

I do not presume to change anything you think, say or do; I file it all away in perfect order, quickly and efficiently, and then I return it to you exactly as you gave it to me.

Sometimes you call me your memory.

I am the reservoir into which you toss anything your heart or mind chooses to deposit there.

I work night and day; I never rest, and nothing can impede my activity.

The thoughts you send to me are categorised and filed, and my filing system never fails.

I am truly your servant who does your bidding, without hesitation or criticism.

I co-operate when you tell me that you are 'this' or 'that' and I play it back as you gave it. I am most agreeable.

Since I do not think, argue, judge, analyse, question or make decisions, I accept impressions easily.

I am going to ask you to sort out what you send me, however; my files are getting a little cluttered and confused. I mean, please discard those things that you do not want returned to you.

What is my name? Oh, I thought you knew!

I am your subconscious.

By Margaret E. White

"Wow," Paul said, "this lady really seems to know a thing or two about this stuff, doesn't she?" Maya replied, "You're not kidding; this is a perfect description of how the inner subconscious and the deeper subconscious work in unison, to deliver out to our behaviour whatever beliefs we've programmed in over time with our thoughts. As it says, 'I ask no questions. I accept whatever you give me. I do whatever I am told, and then I return it to you exactly as you gave it to me'. It can't be any clearer: what we've input via our outer conscious thoughts gets delivered to us via our behaviour, without any alteration or adjustment. 'I co-operate when you tell me you are "this" or "that" and I play it back as you gave it to me. I am most agreeable'.

"Then there is an instruction on how to begin the process of taking control, although we will come to that a bit later on your journey rather than go into it in detail now. But, for now, just listen to what these words are saying: 'Since I do not think, argue, judge, analyse, question or make decisions, I accept impressions easily. I'm going to ask you to sort out what you send me, however; my files are getting a little cluttered and confused. I mean, please discard those things you do not want returned to you. What is my name? I am your subconscious'. Actually, it is the conscious and the two elements of the subconscious that are being described here, the three working in perfect harmony. However, we have to delve a little further into how our beliefs get built, in order to understand how to take control completely of our future health, wealth, happiness and success.

"These words just describe the process of how our beliefs, our deepest and most heart-felt beliefs, are delivered to create the world around us from the inside out. This means that the meaningful and lasting changes that we desire in life, in ourselves, in our relationships with other people, in our health, wealth and the world we live in, actually begin on the inside as beliefs fuelled by emotion and desire. They do not start on the outside and work their way in, which, sadly, is the way that most people, the ones who don't understand how this whole life-changing process works, try to do it, and fail. In fact, that's the way we've all tried to do it at some stage. And we try and try and try, and we wonder why we struggle so much to really achieve anything significant in the life of our choosing. We all try and change the behaviour on the outside because we mistakenly think we can control that, when the reality is that control comes from within. This is a universal law. If we don't understand it and co-operate with it intelligently, it will eventually break us. If we try and break the way the laws work, we will fail. We cannot break the universal law, but we can break ourselves against the law in the process! The result is struggle, suffering, pain, lack, unhappiness, misery, ill-health and all kinds of unpleasantness.

"We need to learn and apply and trust this new way of looking at things and change our internal beliefs first. This way our deeper subconscious, acting as our most loyal and obedient servant, can become our very, very best friend and help deliver every right and proper desire we may have in life. This is because the power available to us through our deeper subconscious is infinite. The sheer scale, vastness, intensity and scope of the intelligent field of creation with which it communes has never been fully grasped, not by any human being that has ever lived. Oh, some have had a glimpse, a peek, but no one has really come close. Let me explain what I mean. Do you know what a placebo is?"

Paul, full of eager anticipation as this lesson progressed, nodded and replied, "Well it's some kind of dummy pill, or something, isn't it?"

Maya confirmed, "Well, there are all kinds of placebos, but you've picked one of the most well-known examples. For instance, if a drug company was considering launching a new drug into the market place, a number of controlled experiments would be needed before official clearance could be given. These would begin with laboratory tests and, if the results were satisfactory, they would then move on to clinical trials, where they would test the drug on people suffering from the particular ailment the drug was designed to cure. As part of the clinical trials, a placebo would be introduced because of the effect the mind can have on healing. Putting it very simply, volunteers are taken from a pool of people that suffer from the particular ailment concerned. The volunteers are split into two equal groups in relation to age, weight, sex, social background and condition of the ailment. One group gets the drug and one group doesn't, but both groups believe they are taking the drug. The reality is that only half of them are actually taking the drug; the other half are taking identical-looking tablets that contain an inert substance, like chalk or sugar, something that will do no harm nor any good to anyone taking it. That is the placebo.

"What is key here is that all the volunteers believe they are taking a drug that has produced good results in the laboratory or for other people suffering from the same ailment. In fact, even the people giving out the tablets and the instructions don't know which volunteers are being given the drug and which are being given the placebo. The principal reason for that is so no accidental indication can be given to the volunteers regarding which tablet they have been given. And do you know what percentage of volunteers who are taking a placebo show significant improvements in their particular medical condition?"

Paul looked bemused but answered, "Well, if they are not actually taking the drug, it will be a very low number, surely? What about 5%, something like that?" Maya smiled and said, "The facts are that it can be anywhere from 14% to 30%! Even though they are effectively taking nothing! This just gives us a glimpse of the power and potential of the mind, when the right beliefs are put there. Let's face it, the volunteers taking the placebo do show significant improvements in their medical condition, and many of them are completely cured, but what is it that makes them better? This is a terrific example of mind over matter, because the actual matter they are taking is a neutral substance, it does no harm and it does no good. Yet 14–30% of people get significantly better!

"This just shows us how obedient and effective our deeper subconscious can be at delivering into the physical realm what we believe deeply in the thought realm, irrespective of what the outside or external circumstances may be, or what the truth or reality might be. In fact, when it comes to health, energy and vitality, as you work with this you will learn that the brain is an incredible laboratory that can produce any combination of chemicals required to cure any ailment that we, as human beings, may develop, including ageing! We are only just beginning to discover the depths to which we can use this for our good and the greatest good of all humankind. We've not yet discovered how to tap into this power on demand but we are getting closer to it.

"The most important message here is this: the deeper subconscious doesn't deliver into our lives what is true; it delivers on what it **believes** to be true! The truth is irrelevant in this context. We have to be very careful about the beliefs we build and the power behind their manifestation."

Paul was flabbergasted, "I can see what you're talking about," he said, "in fact, more than see it, I can feel it. I can feel that power within me, working through me, all around me."

Maya replied calmly, "Most people can, once it is pointed out to them. It's a bit like the 'Fs', isn't it?" Paul nodded in agreement and Maya continued, "In fact, it goes well beyond the realms of our conscious understanding, in terms of the power of our deeper subconscious. For instance, with some Aboriginal tribes in Australia, studies have shown that when the belief in the tribe is very strong regarding certain customs and behaviours, incredible things happen. There have been reported cases of tribesmen disgracing themselves within the Aboriginal society in which they live and being made outcast. Being made outcast means certain punishments are handed out according to their traditions. At the most serious level of punishment, the belief is that, when they are made outcast, they must leave the tribe and sit at the bottom of a specially selected large tree in a clearing in the bush. Everyone in the tribe knows what the outcome will be: within a period of 48 hours, the outcast will die. This belief is so deeply rooted in the psyche of every member of the tribe, that the mortality rate is 100%.

"Nowadays post-mortems are carried out on dead outcasts, and do you know what the cause of death is?" Before Paul could even hazard a guess, Maya went on, "Nothing! Nothing at all! They die of nothing! At least, nothing physical like you would expect, an aneurism or heart attack or something. It's as if they not so much die as just stop living. This can be a bit difficult to follow, but can you imagine having the power up here, in our minds",

Maya tapped her head, "to be able to slow down the way every organ in the body functions, the way the heart beats, the way blood circulates through the body, the way all your major organs function, to the point where they all shut down together, causing death? It's on the outer margin of my comprehension, but I can believe it, can't you?"

Paul replied calmly, "Of course I can. I saw my grandfather do something very similar when my grandma died. He wasn't part of a tribe like the Aborigines, but he had an element of thinking completely conditioned into him. He was a fit, healthy individual for his age, and could do anything around the house. He doted on my grandma, but she, sadly, was not blessed with the best of health, and he constantly said to himself, and everyone and anyone else who would listen, that he would not be able to live without her. When she died, he lasted just 3 months. He just fell apart after his reason for living, my grandma, his wife, had gone."

Maya could see the depth of Paul's feelings; he was hurting. "A lot of people have experienced that with loved ones", she said. "Yeh, I know," replied Paul, "but what I didn't know, until now, was what was happening to my grandfather. He actually brought it on himself, didn't he?" Maya replied with a sigh, "We bring everything upon ourselves. What we're learning about here isn't physical or biological, it's metaphysical and metabiological. The message should be clear now. The deeper subconscious doesn't work on delivering what's true; it works on delivering what we believe to be true. It delivers on belief, not truth!"

Paul was shaken, "So, what you are saying is that we had better be very careful about what thoughts are filling up our minds and what beliefs we are building. Because, eventually, the internal beliefs we have will appear in our real world?"

Maya nodded, "That is exactly what I am saying. The fact that human beings become, on the outside, what they think about on the inside, is one of the fundamental great universal laws. It has been known since time immemorial, and yet, until now, no one has truly grasped its significance in delivering into our lives heaven on Earth, or hell on Earth, simply through our thinking.

"Some of the great spiritual leaders have got close to it and, in fact, every spiritual work ever written says this somewhere. I've picked the book of Proverbs in the Bible as an example, 'As a man **thinketh** in his heart, so is **he**'. Or, in other words, 'What you **thinketh** is what you **iseth**!'" Paul laughed out loud. "OK, OK," said Maya, "I know it isn't quite as eloquent as Proverbs, but the meaning is there all the same. Our thoughts and deepest-held beliefs create the undercurrent that determines the direction in which our lives move. Our lives will continue to move unerringly in that direction, no matter where the winds and the tides on the surface may be taking us!

"The key to happiness, success, wealth, health, fabulous relation-ships, vitality, begins with controlling our thinking and the beliefs they are constantly building. People who wait for circumstances on the outside to change will struggle with taking control of their lives, because they do not understand, acknowledge or use the power of this element of the great universal and unchanging laws. A big step towards taking complete control of our lives is this: human beings **become**, on the outside, what they **think** about most on the inside. **Always have this in the forefront of your mind.**"

Paul was flushed with excitement, "I have really got to grips with this as a concept. It is *so* clear to me. It makes *so* much sense and explains *so* many things."

"Good," said Maya, "we will leave it here for now, because we have had a long session tonight. Reflect on the lessons learned, relate them to events in your own life, and try not to explain this to anyone else at this stage. I know this is difficult to do, because you can see how powerful it is and how much you can help other people. However, it needs to be explained properly, otherwise people won't understand, and their comments may well begin to undermine your, what is still a fledgling, belief in how these great universal laws work. Also, add one more affirmation to the others you are saying day and night: '**My thoughts are an integral part of the power that make up the unseen universal force that is the field of creation**'. Hammer it into your very being to awaken your untapped potential. I'll see you soon." And with that, Maya left.

Chapter Eleven

For the next week, Paul was absorbed with his thinking, and everyone else's come to that. He tuned in deeply to his thoughts and beliefs and found for himself that human beings really do become what they think about most, and that everyone can prove it for themselves if they just study it for a short while. They can study their own thinking to prove it, or they can study other peoples' thinking. Either way, the evidence is incontrovertible, beyond question.

Reflecting on his own experiences, he remembered becoming involved in certain situations when he knew, absolutely knew, that 'it would all end in tears', and surprise, surprise, it eventually did! Every time!

He tried to climb inside other peoples' heads and listen intently to their thinking, and there it was for all to see: their own thinking being projected onto the three-dimensional movie screen called life. 'Oh, relationships never work out for me', some people would claim and, on closer examination, you'd find that they'd had one disastrous relationship after another, and learned nothing from it, and were now heading towards yet another disaster!

Paul was beginning to realise, up until this point in his life, how much negative thinking he had done and by how much he had been, and still was, surrounded by it. He really struggled at times during that week because he felt he was being suffocated by all the negative thinking around him.

He found that his refuge, his lifeline, in the sea of negativity that surrounded him was his affirmation, '**My thoughts are an integral part of the power that is the unseen universal force that is the field of creation**'. It ignited a feeling of well being at his very core, one that radiated out from his centre and kept at bay all the outside negative influences that came in his direction. The feeling was electrifying. He felt safe. He felt invincible.

This feeling created a space within which he could focus upon his thoughts and begin to replace negative thoughts with positive ones. This gave him not only great comfort and even joy, it gave him an enormous feeling of being in control and, therefore, the feeling of invincibility just grew and grew well beyond anything he had previously experienced. As his thoughts became more positive and empowering, he became more positive and powerful. As his thoughts became more constructive, creative and energetic, so did he. The link between the two could be established empirically within a week. He now knew he was ready for the next part of the lesson on understanding and applying the great, unchanging universal laws. At the very moment he thought it, the phone rang. It was Maya, and this time he was not surprised in the slightest that she'd called him when she did.

"Hi, Maya," Paul acknowledged confidently into the arrangement of plastic and metal that was his mobile phone. "I thought it would be you. No, no," he corrected, "I knew it would be you."

Maya answered, "I don't have to ask you a thing. I can tell from your voice that you are ready for the next lesson. Shall I see you at the usual place tonight at 7.30?" Paul answered, "That would be just perfect."

At 7.30 p.m. they met; Maya radiated her usual glow that attracted everyone's attention, and this time Paul looked different. He looked healthy, happy, relaxed and assured, and Maya noticed his glow. Maya commented that he looked different and Paul said it was only a tiny reflection of what was going on inside.

Maya began, "Paul, without realising it fully, you are beginning to co-operate intelligently with the universal force that created everything and connects everything, and the laws that govern how to use it for your highest good and for the highest good of all humankind. You're allowing the universal force to work through you; you've stopped being isolated and separate, and it is visible and tangible on the outside. I and everyone else can see and feel it. This means the fire, stoked with your desire and belief, has been well and truly lit on the inside. This is now an eternal flame that will never be extinguished for two reasons: firstly, because you have been guided to this point, and secondly, and this is by far the more significant, because you have lit your own fire, and that is a monumental step to taking control and achieving your every right and proper desire in life.

"Many people look to other people to light their fires for them, and many do have them lit for them. However, unbeknown to them, they then subconsciously put the fire out with their own thinking. However, you have taken the beacon from me and lit your own fire and now you've begun to fuel it on your own. You have, as a result, taken control, which means you are now ready for the next step.

"What you are going to discover next is how our deepest beliefs get built inside our minds with our own thoughts, our own experiences and with other people's thoughts, opinions and experiences. We are going to examine this at a level that is so deep and straightforward that you will then be able to build any new and desired belief you may want in a way that ensures it will always be delivered for you by your deeper subconscious."

Paul leaned forward and said, "I am all ears."

"Well," Maya said, "understanding how our current beliefs got built into our inner subconscious is a fundamental step towards learning how to take control in the future by only building the beliefs we want. But how did our existing ones get there? Human beings all think on a multi-dimensional level; in fact, it's a three-dimensional thought process that builds our beliefs."

Maya unfolded a piece of paper and pushed it in front of Paul, "These are the dimensions in which we think; we think in words, we think in pictures, and we think in feelings and emotions:

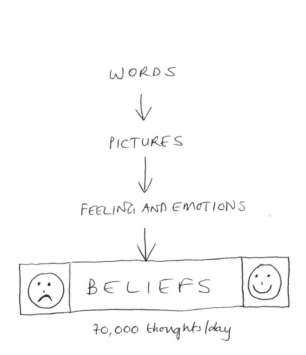

"More importantly, we each individually process a minimum of 70,000 thoughts each and every day. So, if you think of your inner subconscious beliefs or self-image as a canvas for a painting, more than 70,000 brushstrokes get added to it daily. Now, it is also important to understand that sometimes the word-type thoughts immediately give rise to picture-type thoughts because of their very nature. For instance, if I say to you, 'Please don't think of a pink elephant, *do not* think of a pink elephant', what do you see in your mind's eye?"

Paul smiled and said, "Well, a pink elephant, of course."

"That's exactly what I mean," Maya continued. "The words we use sometimes trigger the clearest pictures imaginable and words and/or pictures can trigger really vivid and tangible feelings and emotions. Just seeing a picture of a cute kitten, or a ghastly image of a starving child, can trigger very different feelings and emotions. In fact, you don't even need a picture. Sometimes just the words will do it. For example, if your boss called you at home on a Sunday night, and the only words he uttered down the phone were, 'Paul, I want to see you tomorrow morning in my office at 8.30 sharp; it's about money' and then slammed the phone down, how will you feel for the rest of the evening?"

Paul said, "Well it would be horrible. I'd be worried all night about what he might think he has discovered, even though I knew I'd got nothing to worry about and a clear conscience!"

"That's the point. All our thoughts are stimulated by a whole variety of occurrences, and they can begin in one dimension, i.e. words, and travel through the pictures dimension and into the feelings and emotions dimension. However, the key is that, no matter what dimension of thought they begin or end in, they are all adding brushstrokes onto the inner subconscious canvas that is our beliefs, and are, therefore, being used to reinforce existing beliefs and build brand new beliefs. And, these beliefs, as you know, can be positive and constructive ones, or negative and destructive ones."

Maya pointed to the positive side of the 'Beliefs' and to the negative side, "And, remember, our inner subconscious doesn't have a valve or filter on it that rejects the negatives. It just accepts whatever thoughts we send it, positive or negative, as the truth. And, if we send it enough thoughts about a particular subject, it becomes for us a belief that will eventually turn up in our real world. Remember a point I've mentioned before: whatever we believe with feeling becomes a self-fulfilling prophecy in our lives.

"Not all the three dimensions of thought have the same impact on building our belief structure in our inner subconscious minds. For example, which, in your opinion, of the three dimensions of thought has the greatest impact on our inner subconscious beliefs, words, pictures or feelings and emotions?"

Paul answered quickly, "Well, feelings and emotions, of course, they must be the most powerful of the three dimensions of thought by miles, aren't they?"

Maya nodded and assured Paul that he was correct, "You're right, feelings and emotions are by far the most powerful dimension. In fact, let me ask you something that demonstrates the point: have you ever met someone new who, within the first few minutes of meeting them, has said something or done something to you that rubbed you up the wrong way or really upset you?" Paul nodded and replied, "Yes, quite a few times." Maya continued, "And from that one experience of them, one that affected you at a deep level of feeling and emotion, how long did it take you to get over that experience, which, because of its sheer intensity, had become a negative belief about them?"

Paul replied, "Well, in some instances, I've still not got over it. No matter how close I may get to these people, there is always a nagging doubt in my mind somewhere that there is something not quite right about them."

Maya went on, "Well, apparently, these feeling and emotion-type thoughts can be 90% effective at making a lasting impression on our inner subconscious belief structures. Just from one incident that may have happened and then been repeated in our minds a good few times at a deep level of intensity. Such a thought can very quickly become a life-long belief.

"Picture-type thoughts have the second most impact and are up to 15% effective at making a lasting impression on our inner subconscious belief structures, and word-type thoughts have the least impact. It's reckoned that word-type thoughts are up to only 3% effective at making a lasting impression, providing that no picture or feeling and emotion thoughts are connected with them. Now, what you will find both interesting and revealing is this: when we want to proactively try to change the way someone behaves, or someone proactively tries to change the way we behave, what dimension is usually used?"

Paul responded with a forlorn, "Well, with words, of course. Loads of instructions are thrown at us: 'be more positive', 'stop being sloppy with the detail', 'take proper care of the customers' and the like, delivered to us as spoken words or in a new procedures manual." Maya asked further, "Are they usually well-chosen words specifically designed to create a spectacular picture of what it looks like when the required task is completed? Are they words that emphasise the stunning feelings and emotions that will be associated with its completion?" Paul was aware he was on the brink of another dawning of understanding when he replied, "Well, no, never; well, maybe not never, but rarely." Maya proceeded, "So does the task get done?" Paul concluded, "Well, only begrudgingly or after a load of coercion and threats, and often not to anything like the standard required."

Maya continued, "You see, we've all forgotten what it means to be a human being, to be true *Homo sapiens*. Did you know that *Homo sapiens* directly translated means 'thinking man'?" Paul shook his head, "No, I didn't know that." Maya proceeded, "The only element of your being that makes you human is your mind, everything else you can find in horses, pigs, cows, etc. The only thing you can't is a mind. You see, we are a mind with a body, not a body with a mind. The mind is unique and eternal, the body is not. Let me explain what I mean.

"Ninety-nine per cent of the atoms that make up our body are replaced every year, including those that make up our brain cells, and yet our memories and what is stored in our minds stays with us! So what is real and eternal as long as we exist here? The mind, with all its pictures and images? Or the body, 99% of which decays in its entirety, and passes into the earth each year?"

Paul was stunned by these facts as Maya continued. "Now, don't get me wrong here. It is very important that we look after our bodies because, when our body is healthy and working at its peak, we can help deliver the mind's beliefs and desires more effectively into the physical realm. Have you ever just known, I mean really known, that something is going to happen and then, within hours, days or weeks, it does?"

Paul gushed, "Loads and loads of times!" Maya continued, "And with some of them, it just seemed like a whole series of coincidences, chance encounters etc., had conspired and combined to make some of these things come about?" Paul again gushed, "If I told you about some of them, you would think they are beyond logic, reason or explanation. They are beyond the physical." Maya responded calmly with, "Yes, but nothing is beyond the workings of the great universal laws. Nothing is beyond the creative force that acts as such a loyal and obedient servant to deliver our deepest knowings into the real world for us.

"Therefore, its infinite power is at our disposal, and the outcome is inevitable. But for us to be able to co-operate intelligently and allow the unchanging laws to work for us, we need to abandon such primitive methods of thinking as coincidence and luck. The powers we can and do invoke are indeed beyond the physical. They are, literally, metaphysical. Logic, reason, explanation cannot even begin to describe what is at work with these laws. The laws are beyond all conventional thinking and explanations, which is why there are so many sceptics about its power and effectiveness. They want logical, well-reasoned proof of its existence. To see it, feel it, touch it, measure it, etc., which is nonsense. We don't have the technology currently to do that. We can't yet see something so vast and infinite and eternal. But we can always see the effects of it. It's all around us, if we can just abandon our conventional and primitive thinking for a short while. And there is one way to prove whether it exists or not, and that is to try it! The only proof we need is to put it into action for ourselves and see the results! A little effort and perseverance will prove beyond any doubt that there is a system of practice, within the reach and capability of every human being, that allows each one of us to develop the conditions for us to take complete control of the effects that this universal force can deliver. This is the power to which all things are connected, that resides within, and works through, us so that we can master all the conditions and circumstances in our lives."

"Oh boy," Paul replied, "when do I get the chance to learn it?" Maya smiled at his obvious enthusiasm, "Not quite yet. Before you get the keys that will open all the doors to health, wealth, happiness, joy and success, you need the one key that will unlock the door of the prison cell you are currently in. Before you can hope to learn how it will all work for you in the future, you need to understand why it hasn't worked the way you wished for in the past, OK?"

Paul conceded to this with a nod, "OK," he said, "OK."

Maya explained further, "As you know, the inner subconscious mind is fed, nourished, shaped and formed by the thoughts sent to it in the form of words, pictures or feelings and emotions from the outer conscious mind. And, once these thoughts are accepted by the inner subconscious as a belief, the deeper subconscious effectively instructs all the infinite forces in the universe to work through us to find the resources and circumstances required to turn it into an external physical reality. However, we need to be careful here, because, as we've mentioned before, the inner subconscious mind does not judge or discriminate between all the thoughts, pictures and images. It simply accepts as reality those things that are consistently fed to it in sufficient quantities by our outer conscious mind via our three-dimensional thinking.

"Now, this means that most of our three-dimensional thinking is guided by events that we see and hear on the outside of us, in the physical realm. What we see and hear in the outer world, and especially the thoughts and opinions of other people, are then fed into our central processing unit, i.e. our three-dimensional thinking, and deposited into our inner subconscious minds as real or true. And, for the most part, what do you think that most of the 70,000 thoughts that get processed every day are like? Are they the positive, constructive, dynamic ones that reinforce and remind us of the gifts, talents, abilities, creativity and determination we all possess? Do they focus on the things we want to show up in our lives? Or are they the negative, destructive, discouraging and disempowering ones, that reinforce and remind us how useless and worthless we are, and focus on all the things we don't want to show up in our lives?

"To help you answer this one, let's think of our three-dimensional thinking as self-talk, or a little chatterbox that goes on in our heads all day long." Maya reclaimed the piece of paper she had written on earlier and added a couple of things:

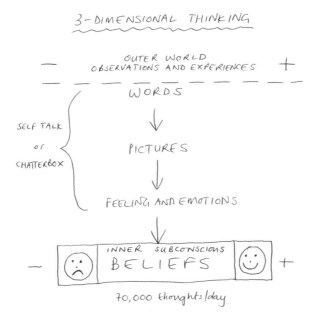

"You see, our outer world observations and experiences, together with things we see, hear and are told, tend to be what we feed into the central processing unit that is our three-dimensional thinking. And if we, through repetitive thought patterns, focus on just a few of those things, those are the ones that get locked into our inner subconscious as beliefs, and then the deeper subconscious automatically swings into action to instruct the universal force and power to deliver the circumstances and situations required to turn those beliefs into a physical reality.

"But, if you are like most people, and you are, and if you are like I was just 6 months ago, and you are, what do we tend to dwell on in our own three-dimensional thinking? Our gifts, our talents; our ability to overcome all the challenges and obstacles that life throws at us? Our invincibility when we really put our minds to something? No! No, no, no! Not a chance! We have a tendency to dwell and focus on our pitfalls, our inadequacies, our embarrassing moments, the stupid things we've done, the mistakes we've made. We are constantly reminding ourselves of our shortfalls and how useless, worthless and powerless and out of control we are! Do you agree?" Paul nodded.

Maya continued, "So, for the most part, the thoughts and opinions of other people that get directed towards us are negative, and a lot of the thoughts and opinions we direct towards ourselves are negative. So is it any wonder most people's lives turn out the way they do? Most people believe that life is negative and a struggle. It is meant to be miserable; no matter what we do, we end up defeated and beaten. They believe that joy, abundance, happiness, health and success are for others, not for them. And, guess what? Once again, whatever you believe with feeling becomes a self-fulfilling prophecy!"

Once again, Paul was taken aback by the simple yet profound message Maya was telling him, "You are absolutely, 100% right! In fact, until the last few weeks when you've been guiding me through all this stuff, I thought I was going mad! Pressure at work, pressure at home, pressure about my finances, worries about my health; my whole mind was a maelstrom of doubts and fears and worries. My self-talk or chatterbox, as you called it, was diabolical. In fact, and you're the only person I've told this, it got so bad just after Christmas last year, I contemplated ending it all. I had completely lost faith in myself, in other people and in the world I lived in. Suicide, for a while, seemed like the only way out, and I felt like that for quite a while. I was still at the bottom of a deep, deep ocean when you got in touch with me again. You have, in many ways, rescued me."

Maya replied modestly, "I don't think rescue is the word. You've come such a long way; no, sorry, we, we've both come such a long way and that type of thinking is well behind us now. There's a really exciting journey ahead for you, learning and mastering the system of practice within the great, unchanging universal laws that will allow you to develop the circumstances with which you can take complete control of your life.

"In a nutshell, the laws operate like this: whenever a thought, picture or image is held firmly in our inner subconscious mind, and there are no conflicting thoughts, pictures or images present, the great, creative force that connects all things, works through us to put its infinite power behind manifesting it externally. The fixed pictures and images firmly held in the inner subconscious mind with heart-felt feelings are the spawning and hatching ground of the actual things themselves! Once they have become real in the thought realm, the whole basis of understanding and using these laws is that anything, and I mean anything, that becomes real in the thought realm is delivered with unerring certainty and accuracy into the physical realm. The great universal laws operate from our inner subconscious mind through our bodies via our behaviour. Therefore, our inner subconscious mind is the master, and our body is the servant. It's the servant that uses our inexhaustible resources to find whatever circumstances are necessary to ensure the outcome. Our body is the vehicle through which our inner subconscious mind functions. It is our instrument of external expression of internal belief, that's all, and a fine one at that!

"And," Maya continued, "you have taken a massive step forward tonight because, if you think about what I've said for a moment, and the process that goes on in our minds, what have you discovered?"

Paul's response was strong, clear and unequivocal, "I've discovered that what we've experienced in our outer conscious world is merely a reflection of the pictures and beliefs we imprint onto our inner subconscious world. And the picture we imprint onto our inner subconscious world is merely an accumulation of all the thoughts we've had over time on the three different dimensions: words, pictures, feelings and emotions.

"This turns on its head the traditional approach to changing behaviour. We need to concentrate and focus on the input; the output then takes care of itself. Marvellous! I've also discovered that feelings and emotions are the most powerful dimension of our thought process when it comes to having an impact on the inner subconscious belief structure, with pictures the next most powerful and words next. However, every single thought has an impact and puts a brushstroke on the inner subconscious canvas, no matter how minute. And I've discovered, big time, that most of the thoughts I have are negative and destructive ones that highlight my pitfalls, inadequacies, shortfalls, fears, insecurities, the mistakes I've made and the daft and stupid things I've done in my life, together with the really embarrassing ones. I now realise two things: firstly that, because of my thinking, I really am my own worst enemy and, secondly, that I am totally responsible for everything that occurs in my life, everything, good, bad or indifferent. I am actually in control of the whole process, although I've not realised it to this extent until now."

"And?" Maya asked encouragingly. "And," Paul said calmly, "my mind has consistently produced for me, in my life on the outside, a generous crop of what I have been sowing on the inside with my thoughts at the inner subconscious level. Yes, even including my ulcers when I was 20 years old!"

Maya looked at him quizzically and Paul elaborated, "Do you remember when I was diagnosed as having ulcers when I was 20 years old? It shook me up pretty badly. I mean, having ulcers at any age is pretty serious, but at 20 years old, it is more than serious, it is potentially deadly! The prognosis is not very good if the condition continues into your 40s or 50s. But, I have now just realised when it all started, and why I have suffered with all my stress-related illnesses in recent years. In fact, I can pin-point the start of all my problems to one specific incident in my past. Do you remember when we were 14 years old and I was going out with Belinda Formby?"

Maya responded, "Do I remember it! You bet! You were the talk of the school. You were both besotted with each other. It was the first, serious relationship in our year." Paul continued, "Yeh, it was, but it was all very innocent really. The odd snog and bit of a fumble was about as serious as it got! In fact, the highlight of our relationship was me walking her home from school every night. And that, on my part, was real dedication to Belinda, because she lived in Cement City, if you remember, which was on the other side of town to where I lived. So to walk her home, I used to go miles out of my way, but she was worth it, because she was gorgeous and our relationship made me the envy of the entire male population at school!"

Maya agreed with a hearty, "That's true!" Paul went on, "Anyway, as time went on and the relationship developed, the walking her home got more and more problematical. Not because of Belinda; she was terrific. It was because she was not the only person from school who lived in Cement City. Loads of others did too, including about 4 or 5 of my so-called mates. They got into the habit of following us on our journey towards Belinda's home. Well, it doesn't take a genius to work out what kind of comments 4 or 5 hormone-riven 14-year-olds were making about us and to us. It was really embarrassing for us both. And, to make matters worse, if you let on that you were annoyed, they'd do it all the more! So we did our best to ignore it. And, for me, that was not very easy, when most of the comments were cheeky, rude, disgusting and even biologically impossible!" Both Paul and Maya chortled.

"Well, this one day in particular after school has stuck in my mind and it's only now, tonight, after our discussion, that the true impact of this on my life has become clear. When I used to walk Belinda home, there was a certain point where we parted. It was at a cross-roads about 300 metres from her front door. There were two reasons for this. One was because at that cross-roads one road took me back towards my home. The second, and main, reason, however, was that it gave me a 300 metre head start on Belinda's father if he ever decided to chase me off for seeing his daughter! This particular afternoon, after we had said our goodbyes and I was crossing the road, Belinda called out asking me to bring my geography homework into school early the next morning so she could copy it, or something like that, and I said OK. The so-called mates of mine, who had not gone more than 5 metres away from both of us for the entire journey home, seized on this. 'Oh God,' they all cried out in a disgusted manner, 'sharing their homework now! Urghh. Cooie, cooie; they'll be moving in together next!' You know the type of thing.

"Anyway, I tried to brush it aside with an 'Oh, get out of it, it's nothing to make a fuss over'. Then Belinda looked at me lovingly and said 'bye, bye' and blew me a kiss; and I automatically blew her one back. My mates went wild: 'Yuk! Did you see that? Blowing kisses at each other now! It makes you feel sick to watch! Yuk, yuk, yuk!' So, feeling somewhat defensive and very self-conscious, I was concentrating on fending off their barrage of insults and lost my spatial awareness; as I turned around to walk away, I collided head first with a lamp post! I hit that thing so hard it nearly knocked me into the middle of next week! Fancy doing that in front of my girlfriend and a group of mates: imagine my embarrassment! Quickly, and in order to avoid any further mocking and jibing, I tried to play it down, even though I was seeing stars. 'Ho, ho, ho,' I said, 'that's nothing! Just a little bump, that's all.' To this day I don't know how I managed to speak. I walked off in the direction of home, acting nonchalantly, until I was out of their sight behind a large wall. As soon as I was out of their sight, I collapsed into a heap on the ground, clutching my head and in terrible pain. But, in as much pain as I was, what do you think I still heard over the wall from my mates, who were now meandering slowly towards their homes?"

Maya replied, "A bit of laughing?" Paul continued, "A bit? a bit? It was hysterical laughing, guffawing and screeching, and as soon as it died down, within a couple of seconds it was back again, with the volume turned up! I was wrecked! I was embarrassed! I was humiliated! I felt stupid and clumsy enough about it happening in the first place, but every time I heard them laugh, I relived the whole of the embarrassing incident in my mind. And, of course, every time I relived it, the initial feelings intensified; the embarrassment, the humiliation, the pain, all increased as I relived and replayed it in my mind. So, after just 5 minutes, I had programmed into my inner subconscious all these negative thoughts and images of how stupid I was, how clumsy and awkward I was, particularly around women. And, not only was this programming negative, it was in the feelings and emotions dimension of thought: the most powerful element. And, from that moment on, as I continued to relive and replay it, I was scarred for life, on the inside anyway, in terms of how any relationship with the opposite sex was going to turn out!"

Maya interjected, "That is a classic example of what you've discovered today, but was that the end of it, after those 5 minutes?" Paul exclaimed, "You've got to be joking! Every step of the way home, I relived it in my mind, without any prompting from my mates' laughter, and every step of the way, in my mind, the whole thing got worse, more embarrassing, more humiliating. My mind distorted and exaggerated the incident all on its own. But then, to make matters worse, when I got home my Mum was waiting for me. As soon as I walked in the house, with a big bruise on my forehead, she asked, with concern, 'Oh, what have you done now, you clumsy thing? You are always bumping into things: you are one of the clumsiest people I've ever known!' Oh thank you, mother dear, I thought. Just what I needed, in case I'd forgotten what a clumsy, awkward so-and-so I was, especially around women! My mother, without realising it of course, was reinforcing my own negative thinking, and adding real substance to my belief. It might only have been words she was using, but they insinuated enough ridicule to trigger spectacular pictures in my mind, and powerful, negative, feelings and emotions. So, more programming was going on from all three dimensions of thinking, all negative. By the time my own self-talk or chatterbox got hold of this reinforcement, hundreds of negative images were being imprinted on my mind every minute.

"Then my Dad came in from work, saw the bruise, laughed, and commented on how awkward and clumsy I was, as did my brother. I reckon that, if I process 70,000 thoughts a day, from about 4 o'clock in the afternoon on that particular day just about all my thoughts in all three dimensions, words, pictures, feelings and emotions, were about what an awkward, clumsy individual I was. So, what did I programme into my inner subconscious before I went to sleep that night? About 30,000 negative images!

"In fact," Paul continued, "I didn't stop thinking about it even when I was asleep, because I woke up throughout the night in a cold sweat!" Maya asked, "You mean you were even dreaming about it?" "Dreaming!" Paul responded, "Let me assure you, Maya, there was no 'dream' involved here; this, to me, was a nightmare! I kept waking up wondering how I could be so stupid and such a clumsy, stupid, awkward person. It strikes me, from what I've learned tonight, that this programming process never stops, day or night."

Maya nodded in agreement, "It never does, and what makes it worse, is that we distort, exaggerate and intensify the images. This simply intensifies the impact it makes on the inner subconscious belief structure. One of my favourite quotes that emphasises this point comes from Eleanor Roosevelt, former First Lady of the United States of America. Surrounded by vicious and acerbic people, she rose above it all; when asked how she did it, her reply was simple and insightful: 'No one can make you feel inferior without your consent'. You have to sanction and believe the negatives other people say about you, in order for it to steal some of the universal life force and for it to become a part of you. When you do this, you commit one of the greatest of crimes against yourself, because you cease to be the real you, the brilliant, unlimited, gifted and talented person you are designed to be. You become a rag-bag of every limiting and destructive opinion that anyone you've ever met has thrown at you, that, for whatever reason, you have decided to keep hold of in your mind.

"When this kind of negative thinking takes root in your mind, you lose your natural thinking ability and your insatiable curiosity to explore and find out more about the world you inhabit, and all the wonderful things you can achieve in it. The intense desire within you for knowledge and experience dries up, because you believe you're not worthy of those things. Your belief that you are useless, stupid, a mistake and an embarrassment, etc., kills your potentiality, and the conscious, learning, unlimited, evolving centre of creative intelligence that you really are will be lost to the world forever."

Paul was agitated and excited at the same time, as he asked, "But Maya, how do we take control and keep in control of our thoughts, when there is so much negativity around and when we are so conditioned to think negatively about ourselves, about other people and about the world we live in? And how do we help the people who are closest to us, my wife, my children? It's such a monumental task!"

Maya said reassuringly, "It's only a monumental task if you think it is! We have to do this one step at a time, one person at a time. However, what promise this holds in terms of what it can deliver for the world and humanity! It's a task worth trying, isn't it?" Paul replied, "You bet it is!"

Maya continued, "Well, before we can sort humanity out, there are a few techniques that you need to learn and master, in order to sort yourself out first. Once you know them, practise them and become brilliant at them, you'll be ready for the next stage of our journey. Are the affirmations you've been doing helping to intensify the pictures and feelings and emotions associated with them, as you say them each day?"

Paul replied that the effect was simultaneously awesome and blissful. Maya continued, "Well if you can make it back here tomorrow night, you can begin the process of taking control. Are you available?" Paul replied, "I am now. I'll see you at 7.30 p.m. here." Maya smiled and said, "I can hardly wait." They left the pub smiling and glowing. The force and power that is unlocked by using the universal laws properly was growing in both of them.

Chapter Twelve

Paul and Maya arrived in the car park of the pub at exactly the same time. It was choc-a-bloc. There was difficulty parking, so much so that they both had to park on a grass verge. The pub was heaving and standing room only; they couldn't even see their usual table let alone sit at it.

Paul spoke first, "Should we leave and go down the road to The Wild Boar? It's always quiet in there." Maya replied, "Er, let's just give it a minute or two." She was calm and relaxed, in spite of the hustle and bustle. Within 30 seconds, the barman rang a bell and exclaimed, "Excuse me everyone! Anyone who's here to attend The Sixties Golf Society Annual General Meeting is kindly requested to go now to The Red Room, which is through these doors on the right, where your captain and committee await you." Within a minute, there were 6 people left in the bar and Paul smiled knowingly at Maya, as they sat at their usual table, which was, by now, empty.

Paul began the conversation, "Maya, I've been buzzing since last night. The more I've thought about what I've discovered, with you as my guide, the more I know three things. Number 1: I am in complete control of my future. Number 2: I am responsible for everything that occurs in my life. Number 3: I have unlimited potential that can be used to achieve any right and proper desire.

"The key, however, is to control what we programme into our inner subconscious minds with our thoughts, because they are what eventually turn themselves into our beliefs. And, as soon as any belief is locked in place in the inner subconscious thought realm, a portion of the infinite life force that flows from us and through us is dedicated to making it happen in the physical realm, whether it is true or not, and whether it is good for us or not. Am I right?"

Maya smiled at the total grasp Paul had of these fundamental and crucial principles. She grinned from ear to ear when he continued with, "In fact, I have just realised for the first time that life is a matter of choice, not chance, as I have always thought. People's lives are an accumulation of the choices they have made regarding what to believe and what not to believe. And this is the scary bit, I've just realised that the truth is irrelevant! It's not what is true that matters. It's what you believe to be true that matters."

"Last night when I got home, I talked to Jackie about this, and she provided me with a great example. A friend of hers, Julie, is a man-hater. In fact, she is a total misanthrope. She thinks everyone in the world is horrible, especially men, and that people are out to take advantage of her, and they are only interested in getting what they want and, as soon as they've got it, they're gone! She comes round regularly to prove to Jackie that the world, the people in it, and men in particular, are like this, by providing example after example from her own experiences and those of friends and acquaintances she has spoken to. And examples from the television and out of the newspapers!

"Jackie is lovely, and always looks for the best in people, and she thinks that the world is a good place and that people are basically good and kind and, if you treat them well and with courtesy, they will always help you, especially men! She is constantly giving Julie alternative examples to consider. They just get rejected instantly by Julie, who retorts that 'people, and men in particular, are just not like that, or, if they are, it is only because you are an attractive woman and a soft touch and that is what they are responding to', etc., etc. Jackie is attractive on the outside, but she is even more attractive and appealing on the inside, because she always looks for, sees and therefore finds the best in others.

"So, the question we were asking ourselves last night was this, which one of these situations is true? Is the world a horrible place full of horrible people, particularly men, trying to take advantage? Or is the world a wonderful place full of decent people who want to help? And the startling discovery that we made was that both situations are true. The world will turn out to be whichever you decide upon. It is each individual's choice!

"It's as if the infinite and vast life force that lies within us all and that flows through us all is bursting to find outlets through which it can channel its full power. And these outlets are our beliefs, our three-dimensionally built, multi-sensory beliefs that we have assembled and chosen to hang in our mental wardrobe. And, whatever we've got in our wardrobe, that is all we can be seen wearing on the streets.

"These beliefs act as conduits by which the infinite universal creative force drives our internal images to become external realities. Nothing can prevent the internal belief externalising itself, because of the power of the universal force. The power is infinite, inexhaustible, vast and available at all times. The degree to which the power is used is determined by the intensity, clarity and depth of the belief. Being certain about something, totally certain, is enough to ensure it will become manifest. And, this is the strange realisation that hit me last night after you and I had talked, it will manifest itself, whether it is good for us or not, and whether it is in our best interests or not. It can't be emphasised enough that the universal force, and the creative power it has at its command, is servile. It applies itself with equal ferocity, subtlety and steadfastness to delivering whatever the belief you hook it to. As you've said before, it's like electricity; there it is sitting behind the socket in the wall, available to all, on tap. You don't need to see it or understand what electricity is, you just need to see and understand what you can do with it. All you need to do is plug an appliance into it, and you get whatever you attach it to. A refrigerator will keep things cold; a cooker will heat things up. The power, the force, the electricity is the same; its effects are determined by what appliance you connect it to. Attach the power to a heart pacemaker or a dialysis machine, and lives are extended. Attach it to an electric chair, and lives are extinguished! Last night I reached another level of learning and understanding of the universal force and how it is controlled and directed by the use of some simple and unchanging laws."

Maya nodded, "Much of the real discovery and understanding takes place away from our guiding sessions. Everyone discovers at their own pace and in their own way and, I have to say, you are a brilliant student."

Paul blushed and said, "Me, brilliant? A brilliant student! Well, that's a first. No one has ever said that to me before. Thank you!" He then continued, "But, I've not finished yet! There were some other things that I discovered last night, too." Maya smiled and said, "Why am I not surprised, Mr Brilliant!?" Paul blushed again, "Well, it is closely related to what just happened between us, Maya." Maya gave a puzzled smile and said, "Do go on." Paul elaborated, "Well, Jackie and I had a big discussion last night about the environment most people are brought up in and live in, and I was remembering what you have been saying about the impact opinions of other people, especially authority figures such as parents, teachers, bosses, etc., have on our inner subconscious beliefs.

"We realised that something major happens from the minute we are born. When we're first born, the input and stimuli we all get from other people is mainly unending praise, attention and affection. We receive total love and unconditional love. Lots of 'goo, goos' and 'gah, gahs'. In fact, when we are tiny babies, we can't do anything wrong. When we cry, we get picked up and cuddled: 'diddums', 'poor baby', 'it will be alright', 'Mummy is here', 'sshhh'. We get reassurance and affection by the bucketful. And babies respond brilliantly to the positive stimulation they get from other people.

"If a baby is sick all over someone's shoulder, it's a case of, 'poor little mite', 'have you got a temperature then? Ahhh'. If a baby gets held up and widdles all over the person holding it, everyone laughs and thinks it is cute. Babies are happily uninhibited, carefree; they are truly human at this stage of their lives.

"But things change as we grow up and become infants, as we start to explore our world, to learn about the world and everything in it; what things feel like, even when they're red hot or freezing cold, what things taste like, even when they're disgusting. All of a sudden the stimuli we get from other people changes. The words change, the tone of voice changes, the volume changes, even the way we get touched changes. 'No!', 'don't', 'naughty!', 'put that down!' As infants, we don't know that we're not supposed to pick up the toilet brush and put it into our mouths, do we? So having someone screaming 'don't' and 'you naughty boy' at the top of their voice doesn't really educate us about what that something is, and why we should or shouldn't be doing something. A few gentle and positive words are what are most appropriate at this point, but people believe that infants, because they can't speak, don't understand, but nothing could be further from the truth, right?"

Maya's look was one of admiration as Paul continued, "In fact, it is usually downhill from here on for infants, children and adults. The more we develop, explore, learn and try new things, a strange phenomenon occurs; the more we do something right, the less praise we get from others, and the more we do something wrong, the more criticism we get! So, apart from the very early months of our lives, from an early age a lot of what gets programmed into us from other people is what we can not or should not do! How limiting is that for us all?"

Maya asked, "Can you give me an example of what you mean?" Paul paused and said, "Oh, I'm sure I could give you a few, if you give me a minute." He was reflective and silent for about 5 seconds before he replied, with a slightly pale face, "Oh, God! There are so many; about my own children. Here's one from last Sunday: James, my 5-year-old son, was playing quite nicely in the lounge. In fact, he was doing a bit of drawing. It was lovely and quiet, which is a rare event in our household. I was reading the Sunday paper, and was engrossed in a story about our local football team. James came over to me with his drawing in his hand, and said, 'Dad, Dad, look what I've done for you'. He showed me a mighty good picture of our house, with a front and back garden, the fence and our family standing outside. In fact, for a 5-year-old, it was a masterpiece.

"Because he'd interrupted my peace and quiet, I was a little irked. So, with my concentration and enjoyment broken, I barked a sharp, "Yes son, yes, that's really good, well done." James, at 5 years old, only related to the words. He didn't catch the tone and inflection, and missed the, 'I am not happy at being interrupted' undertones in my voice. He just heard, 'that's really good' and 'well done'. As soon as praise registers in a child's mind, as approval or a positive stroke or reinforcement, a feeling of being valued, appreciated, loved floods the mind and body. James's automatic and natural response to that was, 'Oh, if you think that was good, wait until you see my next effort!'

"Off he goes and finds a bigger piece of paper and starts to draw our house and the two neighbouring ones. I settle down to read the paper again, while he beavers away, putting his heart and soul in to it. Ten minutes later, he comes to me again with a look of joy, achievement, anticipation and pride, and says, 'Dad! Dad! Look what I've done for you now'. This drawing is considerably better composition-wise and detail-wise but I, yet again, have been interrupted from the enjoyment of my paper, so I respond even more tersely than before, 'Yes, son! That's pretty good as well, excellent in fact!' This time my response is said through gritted teeth, but again James only hears the words, not the frustration and annoyance in the intonation. So again, he takes this as a positive comment, a real compliment. In fact, when it comes to compliments, when you get an 'excellent' from your Dad, it doesn't get much better than that, does it?

"Maybe not, but James knows he can do even better, and so again, filled with a feeling of appreciation, he goes and finds the biggest piece of paper in the house upon which to create a true masterpiece. Twenty minutes later, he appears bursting with pride and lifts up his picture, for which he has drawn the whole road we live in, and all the houses, and says, 'Dad! Dad! Look at what I've done for you now!' By this time, I'm ashamed to admit, I was really annoyed because I'd been interrupted from reading the paper three times. I just blurted out, 'What the heck is wrong with you son, can't you draw anything but houses'. He was crestfallen. I could see all his confidence and feeling of appreciation drain away right in front of my eyes.

"I now realise three things in particular. Firstly that, from a very early age, the more we do something right, the less praise we get, and the more we do something wrong the more rebuke we get! If that comes from people with influence around us, such as parents, teachers, friends, bosses, etc., it destroys the positive side of our associated beliefs. By dwelling on such comments in our minds we begin, through the repetition of the thought, to believe 'I can't do anything right'. Rather than run the risk of constantly not being able to do anything right, we withdraw from a lot of activities, and end up not doing very much of anything at all!

"Secondly, that the vast majority of comments made towards us by other people are negative. Jackie and I last night could not remember one recent compliment or positive comment we had received, either at home or at work. Not one! So, not only is our chatterbox or self-talk negatively wired, we either rarely, or never, get any positive inputs from outer world experiences, or observations from other people. Even though we do the majority of things in our lives, both personal and work related, perfectly well, they never, or at least very rarely, get pointed out to us. It's only the mistakes, etc., that get pointed out.

"And thirdly, words are actually the most powerful drug used by humankind. Well, not so much the words as the feelings and emotions triggered by the words. Words can bear fruit, or words can be poison to people, and most people don't have a very healthy diet! What most people don't realise is the impact words can have when we direct them to others in a careless and thoughtless way, and when we direct them to ourselves in a careless and thoughtless way. And, as I say, it is not so much the words *per se* but what is meant by them at the feeling and emotions level of thinking. I can call you a kitten or I can call you a cat; the words both describe a feline but what they mean to you is totally different. A kitten is lovable and cuddly and a cat can be anything but.

"Jackie reminded me last night of two quotes from the Bible that sum up what I've discovered on my journey with you up to now, and you'll know how difficult it is for me to quote these because I'm such an agnostic. They never made much sense before; they now do. One of these you mentioned to me the other night, and now it has much more significance for me. The other is new to me. In fact, Jackie and I concluded that every spiritual work ever written, whatever the creed or doctrine, probably has similar passages. They're brilliant.

"Quote number 1 is: 'As a man thinketh in his heart, so is he'.

"Quote number 2 is: 'In the beginning was the word, and the word was God' because, from the words we choose, we can build our own heaven or our own hell right here on Earth. It's pretty crystal clear, isn't it?"

Maya was beaming; her student was rapidly becoming a master, "You understand the principles and practices at a deeper level than anyone normally does at this stage of their journey. The examples you are telling me prove it. There is no doubt that, when the system of taking complete control is understood and put into practice by you, you will become a master of all the circumstances and situations in your life. This will enable you to have abundance in every area of your life: health, wealth, success, happiness, relationships, love, compassion, peace of mind, anything at all."

"So, when do I get to discover more about how to use this infinite creative force and the laws that govern it?" Paul enquired with eager anticipation. Maya replied, "At our next meeting. Tonight let's make sure you have completely nailed what we are talking about."

Maya continued, "The primary discovery here is that: 'human beings **become** on the outside what they **think** about on the inside. I know that you know this, but I can't emphasis enough how important it is, and the caveat that goes with it: 'whether it is good for them or not!' You see, as I've said before, our inner subconscious doesn't have a valve on it that springs into action when we send it negative thoughts or programming about ourselves, about other people and about the world we live in. It simply accepts, as the truth, whatever we consistently send it. Our outer world moves towards, and becomes a reflection of, what we think about most through the beliefs we have programmed in our own minds.

"What you have just described, with great accuracy, is the fact that, for the most part, the stimuli that we get from other people is negative and destructive. This negativity is then compounded by what we, in turn, give ourselves, which, for the most part, focuses on our shortfalls, pitfalls, inadequacies, mistakes, the stupid and embarrassing things we've done and the like. So, who the heck is looking after building up the positive side of our beliefs?" Paul shook his head as Maya continued, "Exactly! Nobody is!"

Maya elaborated, "In fact, with so many people their conditioning has been so negative they usually block out or reject any positive feedback they get or, even worse, they turn them into negatives. Have you ever been trained on how to give compliments sincerely, or on how to accept them graciously?" Paul shook his head vigorously, "No, never", he replied. Maya went on, "Now, knowing the power of influence that our comments can have on other people, wouldn't you think that that should be one of the first things we ever learn to do?" Paul nodded in vigorous agreement, "You bet!"

Maya continued, "Most people, if they actually receive a compliment or a positive comment of any kind, reject it by saying something like 'oh, it was nothing'. This means they turn an externally generated positive into an internally processed negative, one that reinforces and builds up the negative side of our beliefs, or self-image as it is sometimes called. Even worse, the majority of people have been conditioned to be highly suspicious of positive feedback coming from outside sources, so they often dismiss them and turn them into internal negatives, thinking along the lines of 'they're after something' or 'they are taking the mickey'. Do you agree? This kind of internal processing also adds to the negative side of our self-image or beliefs."

Paul exclaimed, "You are so right. We all do it, and we all do it all the time. Jackie and I touched on this last night; she asked me how many things I do right at work every day, or rather what percentage of the things I do, do I do right. I estimated it was probably 95% plus. Then she asked me how many of these are commented on by others, especially my bosses. I had to admit it was very few if any of them. She then went on to ask me what does get pointed out and, of course, that's all the things I do that are not quite right. We both concluded that, if you have that culture in an organisation, or a family even, for a year or two, let alone 15 years, it is no wonder that so many people end up believing they are useless, hating themselves, their jobs, their bosses and their partners! But, how do we change it?"

Maya said calmly, "It is actually very simple to have a positive and dramatic impact on our lives. Let me give you an example or two that I witnessed only yesterday when I was playing golf. The first example is, I think, obvious, the second one subtle.

"I was playing Anna, who is a keen and enthusiastic golfer but not very good, or at least not yet. We were matching each other hole for hole in our scoring. On the 17th fairway, after we both had hit good tee-shots, I pushed my approach shot to the green into a deep bunker on the right-hand side of it. Anna then hit the most beautiful 7-iron onto the green and it finished about 6 inches from the hole! Even though I was inwardly cursing, because I was certainly going to lose the hole and probably the game, I called over to Anna 'nice shot'; she replied simply, 'thank you'.

"And, that's it, Paul. It's as simple as that. Giving compliments or positive comments to others is simple. Just catch them doing something right and tell them, and tell them with sincerity. That shouldn't be difficult if you look around. And in response to compliments and positive feedback, a simple 'thank you' ensures the whole good experience is posted onto the positive side of our self-image. The effect can be energising and electrifying. I think it was Mark Twain who once said, 'I can survive for 2 months just on one good compliment!'

"Another way to have a positive effect is to change what we give ourselves in terms of inputs and instructions regarding our beliefs or self-image. An example of this also happened when I was playing golf with Anna yesterday. She had never played at my club before, so she treated us both to three new golf balls as a bit of a 'thank you' for being invited to play. Now, Anna didn't start her round very well; by the 5th hole, she had lost two of her new balls. She was devastated, and told me she can often go for weeks without losing any balls at all. On the 6th hole, which is a short par 3 only measuring 145 yards from tee to green, there is a hellish tee-shot. The green is surrounded on three sides by water and it has really steep banks so, if you miss the green, you go into the water.

"Faced with the tough shot over the water, I saw Anna go to her golf bag and pull out two balls. One was the last brand new one, never yet struck in anger. The other was an old ball she had obviously been playing with for weeks. With both balls in her hand, she took another appraising look at the shot she had to play, and then put the brand new ball back in her bag. She had picked, automatically and subconsciously, the old ball. There was no big debate going on in her head; it was a very subtle decision-making process.

"With the decision made, she walked onto the tee, placed her old, scruffy ball on a tee-peg, had a couple of practice swings and, guess what happened when she hit the ball?" Paul answered, "Well, she put it into the water, of course!" Maya said, "Correct," and continued, "she put the ball straight into the water! And why? If you remember what we have learnt so far, she couldn't really do anything else. Human beings become on the outside what they think about on the inside, whether it is good for them or not! What must Anna have been thinking about, as indicated by the fact that she chose her old ball? She must have been thinking something like, 'It doesn't really matter if this ball goes in the water'." Paul nodded, "Right!"

Maya went on, "By thinking, 'I'd better play with the old ball', she must also have been saying to herself, 'just in case it goes in the water.' So, what was she picturing herself doing? Yes! Putting it in the water. In fact, immediately after hitting the shot she looked at me and said with frustration, 'I knew, I flipping well knew, I was going to do that!' Well, of course she did! She knew, subconsciously, what she had chosen to focus on in her mind: putting the ball in the water and not putting it on the green was going to happen, and it did.

"She predicted the outcome with her decision to use the old ball and the thinking that went with it. In fact, she preordained it with her thinking, and the pictures and feelings and emotions associated with her thinking. We can and do set ourselves up for failure sometimes without even consciously realising it! I've mentioned this before, and now you'll understand what's behind it. How many times have you done something like that in your mind when you *knew* it was going to end in tears, or disaster of some kind, and how many times were you right? "Paul nodded knowingly, "Every single time. I was right about every one of them!"

"I think you've got to the end of the first part of your journey; you've got your foot off the brake! People who are successful at using the infinite universal force, using the laws associated with it, have a wonderful ability to see and feel the results and outcomes they want, not the results and outcomes they don't want. Nor do they see all the problems in between. When we focus on the things we don't want, and the problems in between, guess what we are bringing into our lives?"

Paul had a eureka moment, "Well, what we don't want, and all the problems in between, of course!"

Maya continued, "We must follow a system to use these great universal laws to our advantage, one that eliminates all negative thinking from our minds, in order to stop negative outcomes in our lives. The system can be practised and mastered; it's simple but not necessarily easy. All truly successful people follow it, in a manner that is consistent with their own particular style and personality. Without following it, there can be very little lasting success, happiness, wealth, health, etc.

"The system of practice is hard to master because of a couple of conditioned responses that have become endemic in our culture.

The first of these is that, when communicating with people, we often tell them the opposite of what we want them to do. Supposedly to get them to do what we do want them to do! Let me illustrate what I mean. Do any of your children have untidy bedrooms?" Paul answered instantly, "Are you kidding? All three of them have!"

Maya continued, "Let me explain why you never get them to tidy up their bedrooms on a permanent basis. I bet you say to them, like most parents do, something along the lines of: 'You! In this bedroom now! Is this your bedroom? It doesn't even look like a human lives in this room. It looks like a pig sty. In fact, a pig wouldn't even live here! It's an environmental health hazard! If the environmental health officer came around here today, they'd torch the place! You are the messiest kid I've ever known, now get this lot cleaned up!'"

Paul couldn't help but laugh, "You must have been listening in on most of the conversations I've had with my children recently about tidying up their bedrooms. All our conversations about tidying up go something like that!"

Maya responded, "Every parent seems to do it, to a degree. But think about the impact this may be having if, as we have discovered, human beings become what they think about. What have the words used here got the children thinking about? What pictures have been painted? What images have been produced in the mind of the child on the receiving end of this?"

Paul could see where this was going, "Well, the ones you don't want: the ones about being a pig, and disgusting, an environmental health hazard, the messiest kid in town." "Exactly," said Maya, "the opposite of what we want. So, do the bedrooms get tidied on a permanent basis? No! They may get tidied up straight after the confrontation, and stay tidy for a short while, but eventually, over time, the bedrooms will revert to reflect the picture or image we just painted in the children's minds! Within a day or two, the bedrooms will be trashed again!"

Paul continued, "I experienced another example of this very thing this morning, when I was driving the children to school. Two of them were in the back seat messing about and making a fuss as usual. Ten minutes passed before I realised that James had opened a can of fizzy drink just before getting into the car and was drinking it while mucking about. As soon as I noticed the can open, I said, 'You are going to spill that for sure, now watch it!' Within 5 seconds, it was all over the place! Ye gods! I made it happen by painting the wrong picture!"

Maya went on, "We've got to get into the habit of telling people what we want, not what we don't want. This is tough, because of our programming; we are programmed and conditioned to do the opposite. Once the wrong picture or image is deposited in our inner subconscious mind, the delivery of it is on its way; our deeper subconscious sees to that. It's automatic. It's a certainty. In fact, as you know, anything we programme into our inner subconscious mind takes root, is processed and automatically delivered to us via the power that the deeper subconscious invokes."

Maya continued, "Which brings us nicely to the second of our conditioned responses that have become endemic in our culture. This is an exercise that involves learning about learning."

Paul looked puzzled, "What? Learning about learning? I don't know what you mean."

Maya smiled at Paul and said, "It is all about our inner subconscious and deeper subconscious working together in harmony to handle the automatic functions on behalf of our minds and bodies. There are two types of automatic functions that get handled. The first set of functions is the natural ones, such as eating and digestion, sleeping, heartbeat, temperature control, breathing, walking, and the like. Thankfully, we don't have to press a button every time we want our lungs to work, it just happens automatically. If you were to run around the car park and then sit down, your lungs would be working overtime without you having to reset the dial.

"The second set of functions that our inner subconscious and deeper subconscious handle automatically for us is the learned ones. Any ideas what I mean by learned functions?"

Paul volunteered, "Erm, well things like language, speaking, writing, reading, your times tables, I guess." Maya continued, "Yes, you guess really well. Any others?" Paul continued, "Well, anything that you learn must be included. Things like driving, playing a musical instrument, work skills, using a computer, social skills, eating with a knife and fork, sports even, how to play golf and the like."

Maya smiled and nodded, "You've got the idea! But how did we learn to do any of those things to the point where they become totally automatic to us?" Paul looked puzzled again, and so Maya helped him out a little, "Do you remember how you learned how to write? Or read? Or remember your times tables?" Paul's puzzled frown lifted as Maya went on, "Yes, **repetition**, followed by **repetition** followed by **repetition**. Let me ask you something else, can anyone ever learn how to do anything to the point where it becomes totally automatic any other way?" Paul shook his head, "I don't think so, can they?"

Maya confirmed, "No, definitely not. However, this is one of the big problems with people learning new things, especially when we become adults, because we've forgotten what learning, real learning, is like. It's as if someone has sold adults a bill of goods that says, after a certain point or event in their lives, everything is supposed to be easy, really easy. So, when we try anything new, if after two or three goes at it we are not experts or black belts in it, whatever it is, we put it in the too-hard box and start telling everyone that it's not really our thing! If anything kills our ability to use more of our potential, and to become all we were designed to be, it's that kind of thinking and doing. And the problem is that that attitude is *everywhere* in the adult world! For instance, do you remember driving here tonight to meet me?"

Paul responded positively, "Well yes, of course I do!" Maya disagreed, "I actually doubt that very much. You may well remember bits of the journey, but I don't think you'll remember driving here. Driving has become so automatic to you now, you've probably forgotten what driving is actually like. Let me clarify this for you. I know you are a proficient driver now, but what was it like when you were first learning how to drive a car?"

Paul replied, "It was a nightmare. It was horribly frustrating, embarrassing, humiliating, even frightening at times." Maya asked, "So there was a considerable price you had to pay?" Paul nodded and said, "I'll say there was, a very considerable price to pay!" Maya then asked, "So why did you pay it?" and Paul replied, "Well, the thought of having my independence, my own car, to come and go as I please, was a big incentive." Maya continued, "In other words, the promise was bigger than the price you had to pay to get it, right? You were willing to pay the price, because the promise was worth it! All the pain involved in learning how to use the clutch, the gears, get those mysterious bite points right, the embarrassment of stalling the car at traffic lights, kangaroo-jumping and rolling backwards on hill starts, etc., all that was worth it." Paul agreed, "100% worth it!"

Maya went on, "It comes back to the question of how you learnt to do all those things to the point where they were totally automatic to you. The only way human beings learn how to do something to a level that is totally automatic, free-flowing and permanent is practise, practise, practise. Lots of it.

"Did you know that learning how to drive is probably one of the last things most people learn to do properly as adults? After that most people seem to believe, because they are now adult, learning is different and everything new they learn is supposed to be really, really easy! But it doesn't get easier and it doesn't get harder: it is just the same as it always was. Learning to do anything to the point where it becomes totally automatic, and therefore easy, is always going to be hard. Everything is hard before it becomes easy.

"It's as if most people are on the ground floor of a building that houses magical success on the top floor. Most adults have been duped into believing there is an express lift that will take them to the top floor in no time and with no effort, apart from stepping inside and pressing the button. Life's not like that; learning's not like that. It never has been, and it never will be. But in the quick-fix world we live in today, people want to believe there are short cuts. There are not. The successful people in the world, truly successful ones, seem to be able to read a sign above the express lift, a sign that is totally invisible to the unsuccessful majority, and it reads: 'This lift is out of order. If you want to get to the top of this building, to the floor that houses success, you have to do it the good old-fashioned way, take the stairs'! It's all about hard work and application, not short cuts; hard work and application combined with a desire to get better every time you try!

"I don't know a single person who became good at something without working really hard at it and making plenty of mistakes in the process, whether it's taking free kicks in football or becoming an expert with computer spreadsheets. I read the other day that a child, on average, falls over more than 1000 times before he or she ever learns how to walk! Imagine if a child learning how to walk had an adult's conditioned mindset about what it is like learning to do anything new! Ye gods! After 3 or 4 unsuccessful attempts, the child would give up and say to its mother, 'Oh you can forget this! It's way too hard!' The mother might implore the child to keep trying, and the child reply, 'But Mum, I keep falling over. I'm not trying anymore!' One final plea from the mother: 'Oh please, Gary' just try one more time! After all you are now 43 years old!'"

Paul laughed out loud and said, "I get your point, Maya."

Maya went on, "So now, do you want to know how to take complete control of every circumstance and situation that life throws at you?

172

Of course you do! You wouldn't be human if you didn't. However, I think you should take a day or two for everything we've discussed tonight to really sink in. Then I will explain how to obtain the keys to the kingdom of success. Is that OK?"

Paul nodded his OK. He was a little disappointed they were stopping there, although he did realise that the only way to cope with the powerful material that was being revealed to him was to take it steadily.

Maya added, "However, there is one thing in particular I want you to observe and practise before we get back together again. I want you to observe how much sarcasm, teasing, cheap shots, put-downs and mickey-taking people use in their daily vocabulary. And, once you have observed and noted the words and phrases used, I want you to completely eliminate them from your own vocabulary, OK?"

Paul immediately saw a problem, "But, if I eliminate all those things from my vocabulary, I might not have any vocabulary left! At least, not at work. There will be no fun to be had!" Maya smiled and said, "With a little practice, you will master this pretty quickly, but why do you think I'm suggesting that you observe and practise this? And it's not because I am a killjoy!"

Paul shook his head in bemusement and Maya continued, "Well, there are 2 reasons. Number 1: by definition all sarcasm, teasing, name-calling, put-downs, cheap shots, etc., are all negative, massively negative. Number 2: such cheap shots, etc., are all personal and, therefore, affect us at the feelings and emotions level of thinking, which as you know has the greatest impact on building beliefs. So, in many ways, such vocabulary is a negative double whammy because it can completely destroy people's self-image and erode their confidence and belief in themselves."

Paul protested, "But surely it's all just a bit of fun and no one takes it seriously?" Maya continued, "You may think that, but people do take such comments seriously, a lot more seriously than you may initially think. You remember the nick-name you had at school?" Paul blushed and said, "Don't bring that up; it's taken me years to try and forget it!" Maya explained further, "Don't worry, but just think about what would happen if anyone at work got to find out what it was." Paul replied, "They would mock me mercilessly, I'd be ridiculed to death. But they would be saying it as a bit of fun, so I would rise above it. It wouldn't actually be like when we were at school."

Maya replied, "Are you quite sure of that? All the old feelings of embarrassment, humiliation and rejection would come flooding back and, even though you've probably learned over the years to laugh it off, it would still have a devastating effect on your self-image because your doubts, fears, shortfalls, pitfalls and inadequacies would begin to surface again. Let's not dwell on it now, just do this exercise over the next few days: observe and practise. OK?"

She went on as Paul nodded in agreement, "I'll call you in a couple of days to see and hear how you've got on with this and everything else we've learned tonight. You have started the process of taking control, Paul, even though it may not feel like it yet. The first step is to stop sowing seeds of negativity in your own mind. Combining this with eliminating thoughts associated with your fears, doubts and shortfalls means you are not attaching any of the universal force that flows through your life to the negatives. This means that all the universal force and power that comes from you and flows through you can be channelled and directed towards manifesting the things you want in life, not the things you don't want."

Paul and Maya left the pub together and drove off in different directions, although they were now travelling down the same path.

Paul had never felt so good, so energised, so uplifted, so inspired. It was wonderful to know that he was in control and that life is a matter of choice and not chance. What joy! What bliss!

Chapter Thirteen

For the next few days Paul was amazed, as he simply observed. Even though, after the previous lessons with Maya, he had learned to change negative thoughts into positive ones the instant they appeared, he was amazed just how many sarcastic, name-calling, put-downs, cheap shots and mickey-taking comments were aimed directly at himself. He was also surprised how often they came from the people who were closest to him!

Even his wife, who he thought was one of the most positive and supportive people he knew, did it all the time, obvious on occasions, subtle on others. When he got home after his last meeting with Maya, he was greeted with 'How nice that you've decided to grace us with your presence, to what do we owe this honour?' The following evening he got home from work to find Jackie helping their eldest child with his homework, and all he heard were comments like, 'Well you're just like your father, because he was never very good at maths either. It must be in the genes!' Good grief!

At his golf club, down his local pub, most of the comments were sarcastic or cheap shots. He also discovered that if you said anything about it, or showed that you were affected by it at all, the barrage intensified! He found this to be especially true with friends.

At work it was terrible. Everyone had nick-names and, Paul realised, they were all related to some embarrassing event or meant as some kind of put-down. His own nick-name had changed, since he had developed his new attitude and his subsequent good performance, from Tortoise Man, i.e. hiding from any trouble, to Teacher's Pet! He noticed that there were no nicknames like Superstar, or Mr Go the Extra Mile!

He mused over whether these sarcastic comments and cheap shots were designed to hurt, but couldn't really come to a firm conclusion. As most people were guilty of the practice, it was probably part of their conditioning. And it might be that their comments were made in all innocence, but they could touch on very sensitive issues.

Two reactions to all these negative comments were commonplace. The first was a 'did he mean that or not?' This was usually attached to a more subtle put-down. A colleague in his office, who was somewhat overweight and very sensitive about it, went on a fitness campaign and did really well to lose 25 lbs in 3 months. The only comment from the office black belt in sarcasm and put-downs was, 'Neil that is a fantastic achievement. Now you've only got another 35 lbs to go!' Neil was disheartened by this, but couldn't let it show for fear of more of the same.

The second reaction was to 'get the bast***s back' by retaliating with more sarcasm and mickey-taking. 'Very positive', Paul thought. He concluded that, with all the negativity around generally, all the sarcasm, teasing and cheap shots, it was not easy to remain positive all the time. Negative comments could affect a person to the extent of taking over their thinking. He realised that just one personal put-down could send someone's thoughts spiralling into a negative abyss. The old adage 'no man is an island' came to his mind. In an ocean of negativity, it is easy for a person's positive self-image to become eroded, drowned and ripped apart by other people's comments!

Paul realised that if you take on board just one negative comment seemingly directed personally at you, it can put all kinds of doubts in your mind and completely undermine your confidence. He examined how he let the impact of sarcasm, teasing and put-downs affect his individual self-talk, causing doubts about his gifts, talents and determination to take over. 'When I'm in this mental state,' he asked himself, 'if I had a friend who talked to me like I talk to me most of the time, would he or she be a friend for very long?' The answer was obvious, and the solution even more obvious. 'I'm going to stop beating myself up because of other people's unkind comments, opinions and observations that they pass off as a bit of harmless banter.'

Paul also realised that, while he had been shown how human thinking processes work and he knew what he needed to do, he didn't yet know how he could fully protect himself from the negativity people hurled at him. And the negativity did seem to be endemic in the culture of today.

'How can anyone engage in sarcasm, teasing or cheap shots once they understand its potentially devastating impact on other people's self-image, beliefs and confidence?' he thought. 'Especially if it is with your own family and loved ones?' He remembered one of the phrases he used regularly when his young children were playing up a little, which was 'If you are not good, when the Baby Buyer comes around, we're going to sell you back to him, but we won't get much for you!' He was mortified! Why don't people explain to each other how all this works and how it kills people's potential and people's sense of worth and value early on in life?! He decided it wasn't so much a conspiracy as sheer ignorance, in the true sense of the word 'ignore once': let's just ignore it. Have people really got no idea of the impact of this stuff? Who in their right minds would do it if they did? 'Lots', Paul concluded. And why? Because putting other people down and eroding their confidence means the perpetrators don't need to do much to look better!

Paul decided he was only ever going to offer positive comments to people from now on, and only surround himself with people who did the same; although he realised he might have to change his job, even his friends! He now knew the extent he would have to go to to create a positive environment within which it would be easy to control his own self-talk. Without doing that, he knew he would be swimming against the tide of negativity forever, and would eventually be overwhelmed by it and doomed back to the life of misery, failure, struggle and unhappiness Maya was helping guide him away from.

He then found that eliminating sarcasm and the like was a lot easier than he'd thought it would be. Like developing all new habits, it just needed practice and persistence. He was amazed at how the behaviour and performance of people around him improved almost instantly when he changed his comments to them from negative to positive. He was annoyed with himself for not realising this sooner. His son's maths improved beyond recognition after a few positive comments such as 'you've come on in leaps of bounds' and 'I didn't know you were so good at geometry'. This gave Paul a tremendous sense of power and control. He felt as though the next stepping stone to unlimited health, wealth, happiness, success and abundance of any sort had been well and truly laid and cemented down. He had never been happier in his life. His feelings of power and control grew daily, as a result of practice and discipline.

Whatever he experienced and observed, he came to the same conclusion every time; whether people see success or failure in their minds, in their imaginations, if the thoughts are repeated often enough they are the forerunner of actual success or failure. Children don't expect to fail until their parents, peers and other people repeatedly show them how to! Through sarcasm, teasing, put-downs, cheap shots and mickey-taking, people are taught to dwell and focus on past mistakes. Because everyone is in this together, the thinking patterns of the whole world need to be changed, but the start of the journey begins with an individual making a choice, a choice to take control of his or her external environment as much as he or she can, because what people see in their imagination rules their world.

'My thoughts really are part of the power of the universal creative spirit', he concluded, as he recalled his affirmation, and he knew exactly what that meant. He also knew, probably for the first time, the sheer scale of how many of people's thoughts are negative, destructive and derogatory about themselves, other people and the world in which they live. Paul realised that people must learn to eliminate all those negative thoughts and replace them with positive, empowering thoughts. By doing that they could direct all the power of the universal laws that work within them and through them towards positive goals; that way humans would become unstoppable. 'Oh yes!' Paul thought, 'obstacles may come our way, but none of them, and no series of them, will ever be able to permanently thwart the human spirit once it is fully ignited.'

One negative thought did cross his mind: 'Surely it can't be that simple?' 'But why not?' he chided himself. Since he had changed his thinking in recent weeks, his world had changed positively and profoundly for the better. Yet his universal human spirit had only just been kindled. In fact, he was still only scratching the surface. He'd hardly started on his journey towards being in control, towards abundance, unlimited happiness and success. It all seemed so clear now, so simple, so powerful, so exciting, so certain. His final conclusion, just before Maya rang him to arrange their next session, was, 'The secret of enjoying any kind of abundance in life, is, therefore, that there is no secret! It is simply about creating positive beliefs in our minds to act as conduits by which the infinite creative power, that lies within us and flows through us, can be channelled and directed. Wow! Isn't this the mechanism by which all wishes, no not wishes, desires, heart-felt desires, are fulfilled? Isn't this what humans have been searching for since time immemorial: success, health, happiness, abundance, caring, sharing, peace, energy and vitality on demand; on purpose; on tap?'

Paul felt a calm, a tranquillity, a bliss beyond anything he had ever felt before. While he wasn't yet fully in control, he felt ready to take control, and he could see and appreciate the way that Maya had prepared him for this, with the affirmations and the understanding of the processes at work. Paul also understood that using any techniques that Maya might now share with him, without going through the right preparation first, would be a waste of time. The inner voyage of enlightenment and understanding was equivalent to the germination process in a seed, which is done for the most part in quietness and darkness, unseen and unheard. 'Now the roots are firmly established, it is time to blossom', he thought.

His train of thought was disrupted by his mobile phone ringing, as he sat on a bench in a park close to his office. He had begun to take half an hour at lunchtime to take in all the beauty the world has to offer. For example, he had just noticed, for the first time ever, the beauty in the detail of a clump of snowdrops. Before, he'd always been too busy or distracted to observe such beauty fully. Lately he seemed to relate to things from the inside, rather than at a fleeting, superficial level; they were not separate from him, he was part of them and they were part of him. He began to feel that everything in the universe was connected to everything else, by some intelligent and creative force field that was almost tangible. He realised that everything in the world, in the universe in fact, was a different expression of the same creative force and infinite, intelligent power, different in form yet connected in a living, vibrant way.

He said 'hello' into the phone, knowing without checking that it would be Maya. She sounded strong and calm as she said, "Hi, Paul, it's Maya. How are you?" Paul responded positively, "Do you know something, Maya, I was just thinking about that, and I am on top form. I couldn't be better!" Maya said, "Good! I'm so pleased to hear that. Tell me, what do you know?" Without hesitation, Paul replied, "I was just thinking about that as well, and I know that the world seems to be different now compared with just a few days ago. I am seeing and appreciating even simple things in a different, 'enhanced', way. Seeing and appreciating shapes, colours, smells, feelings at a different level. I feel I am connected to, and communicating with, the world in a different way. It's truly sensational."

Maya enquired, "Do you know why that is?" He replied, "I've got no idea. I just know it is different." Maya explained, "The main reason is that you have obviously observed and practised identifying the negatives that come at us from all kinds of directions, and learned not to give any of them any of your energy and life force. So your senses and feelings are allowing the creative, intelligent spirit that flows from you and through you, the source of energy of all things that connects all things, and all its power, to be directed towards positive channels and outlets. And, as a result, the whole world for you does not just look different, it is different! We now need to meet so I can show you how to master channelling and directing this infinite power, so that you will be able to accomplish any chosen, right and proper desire you may have in life. When can we meet?"

"As soon as possible, please", Paul implored. "What about tonight?" Maya asked, "although can we meet at 6.30 p.m., because I have someone to see after you?" Paul spluttered, "I'll make sure I can make it. See you in The Old Fox at 6.30."

Chapter Fourteen

When Paul arrived at The Old Fox, he could see through the window that Maya was already sitting at their usual table. She was scribbling into a notepad, and finished just as Paul entered the pub and walked over to her. She radiated her usual warmth and goodness and positive vibes. Everyone else in the pub seemed dull and lifeless. Maya greeted Paul and said, "You've noticed something, haven't you?"

Paul nodded and said, "Yes, but I don't know what it is. I just know something's there." Even though he knew no one other than Maya could hear what he was saying, he now realised that everyone's attention in the bar had been drawn towards him from the moment he had walked through the door. Maya continued, "They've noticed it too! All of them!"

Paul quizzed Maya, "What is it?" Maya replied in a very matter of fact way, "It's the universal power, the infinite, creative, intelligent power, not just being in you but now flowing through you. You have obviously practised getting rid of the self-imposed barriers that prevent the flow: the doubts, the pitfalls, the shortfalls, the inadequacies that other people hand us that we then reinforce solidly in our minds. You've dumped all that stuff, so the power freely radiates from you and through you; the process has begun."

Paul enquired, "Is that why everyone else appears so dull and lifeless?" Maya responded back, "What do you think?" He didn't have to answer. Maya continued, "Do you see those three men standing at the bar? Well, they arrived about half an hour ago for a swift half after work. They weren't radiating much universal power when they walked in, and they have done nothing but take the mickey out of each other, their partners, their children, their work, etc., since then. As negative after negative comment piled up, you could see what little there was of their radiating life force getting choked to the point where it was almost completely extinguished. It also visibly sapped any power that was being radiated by the people around them; except from me, of course!"

Paul was curious, "Why not you? Surely it affects everyone?" Maya nodded, "Well, it affects most people. It even affected you. You were radiating universal power strongly as you walked in, and you still are, but it is no longer quite as powerful. Some of your life energy has been stolen by these people with their negativity." Paul was puzzled, "Well, why has it been stolen from me and not you? Oh, no, don't tell me, because you've learned some techniques in your journey towards enlightenment that I don't know about yet? Yes? Am I right?" Maya smiled and said, "You are, as usual, spot on." Paul asked immediately, "So, what is it then?"

Maya responded, "That's why we have met tonight, to start the process for you, but first, as ever, you must understand what the process is. Let me ask you a simple question. Where is the only place where there is no darkness?" Paul couldn't immediately come up with the answer, so Maya volunteered, "The only place where there is no darkness is the ultimate source of a light, like the sun. It's radiating so much light outwards, because it is a source, that no dark can ever get in; until it stops radiating that is! And that's what you must learn to do, to radiate with intensity. Once you learn how to do this, and become an ultimate source of light, no darkness can ever affect you, no fears, no pitfalls, no inadequacies, no shortfalls. You become an invincible and unstoppable being with infinite, creative power flowing along the channels and conduits opened up by your positive beliefs. This unlimited power allows us to operate at a multitude of levels in the mind; it is this that makes us unstoppable. We operate at the intuitive level, and the inductive and deductive levels. The fact is, the deeper and quieter we go inside ourselves, all sources of higher intelligence become available to us."

Paul nodded, but only half understood what Maya was saying. Maya sensed this, so began to explain it bit by bit, "It's important to know that an integral part of becoming a 'sorcerer' in the true sense of the word is to radiate positives so strongly that nothing negative can get in. You must also be sure that you are radiating what you want in life." Paul said, "But surely we all know that! Isn't it just that the negatives from others and from ourselves get in the way?" Maya continued, "Well, it's not quite that simple. The universal force and power that is in us and flows through us is infinite. It is obedient but needs precise and accurate direction, otherwise the force and power tends to get scattered and diffused. It's like watering the garden with a hosepipe that has got loads of holes in it and no nozzle attached. No matter how much water pressure is available from the tap, you'd be lucky to get a dribble of water out of the end, let alone a powerful jet!"

Paul responded with, "Yes, that's what I mean. If you patch up all the holes, all the negatives, the power returns to the end of the hosepipe, and whoosh!" Maya said, "Not quite. The power at the end of the hosepipe improves for sure, but to reach the far corners of the garden, the power needs to be channelled further and directed with a nozzle, or the end of your thumb."

Paul nodded in understanding and Maya continued, "Let me show you an example." She tore out a blank piece of paper from her notebook and wrote the word 'Success' on top of it, and handed it to Paul. "Now," she said, "is success something you want to achieve in your life?" He responded, "Isn't that something everybody wants to achieve in life? Surely it is a basic aspiration everyone has? Although I suspect that it means different things to different people." Maya nodded and said, "Yes, of course it does. But what we are interested in here is what it means to you. Just take a couple of minutes and write down for me what the elements of success are, so far as you are concerned. I don't want a definition of success, but what you think are the elements of success."

Paul's head was spinning with so many jumbled thoughts that for a moment he couldn't focus, but then he wrote down 'Happiness', followed by 'Recognition', 'Respect' and 'Achievement'. After that his mind was blank; he couldn't work out whether this was because it was overloaded or there was nothing more there. He didn't know if his mind was in the middle of a hurricane or becalmed, "I thought this was going to be easy", he said, somewhat apologetically, to Maya.

"Well," said Maya, "consider whether someone has turned the tap off, or the hosepipe is leaking so badly that very little is dribbling out of the end. You should know that the tap can never be turned off at the source, there is a constant and infinitely powerful flow. So, you must still be holding negative thoughts that are sapping the power." Paul objected, "Yes, but I've eliminated the negatives as much as I can!"

"That may well be so," Maya continued, "but are you directing the power towards what you want out of life? If your elements of success, as indicated by the words you've written down, are anything to go by, then clearly not! If we move towards, and become like, the pictures in our minds, how clear is the picture in your mind of what success looks like? Paul shook his head and replied, "Well, obviously not very clear at all." Maya went on, "You see, if the picture is vague and fuzzy, so will be the outcome! All success starts with a crystal-clear picture of the outcome in your mind. You then need to energise it further, by attaching feelings and emotions to what it will be like once you have achieved it, and by attaching the intensity of desire. We will cover that in more detail later; for now, let's work on the words and pictures and a structure that will help funnel and channel the unlimited, creative force towards achieving anything you desire, without limit. Is that OK?" Paul enthused, "You bet!"

"Right," said Maya, "the list I am going to share with you, highlighting the elements of success, is not my list. It's not one made up from my thoughts. It has been compiled from centuries of studying the world's most successful people from all walks of life. These people include business tycoons, such as Andrew Carnegie, who spent the first half of his life becoming the richest man in the world and the second half of his life giving all his wealth away to worthy causes. They also include people like Mother Theresa of Calcutta, for whom compassion and helping those suffering in abject poverty was all important, statesmen of stature, such as Benjamin Franklin and Nelson Mandela, and the world's top sportsmen and sportswomen. The characteristics of people who have excelled in their field, who have succeeded at all kinds of different levels in their lives, have been used to compile this list."

Paul was fascinated as Maya began to write her elements of success under his earlier words:

1) Peace of mind
           Freedom From   * Fear
                                  * Guilt
                                  * Anger/Regret.

She explained, "These three things, fear, guilt and anger/regret, are the three biggest mental cancers of the present day. A lot of people would probably say having a lot of money is an element of success in today's world. However, without peace of mind, money means very little. A most apposite example is Howard Hughes, who at one time was the world's richest man. However, he lived the last 20-odd years of his life in a hermetically sealed environment, because he was terrified of micro-organisms. This fear was so intense and deeply rooted that it was impossible for him to live a normal life and enjoy his wealth and good fortune.

"History is littered with examples of people who couldn't enjoy their existence on this abundant planet because they were racked with guilt about things they had done in the past. It is also littered with examples of people who didn't live life to the full because they were so consumed with anger or regret over things that had, or had not, happened in the past. The reason we call them mental cancers is because they are so pervasive; they steal all your life force, leaving very little or nothing to help bring you joy, happiness, success, propriety and the like. Peace of mind, therefore, is the first of six fundamental elements of success in life. Without it life can mean very little."

Maya took pen to paper again and this time wrote:

2) High levels of health, energy and vitality.

"I know lots of people, with lots of money, who would give it all up tomorrow to live one week of their lives with high levels of health, energy and vitality. The words chosen here are very specific. A dictionary definition of health is 'lack of illness' and most people don't just want to be not ill, but alive with boundless energy and vitality! The kind that keeps us going all day, and all night if necessary! Without this we, literally, have nothing."

Maya's hand moved towards the paper again, and Paul watched in eager anticipation as she wrote:

3) Loving relationships.
   Mature, lasting, shared.

Maya elaborated, "As human beings, our feelings and emotions are the immediate drivers of our behaviour. We, as you know, are emotional creatures, and make decisions emotionally. We justify them rationally, of course, but we make decisions emotionally. It would be naive to believe anything different. The biggest emotional need we have is to be loved. I'm not just talking about love on an intimate level; I mean love in all its aspects, at every level; respect, recognition, appreciation, etc.

You see, love is the food of our souls. We need love from the day we are born in order to thrive.

It's well known that in the 19th century up until the 1920's most babies that were abandoned and ended up in institutional care died. This was not because they weren't fed, clothed or bathed; it was because they weren't loved. After the 1920's when abandoned babies were cuddled, stroked, sung to, hugged, kissed etc … they thrived!

Even today, and you can ask any doctor in any hospital and they'll tell you that a poorly nourished baby that is loved will fight harder to live than a well nourished baby that is emotionally neglected.

"And we never grow out of our need to be loved. We are emotional creatures, and our biggest emotional need is to be loved, respected, admired, recognised and valued by others and ourselves. Without that, all our talents, gifts, skills and unlimited abilities simply wither on the vine and never come to fruition. The world and all the people in it will never get to see what we have to offer, if we don't love ourselves enough to work on the gifts and talents we all possess."

Paul's mind raced with all the strategies and tactics he had used all his adult life to deny himself this basic human need, to cover up the hurt he felt when he didn't feel loved or when he knew he hadn't earned it. The upshot of it was, he had convinced himself he didn't need it anyway; it wasn't macho. It was a double-edged sword to realise this. He had deluded himself for so long that being loved didn't matter, but it was now a release to acknowledge that, deep down inside, he had always known it did. He smiled to himself as he made up his mind to concentrate on developing strategies and tactics in his life to attract love, respect, admiration and the sense of being valued. He smiled because he knew that it would be simpler, easier and a lot more enjoyable than the tactics he'd been using in his adult life up to now. He also realised that, by adopting a different approach to love and being loved, the true treasure was not the end result, i.e. being loved, respected, admired and valued, but the kind of person that you become in the process.

Maya asked if Paul was ready to continue. "Oh yes," he said, somewhat apologetically, "I was in a little world of my own for a minute or two then, sorry. Do go on." She said compassionately, "Most people have a big 'ah, ha' moment at this point." Paul replied, "It was probably the biggest 'ah, ha'' moment I've ever had in my life. Anyway, enough of that, what is number 4?" Maya returned to the piece of paper and wrote:

4) Financial freedom.

She explained, "Whether we like it or not, money is the mechanism humans have chosen for the exchange of goods and services in our society. To be financially independent, to not have to worry about where the next meal is coming from, or how to pay the bills, or what is going to happen if you get sick and are unable to work, is one of the key elements of success. The choices and options this gives people to channel their gifts and talents in a direction or directions of their choosing is electrifying, especially when it comes to the use of our most precious asset, time. There are many people I know who earn fabulous amounts of money and have a terrific lifestyle but a dreadful quality of life. These people are not financially free. In fact, they are trapped. Trapped into chasing more money to finance a lifestyle they can't really afford, which means their quality of life gets worse, not better. How sad is that?"

Paul replied philosophically, "It must be about the saddest place in the world to be."

Maya continued, "Now financial freedom means different things to different people. My father, as you know, is a proud pensioner. He has been retired for years and lives a simple yet fabulous life on a very modest yearly income. If you gave my father an extra £10,000 per year, he wouldn't know what to do with such outrageous wealth and fortune. In fact, I can tell you exactly what he would do with the extra £10,000. He would give half of it to me, and the other half to my brother! He lives a very fulfilled life, pursues his hobbies and goes on holiday abroad every year. He couldn't want for more, he says. His approach to life and happiness is very simple: it is not about having a lot, it is about being content with a little. Anyone in this country who isn't content with what they've already got will never be happy. Never!

"Now, to other people, earning £100,000 per year is only just enough to keep the wolf from the door. They are usually the people chasing the expensive lifestyle they can't really afford, who have a lousy quality of life and are stressed to hell. And there are other people who are earning £1,000,000 plus and it isn't enough! We live in an incredible country: anyone here who earns £10,000 per year is probably regarded as poor! Yet about 85% of the world's population would find that really peculiar. To 85% of the world's population, £10,000 per annum is wealth beyond their wildest dreams. The average income for many families in Bangladesh, Africa, India, China, etc., is less than £100 per year! We have to decide, as individuals, what level of income, money in the bank, pension and the like, would give us financial freedom. Are you OK with that?"

Paul nodded approvingly, "It's more than OK. In fact, it's KO! It's knock out! All my life I've been chasing, chasing, chasing, and I've not known what I'm chasing, or how far away the finishing line is! All I know is that up to now, the faster I seem to go, the further away the finishing line seems to get. From what you're saying, it seems that I have to determine where the finishing line is for myself, and then set my own pace and direction accordingly. Is that right?" Maya smiled and said, "Yes, sort of."

"Anyway," she continued, "let's move onto the next element of success", and wrote:

5) Worthy goals and ideals
   - Sense of purpose/meaning

"Successful people have crystal-clear pictures in their minds of where they are heading. They don't leave it to chance. They know that life is a matter of choice, not chance, and, therefore, decide ahead of time what they want, and, more importantly, what they need to become to get it. This is not only in a personal sense. They also decide to be part of something bigger than themselves, whether it be a company, a charity, a football club or a local scout group!

"Having a 'why' to get out of bed in the morning will help you or anyone cope with any of the 'hows' that go with it. The why, providing it is a worthy why, will help pull you or anyone through the tough times and the struggles that usually go with achieving any worthy goal or objective. This is such an important element that we will dedicate one of our future meetings to guide you through a goal-setting master class, which will show you the rules to follow to ensure that every right and proper goal you decide upon will be realised. There are certain things you must and must not do to make the unlimited universal force, that is available to us all on demand, work for us. That way you can literally work miracles with any aspect of your life."

Paul responded, "I can't wait for that session!"

Maya smiled and then started to write as she said, "Finally, number 6 is:

6) Personal fulfilment.
   – knowing you are using your
   full (?) potential.

"Really successful people habitually dig deep and use as many of the gifts and talents with which we've all been blessed as they can. Some of these gifts and talents are on the surface, some are more deeply buried, but they are there all the same. Using them gives a feeling of exhilarating power and control.

"Successful people know what you now know, that there is no force, power or set of circumstances on the outside of us that is greater than the force, power or set of resources available to us on the inside. They know that the history of humankind is littered with examples where the human spirit has triumphed over all kinds of adversity. Not instantly, but eventually. They also know that some of those triumphs have not only utilised the creative power and force within us, but also that which flows through us. These powers and forces sometimes transcend human potential. It's beyond the physical, it's metaphysical. It makes the impossible possible; it turns dreams into realities; thoughts into things.

"As we have discussed before, our unlimited power and resources need conduits along which they can be directed and channelled, so that they can express themselves externally. These conduits, in this instance, take the form of our desires, i.e. our goals and objectives. These don't need to be huge, such as creating and building the world's most successful company, or eliminating world poverty. They can be simple, such as helping tend to the poor and sick in the community, or becoming the best husband or wife, father or mother. It can be keeping your body fit and healthy in order to serve others. No goal or objective is more or less important than any other, they are merely different. There is certainly no hierarchy or differentiation in the way our unlimited and infinite resources are thrown behind manifesting every right and proper goal or objective. However, there are rules that need to be followed in order to be in total control, and to become unstoppable in achieving anything upon which we set our heart and mind. These rules will be covered in a later session. For now, I want to finish off this particular learning point in relation to success. Are you alright with this? You look slightly uncomfortable."

Paul's response was slightly embarrassed, "Er, no, no. I, I am very comfortable with it. I was just reeling a little from what you have just said about no goal or objective being more important than others. I've always been told that you need to set big, ambitious goals and objectives, all of which should be very 'me' centred, and that's the way you succeed. Walk all over people, knock them out of the way, do whatever it takes to succeed, no matter who you hurt!"

Maya nodded with understanding, and added, "Nothing could be further from the truth. Goals and objectives work best when they are simple and other people-centred. Someone once said 'You can have anything you want in life, if you help enough other people get what they want in life'. We'll cover this in detail later. But the kind of warped thinking you've mentioned is one of the main reasons that people don't set goals and objectives, they think they've got to be big and earth shattering, and then there is the added trepidation of what you've got to become as a person in the process! So people often run away from setting goals and objectives. The music that is in everyone, waiting to be played to the full, dies with them. How sad is that?

"The goal-setting master class that we'll cover in a later session will, believe me, blow your socks off! In the meantime there is one other thing we need to discuss about success." She now wrote alongside 'Success':

SUCCESS — is a journey and not a destination.

Maya pointed at the statement she had written, and asked Paul what he thought it meant. He mused for a while and replied, "Well, I've heard it said many times but I've never really stopped to think what it meant." After another pause, he suggested, "Does it mean that this goal-setting thing never ends? Does it mean that it is on-going?"

Maya smiled and nodded in approval. "It means exactly that. It means that, once you start on this path, the path that leads to unlimited prosperity, wealth, health, happiness, success, bliss, or anything your heart desires, it is endless. In many ways, all goals and objectives are self-defeating, because when you've achieved something special to you, there is always another something special to achieve. Now, when *we* are in control of creating our own goals and objectives it's exciting and electrifying. Sometimes when other people are forcing goals and objectives upon us that we don't believe in, it can be stupefying and debilitating. In a work environment, if goals and objectives are not communicated properly, and in most work environments they are not, the general reception from people is 'oh no!' rather than 'oh boy!' Even worse than that is when people gang together with the cry 'you keep moving the goal posts!' against the leaders of an organisation. Therefore nothing changes at anything like the speed it needs to, and the organisation and the people in it, including customers, all suffer. Does this sound familiar?"

Paul nodded and laughed, "It certainly does." Maya continued, "The really important message in the '**success is a journey and not a destination**' statement is that, if we are never going to get there, what do we need to do with the journey?"

Paul was only unsure for a second or two, then replied, "Well, enjoy the journey, of course!" Maya asked encouragingly, "How much of the journey? Which parts of the journey?" and Paul enthused, "Well all of it, of course, every single part of it!"

Maya continued, "This is massive; this is immense; it is bigger than a big 'un when it comes to having a fabulously rich and robust philosophy on life, and understanding what life is all about. You see, so many people think that success is only about achieving things, and big things at that; big, important goals and objectives. And that achievements, or arriving at a destination, are the only thing that matters, no matter what it costs. How many people do you know who say things like 'When I get this, house, car, promotion, amount of money invested, relationship, I'll be really happy'? And, guess what? When they do get it, and occasionally people do, guess what? They're not happy! Why do you think that is?"

Paul offered, "Well, is it because they are greedy and always want more and more?" Maya replied, "Mmm, it's a very valid answer, but it's not the main reason. Many people, in order to achieve some objective or other, have had to dig deep and use some of their hidden gifts and talents or use them in ways they've never had to before. When this happens, even more hidden gifts and talents are discovered. This usually spurs people on to asking themselves what else they might be able to achieve. This is not a problem in itself. The problem is that if we only allow ourselves to be happy when we reach a destination or, in other words, allow our happiness to be driven purely by the achievement of goals and objectives, we will never be really happy or successful! The reason for this is that there will always be something else to strive for. It's like knitting fog!

"Many people, when they've achieved a goal, immediately move onto the next one. And, as they are moving towards achieving the next goal, they become all too fixated and consumed by just its achievement. Nothing else matters, these people have no time for anything, or anyone, else. They are rude, aggressive and short tempered. They can't sleep, they work all the hours God sends, but they miss the most important meaning behind '**success is a journey and not a destination**', which is: if we are never going to get there, we *must* enjoy the journey, every aspect of it, the good bits and the not-so-good bits. The true treasure in achieving any goal is not in what you get from it, it is in what you become to achieve it! If you have a goal to become a millionaire, the true treasure is not in having a million pounds sterling in the bank, it's in the person you've become to accumulate such wealth. Any millionaire who's earned that sort of money will tell you that you can take all their money away tomorrow, and they'd have a million pounds again in a couple of years! And, they'd love every minute of getting it!

"So many people put off their enjoyment and happiness by thinking it lies somewhere down the track, in the future. People forget to be happy in between the happenings! One of my favourite sayings is 'There is no way to happiness, happiness is the way'. It's about enjoying the journeys, all of them. It's about enjoying the challenges and the obstacles. No one goes through life tip-toeing through the tulips all the time but, even if they do, they should stop off occasionally to enjoy the view, taste the fresh air and savour the feel of it all. Happiness is in the moment, the here and now, and it's in every moment. We need goals and objectives to channel our awesome power, but we need the good sense to stop occasionally and smell the flowers on the side of the road!"

Paul was perturbed, and asked, "But surely you can't enjoy it all, not the really bad stuff, can you?" Maya replied, "No, no, I am not saying that, but sometimes we need the bad stuff to help us realise how good the good stuff can be when it comes. Was it William Faulkner who once said, 'Given a choice between grief and nothing, I'd choose grief'? Because at least with that you still feel alive and realise the blood is coursing through your veins, but with nothing, there is ambivalence, apathy, nowt!

"Someone told me the other day of the results of a study that showed unsuccessful people define success as 'being able to do what you like'. It went on to say that no really successful person would ever say that. Successful people use the same words in a different order: 'success is not "being able to do what you like" it's "being able to like what you do!"' In fact, it goes a stage beyond that: 'success is being able to *love* what you do!' I'm only just coming to terms with some of this myself, and it has already transformed my life.

"The fastest way to happiness for any human being is this: fall head over heals in love with your job. Yes!" Paul looked nonplussed and Maya went on, "Yes, every aspect of your job, the good stuff and the not-so good stuff. Let me explain why I say job first, and not partner and family. Most people spend most of their conscious waking hours at work, thinking about work or talking about work. So, what people should do is to look at work in a new light, in a seeing the 6 'Fs' kind of light, and look at the whole picture. Most people are amazed to find that there is a lot to fall head over heels in love with in their job, they just couldn't see it before!

"If, when you do look at your job in a new light, you genuinely can't fall head over heals in love with it, you may need to make a really tough decision. The decision should be to go and find a job that you can fall head over heals in love with. Do you know why?"

Paul shook his head so Maya continued, "Because you're too valuable and life is too short! Let's face it, if you've got any dignity in yourself as a wonderfully gifted, fully functioning human being, why should you settle for anything else?"

Paul spoke now, "Well, you know, I have changed my attitude towards work enormously since you've been guiding me and my life has already changed beyond recognition, so I don't need any convincing on that one!"

"Good!" Maya said. "Now the next step to happiness is to go and fall head over heels in love with everything else in your life, your partner, your kids, your friends and neighbours, your relatives, the whole lot, and again, if you can't do that, you may have some more tough decisions to make."

Paul was struggling a little with some of this, "Yes, but while you can pick your friends and work colleagues, you can't choose your relatives. We've no choice who they are." Maya agreed, "You've no choice at all, but you do have a choice about how much you see them and how much influence you allow them to have on you. Life really is a matter of choice, not chance. We need to make the right choices to be truly happy and successful.

"What I would like you to do before our next meeting is to think, really think, about what you want out of life for it to be truly successful for you and those you love. Will you do that for me? I found it useful to write down on one piece of paper the 50 things I want to get out of life in the next 10 years. It got my creative juices flowing. But don't restrict yourself. Write down the things you want, not just the things you think you can get. OK?"

Paul replied, "The process has already begun." "Terrific," said Maya, "We'll call it a night now. The next time we meet, you'll be ready to learn how to take control of the process of your life in its entirety, so that nothing is beyond your reach. How do you feel?"

"Exhilarated, exhausted and powerful beyond measure, all at the same time", Paul said. "Get used to it," Maya said, "the best is yet to come."

They left The Old Fox together and drove off separately down the same road.

Chapter Fifteen

During the next few days Paul felt the most excited and frustrated he had ever been in his life. He sensed the vastness, intensity and sheer power of what lay within him and flowed through him. He knew beyond any shadow of doubt that this awesome force, available to anyone on demand, could, when used properly, turn every right and proper desire into a reality, which meant guaranteed success! 'That's exciting! It's as exciting as anything gets in life', he thought.

However, Paul also realised that he had no really clear pictures in his mind of what success looked like for him, his family, his career, his health, his wealth, his happiness and peace of mind. He could see the odd glimpse, but nothing more than vague hopes and wishes that flashed across his mind on occasions. He had no burning desires as such. Yes, in recent weeks, with Maya's guidance, he'd tidied up his mind, especially regarding his attitude towards work. And, he reflected, the change and improvements there, together with a positive momentum, had been breathtaking. But much of his focus was defensive, to stop himself getting really ill or depressed. As he thought about it, he realised that his actions were more akin to running away from something he feared rather than running towards something he desired.

He smiled to himself, as he thought how human kind had perhaps been running away from things since its earliest beginnings in order to survive, so he was in good company. 'Not a very modern man', he thought! Fear may be a great motivator, but desire, a burning desire, to create something wholesome that benefits yourself and other people, would be an even greater motivator. But, you need faith and belief in your unlimitedness to turn the motivational power fully on.

A big realisation was that human beings are not simply creatures, they are creators! Instincts are one thing, and should never be forgotten or ignored, but desires in the form of goals and objectives, together with the certainty of their fulfilment, is quite another. They should be nurtured and managed properly. 'It is this that makes us truly human beings, and not just human doings,' he thought. 'This moves us from a position where our actions are dominated by instinctive responses to outside influences and images, to one where our actions are determined and dominated by our responses to internal pictures and images that we have chosen to put into our minds.

'So, if we could learn to deliberately plant pictures and images of what we want, in terms of desires, goals and objectives in our minds, then our response to these inside influences and images would determine and dominate our actions. What a revelation! Isn't this the secret of a fulfilling life that seems to have eluded the majority of humankind? We let outside influences and events imprint themselves on our beliefs and self-image which, in turn, dominates our behaviour and actions. We should choose what to imprint internally on our self-image and let that dominate our behaviour and actions!' Paul cringed when he thought of all the occasions he had let external events alter or obliterate the things he wanted in life. He now understood why his awesome power and energy had more often than not been scattered and diffused, with the result that he never got anywhere fast! The result in fact was misery, poverty, ill health and unhappiness, as all his power and energy was put behind turning those pictures into a reality for him.

He was uplifted and enthused at the thought of choosing positive internal pictures and images for himself. How good it would be to channel and direct his entire energy and creativity to turning those images into an external reality in double-quick time. 'Wow,' he thought, 'this is power, this is control, this is awesome. This needs to be used wisely'.

He was glad these thoughts were racing through his mind while he was lying waiting for the alarm clock to go off. It was such an intense awakening to the sheer scale of the creative forces that open the way to achieving desires, goals and objectives that, if he hadn't been lying down already, he might have fallen down! He had a fabulous feeling of power and control while he showered that morning! However, he did still have the task of deciding what he wanted, and that was a lot harder to figure out than he'd imagined. What did he want? Really want? It was tough, because up until this point in his life he had thought life was a matter of chance, not choice. Faced with unlimited choice, for a while his mind suffered a kind of paralysis. 'Paralysis by analysis', he called it.

After his first couple of meetings at work that day, he had an hour to himself. He concentrated hard with a blank piece of paper in front of him. He wrote on the top of the paper:

> 50 things I want out of life in the next 10 years (not things I know I can get, things I want)

He concentrated even harder, but nothing was forthcoming. As soon as an idea came into his mind, it immediately seemed to evaporate. It took him a while to figure out why. Every time an idea came to mind, two dominant thoughts swamped it. The first thought was, 'Don't be stupid, you'll never be able to get that!' as his old beliefs of limited ability and inadequateness came flooding back. The second thought was, 'Who the heck do you think you are to have that?' as his old belief of being unworthy re-appeared.

It was as if there was a real, unlimited Paul that wanted to get out but it was being shouted down and put off by the conditioned, limited Paul. On the one hand he couldn't understand this, but on the other he could. These were the negative ways of thinking that had dogged him, as they had most people, all his life. In order to silence the old conditioned, limited Paul, the naysayer, the devil's advocate who seemed to undermine every right and proper desire that came into his mind, he needed to confront these thoughts head on, understand their motives and tactics, and vanquish them once and for all.

After staring into space for what seemed like an eternity, a blinding revelation hit him regarding the major motives and tactics of the conditioned, limited self. The tactics were to present statements and questions that would steal all the energy and creative force at his disposal. These statements and questions had to be answered, thereby deflecting energy from focusing on the actions needed to achieve desired goals and objectives. It's as if the conditioned, limited self makes a statement, or asks a question, such as 'Don't be stupid, you'll never be able to do that!' or 'Who the heck do you think you are to have that?', and the combined subconscious is forced to put all its resources into providing answers to 'Why you never will' and 'Why you don't deserve it'. The list of questions can grow, and so the dream is washed away, the energy and enthusiasm drowned, and feelings of total inadequacy and worthlessness fully restored!

Paul discovered that the primary motive behind the tactics of the conditioned, limited self was to prevent him from seeing or accepting his unlimited potential. He now understood why he often said, 'I don't like myself sometimes'. He smiled as he tried to figure out who the 'I' was and who the 'myself' was in that statement. 'Was this positive proof that there is a "big I" and a "little myself" in all of us?' He decided it was.

'The amount of negative conditioning we have in our lives means that we often deny our talents and abilities out of so-called modesty, but the reality is that it's out of fear. For us to acknowledge and accept our unlimited talents and abilities, we need to commit to using them and becoming all we are designed to be. At the end of the day, no-one can use those talents and abilities but ourselves. We just need to accept what we really are, the "big I", and tune in to using the creative powers and unlimited forces that we possess. Many people wait all their lives for someone else to come along and "turn them on".' Paul knew he hadn't been that bad, at least he'd been searching all his life. 'What a terrible philosophy and plan for a life! What would happen if no-one turned up to turn them on?'

Maya had shown up because he, no they'd, been searching. Paul was already 'turned on' to finding something; Maya was now 'tuning him in'. 'She wasn't some kind of external motivator there to "turn him on", she was merely enlightening him and helping him tune himself into the universal power at his disposal. Anyone could do it', he thought. 'Anyone could accept their limitless power. So, why don't they? Could it be because they then wouldn't have any more excuses for not achieving more in their lives? Maybe that would be just too much responsibility for most people to handle', Paul mused.

He opened his desk drawer and pulled out a quote from Nelson Mandela's inauguration speech as President of South Africa, in 1994. He had kept it for some reason and now he knew why, it read:

Nelson Mandela – Inaugural Speech 1994

Our deepest fear is not that we are inadequate.
Our deepest fear is that we are powerful beyond measure.
It is our light, not our darkness, that frightens us most.

We ask ourselves, 'Who am I to be brilliant, gorgeous, talented and fabulous?'

Actually, who are you not to be?

You are a child of the universe.
You playing small doesn't serve the world.
There is nothing enlightening about shrinking so that other people won't feel insecure around you.

We are born to make manifest the glory of the universe that is within us.
It is not just in some of us; it is in everyone.

And as we let our own light shine, we unconsciously give other people permission to do the same.

As we are liberated from our own fear, our presence automatically liberates others.

As Paul reflected on the words and the wisdom and power they contained, he was completely amazed. This guy knew a thing or two! Then, of course, he would have done. Being locked up for 27 years and never letting go of his picture or dream, and seeing it slowly turn into a reality, would have given him an unshakeable faith. And he'd certainly want to share it with others, wouldn't he?

With this little bit of inspiration to oil the wheels, Paul let the 'big I' dominate his thoughts and silence the 'little myself' and returned to writing a list under '50 things I want out of life'. Now a river of words appeared. He started with things like being healthy and happy, then ones like taking the kids to Disneyland in Florida and providing them with a first-class education. Seeing the pyramids in Egypt and having a brand new car came next, followed by being able to retire at 50. The flow became a flood: learning to play the guitar, writing a book, speaking French fluently, taking care of his parents in their old age, becoming head of his department at work and creating 200 new jobs, playing golf at the Old Course at St Andrews, helping out at the old people's home around the corner. In no time, there were 96 things written on the piece of paper in front of him! He felt euphoric.

Just then his phone rang, and as he answered he noticed that his voice was strong and his tone enthusiastic. It was Maya, "Hi Paul, I've just been thinking of you. Are you ready for our next get together?"

Paul replied, "Well I certainly am now. I had some real difficulty deciding what I wanted out of life, and I have had to exorcise a few demons, but I now have a list. Is that normal?" Maya laughed as she replied, "I know I had difficulty at first too, as have most other people I know who have been guided or who are being guided. It's not so much normal, more like to be expected. Can we meet tonight? Or would tomorrow night be better for you?" Paul answered firmly, "No, no, tonight would be great. Usual place?"

Maya surprised him with her answer, "No, I have a table booked at the Yang Sing Chinese restaurant in town. So, if you're up for it, I'll treat you to the best Chinese meal in the country. What do you say? The table is booked for 7 o'clock" Paul responded, "You bet I'm up for it! I've always wanted to eat there, and never got round to it." Maya cheekily asked, "It's not on your '50 things I want out of life list' is it?" Paul replied, "Well, it's not in my top 50, but it is number 91! Amazing!" Maya closed with, "I'll see you at 7, bye."

Chapter Sixteen

They both arrived at the door of the Yang Sing together. The smells, the noise, the atmosphere, were unique and enticing. They were shown to their table. After a little small talk, Maya asked Paul, "So, what were the demons you had to exorcise?"

He explained, "Basically they were negative feelings of doubt and unworthiness that seemed to devour every positive thought I had about what I wanted out of life. Once I had banished them, ideas of what I wanted began to flow, as did the energy and the power required to make them come about. It was incredible. As soon as I focused on what I wanted, the means to their achievement began to present themselves as well. The energy and power that came from me and surged through me was tangible; I was euphoric, even!" Maya nodded and said, "And do you know why that happened?"

Paul also nodded, "I think it was because I diverted the energy and power flow from the fear conduit to the desire conduit. I wasn't going to be shouted down by the conditioned, limited me that is fear. So I let the big, unlimited me loose, the one that is desire, and, oh my word, it is big and unlimited!" Maya laughed at Paul's enlightenment, his enthusiasm and his way of expressing the significant steps he had taken.

Maya added, "We can take this up a notch now, in order for you to take control fully. As you know, it is a step-by-step process and we still won't be covering how to set and achieve any goal and objective you choose in life just yet. We'll cover some sound advice on the areas in your life you should focus on, and some pointers on where to start this process. So, going back to our hosepipe analogy, is the nozzle OK? Have you got some focus?" When Paul agreed, she went on, "We have to make sure all the holes that could potentially appear anywhere along the hosepipe and lessen the flow are patched up first. And then we need to make sure you know how to avoid creating any new holes in the future, in order to keep the power full on.

"The way to begin the process of taking control is by understanding something we call the self-talk cycle." Maya took out a piece of paper and drew on it.

"It works like this," she pointed at the top box, "It all begins here, with our self-talk, with the minimum of 70,000 thoughts a day we have in word form, picture form and feelings and emotions form. These thoughts are constantly building and reinforcing our self-image and beliefs because, don't forget, our inner subconscious accepts all the thoughts we send it as the truth.

"Once these truths build up and are accepted as our beliefs, this effectively determines what shows up in our real world as our behaviour, or our real performance. Then the way we behave or perform goes back and feeds our self-talk. It's a vicious cycle." Maya's finger circled just above the piece of paper on the table:

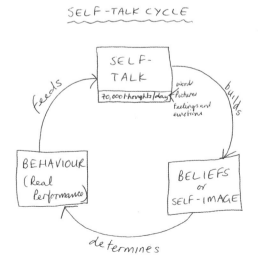

207

"So, if we begin a task with sufficient numbers of, or intensity of, thoughts like, 'Oh, I don't think this is going to work', to build a belief of doubt and uncertainty in the subconscious self-image, it becomes more than likely that it won't work, or at least not in the way it was intended. And then, when it doesn't work, the failure feeds the self-talk with thoughts like, 'Oh, well, I'm never going to try anything like that again!' Unless and until this negative thinking pattern is broken, the cycle of failure could become self-perpetuating.

"In order to improve any aspect of our behaviour and performance in life, we need to be able to break into this cycle at some point. It's all too easy for us to allow our lives to slip into ever-decreasing circles of failure, misery, ill-health, poverty and the like. Most people, when they try and improve any aspect of their lives, tend to grab hold of their behaviour consciously and try and act the way they want to be. For instance, people who believe they are shy may try very hard to behave in an outgoing way. However, because our long-term, automatic and free-flowing behaviour is determined by our beliefs, these beliefs act like an autopilot. The autopilot is pre-programmed to take us in the direction, in this instance, of being shy. So when we try and act in an outgoing way there is tension, there is conflict and constant resistance, because the external behaviour doesn't match the internal belief. As with any autopilot system, there is a manual override, which is what grabbing hold of the behaviour is. The problem is that, while consciously we can continue to try and act in an outgoing manner, our subconscious autopilot, which is our belief, is constantly pulling us back to where we know we belong, i.e. being shy. Try as hard as we might, eventually we get tired and exhausted and stop consciously trying to be something that we know we're not, and we go back automatically to our old pre-programmed behaviour of being shy."

Maya put a cross through the box marked 'Behaviour/real performance' on the paper; she tapped the box with her pen, and said, "So, you can't change the way you perform on a substantial basis by simply grabbing hold of your behaviour, trying hard and holding onto it for grim death, like most people do. It simply doesn't work. It doesn't lead to automatic, long-term and free-flowing changes in performance, not if you're behaving in a way that you know, deep down, you don't believe in.

"The other thing to understand is that," leaning forward she put a cross through the box marked 'Beliefs or self-image', "we can't break into this cycle via self-image either! It is impossible to climb into the mind and remove the offending neurone cells that contain the negative and destructive beliefs. We don't have the technology to do that yet. Nor can we go shopping and buy a brand new brain full of new, positive beliefs!"

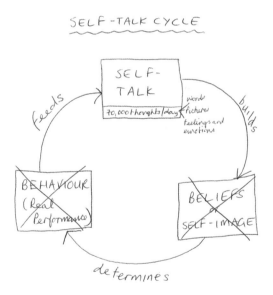

"What we can do, though, is take control of what builds our beliefs, our self-talk: the word-type thoughts, the picture-type thoughts and the feelings and emotion-type thoughts that build our beliefs in the first place. This is the only place where we can effectively break the vicious cycle and begin to take control, control the thoughts that build the beliefs in the first place."

"And it's really convenient, some would argue it is more than just a coincidence, that our thoughts are just about the only things in life over which we have complete control! Nobody can make us think anything we don't want to think! People may try; other people constantly try and print outside influences on our self-image and beliefs all the time, but they can only succeed if we allow them to. People will tell us all the time that we are this or that, and that other people are this, that or the other, and the world is this, that or the other, and we believe them! Our lives, other people and our world then become a reflection of the beliefs that others have given to us and we've accepted. We become prisoners of the beliefs we have acquired. We need to break free, in order to become our real, unlimited selves."

"The key to breaking free and taking control is not at the output end, by constantly changing our behaviour, and then crossing our fingers and hoping we get lucky, so that somehow the desired new behaviour sticks. That approach is as futile as it is stressful. The key to taking control is at the input end. Carefully choosing the word-type, picture-type and feelings and emotion-type thoughts that build the beliefs that represent what we want, that is the key. Taking control of our self-talk is what success in any area of life is all about. Constantly programming in what we want and the outcomes we want, is the way to take control. The frequency and intensity of feeling associated with the programming will determine how quickly our word-type thoughts, our picture-type thoughts and our feelings and emotion-type thoughts build new and improved beliefs in the subconscious self-image. Once these beliefs are locked in and the autopilot takes over, the desired behaviour, performance and outcome become inevitable. Beliefs, heart-felt beliefs, create our connectedness with all things, and they serve to marshal all the forces in the universe to work in harmony with us to turn belief into reality. Fact!"

Paul was taken aback by the force of Maya's last comment. She continued calmly and with absolute authority, "Trust me on this!

And the 70,000 thoughts we have a day are plenty to do this with; we don't need more. We just need to focus and concentrate our thoughts on what we want, not on what we don't want! It's simply about control, control at the self-talk or thought level. Do you see what I mean?"

Paul nodded and said, "It adds a great deal more to the spiritual text we've talked about before: 'in the beginning was the word, and the word was God'! Words, or at least the meaning we associate with the words that go on to make up our self-talk, are really, really powerful, aren't they!"

Maya agreed, "As we've said before, words are the most powerful drug used by humankind. There is no question of that. Our self-talk builds beliefs in our minds that can bear fruit or be pure poison. With the self-talk we choose to feed ourselves, we make our own heaven or our own hell, right here on Earth!" Paul had heard that before, but it had never meant as much as it did now; it struck a deep chord with him. He made himself a solemn promise to take complete control of his self-talk. He took a vow, not a vow of silence, but of right talk. He nodded to himself in full agreement with his vow and smiled.

Maya explained further, "You see, winners and losers have got very distinctive self-talk. The words that people use day in, day out, tell us all we need to know about them in terms of what's going on in their lives and the direction their lives are taking. The words people use are windows into their souls. All we need to do is sit back and listen! So, what do you think a winner's self-talk sounds like?"

Paul thought for a moment, and replied, "Well, it will be positive and upbeat all the time, always reflecting the kind of can-do, want-to attitudes that these people possess." Maya asked further, "You're absolutely right, but do they have positive self-talk all the time? What about when the chips are down and things seem to be working against them?"

Paul suggested, "Well, that is probably the biggest difference between winners' and losers' self-talk. When the chips are down, that is when winners' self-talk moves into overdrive; they are even more upbeat. They say to themselves, we can get over this no matter what!"

"You're spot on again, Paul," Maya said, "winners have a wonderful ability to focus on what they want and what it is going to look and feel like when the desired outcome has been achieved. They constantly feed themselves, and others, positive self-talk about how, if they try long and hard enough, they will succeed. They also possess an unshakeable belief that all the forces in the universe will conspire to not only show them the way to succeed, but also find the resources to do so!

"Losers, however," Maya continued, "seem to have the ability to do the opposite. They feed themselves, and others, self-talk about the desired outcome being impossible, how it's never been done before, how difficult it would be. They focus their self-talk on the pitfalls, shortfalls and inadequacies that they and others have. They focus on these problems with such intensity that in their minds the problems become insurmountable! Everyone stops trying and, lo and behold, they've all failed to achieve something, again! In fact, it is more than a vicious cycle. It is more of a vicious spiral. It becomes a self-talk spiral, where the words, pictures and feelings and emotions fed into it determine whether the spiral goes 'up the way' or 'down the way'. Maya completed the diagram she had started earlier:

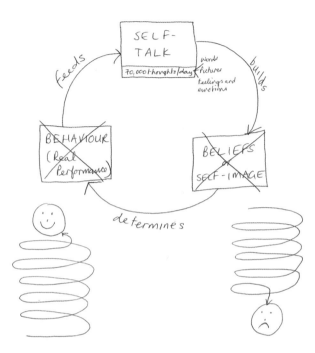

SELF-TALK ~~CYCLE~~ SPIRAL

"You see," she elaborated, "study after study shows a clear link between the range, richness and focus of our vocabulary, and the success we enjoy in life. For instance, the prison population in every country in the world has the smallest range and richness of vocabulary of any segment of the population. The range is limited, the richness is limited, so painting winning pictures together with associated positive feelings and emotions is limited. The cell walls or perimeter fence they physically find themselves behind are merely a reflection of their mental prison. We can be as confined and limited as our smallest dominant thought, or as expansive and great as our largest dominant aspiration. We choose.

"As you know, however, it is more than words. It is the meaning that we associate with the words that determines whether the self-talk spiral goes up or down. For example, in Ghana, within the Ashanti tribe the tradition is that people are given a middle name that reflects the day of the week upon which they were born. However, it's not just the name of the day of the week that is important, Paul 'Wednesday' Adams. It is the meaning associated with the name that is important. Just as here in the UK, they have a sayings along the lines of 'Monday's child is fair of face; Tuesday's child is full of grace; Wednesday's child is full of woe; Thursday's child has far to go', etc. The meaning associated with Wednesday in their language and tradition is troublemaker! So, imagine the impact that has on anyone's self-talk spiral, to have yourself, and others, telling you you're a 'troublemaker' from the day you're born! There are more than 50,000 crimes a year in Ghana, and more than 50% of them are committed by people born on Wednesdays!"

Paul was stunned, "Blimey! And this all links back to what we were saying earlier about the names we call people and the words, or rather the meaning associated with the words, that we use for people, children in particular. Just how powerful is this stuff?"

Maya interrupted, "But the key here, to taking control, is to control what we feed ourselves to determine in which direction we set our own self-talk spiralling, up or down. We can't control what other people say to us, but we can control what we do with it! If our thought process is one of the very few things in our lives that we have complete control over, and, if there is a big guy or gal in the sky somewhere who made it that way, do you think he or she might be trying to tell us something?" Maya leaned over and her hand circled the paper, index finger extended, "You'd better control it," she tapped the 'Self-talk' box, "because, if you don't control it, it controls you!"

It all made perfect sense to Paul and he felt uplifted, "I feel more euphoric, more powerful and more in control every time we meet, as you open up another level of understanding for me. In fact, it is all so simple; the keys to happiness, success, wealth, health and the like, are available to everyone. None of what you're asking me to do is beyond the ability of anyone on the planet. This could cause a seismic revolution in human consciousness if enough people begin to master it. We could really change the world for the better!"

Maya laughed and said, "Hold on, Paul! Let's just start with changing your world first. It may be, as you say simple, but let me assure you it isn't easy. Let's just think about some of the words and phrases that distinguish winners from losers, should we? This will be a fascinating and eye-opening lesson." Maya handed Paul a piece of paper headed, 'Winner and loser self-talk.' "There are two columns. Just read down them and see if you can recognise any of the phrases." The piece of paper looked like this:

Winner and loser self-talk	
Winners say	*Losers say*
Life is good to me	Nothing ever goes my way
I'm amazed at what I get done these days	I don't have the energy I used to!
I'm the luckiest person alive!	The only luck I ever get is bad luck!
I'll find time to do it	How do you expect me to find time to do it?
Let's get to the heart of the matter and sort it out …	I can't seem to get to the root of the problem
I haven't expressed myself clearly	You just don't understand …
I dislike that intensely!	I hate that and everyone and everything
We have different views on things	I'm not changing my mind
I'm OK, but there's still room for improvement	I'm not as bad as the others. Have you heard about such and such?

Tell me what you think; give me your opinion. If you were me, what would you do?	*I have said it again and again, now just get on with it and do it!*
There must be a better way	*We've always done it this way*
It's difficult ... but it's possible	*It's possible ... but it's difficult*
Everytime I make a mistake, I use it as a learning opportunity to grow and develop	*I seem to get everything wrong these days.*
Let's make it work this time	*There's no point in trying again*
Let's work on a presentation for management	*Management will never agree to that*
I'm always on time for everything	*I am always late for everything*
You learn something new everyday	*What about all my years of experience?*
My weight is always consistent and acceptable	*I can lose weight, but I always put it back on again*
Let's make it work this time. A solution already exists, it's just waiting for us to find it	*There's no point in trying again. Everytime we've tried, we've failed*
Let me help you. Between us we can succeed	*That's not my job! It's more than my job's worth to get involved.*
That sounds exciting	*Why keep changing things?*
I've learned who you can trust these days	*You can't trust anyone these days*
Let's go do it!	*You go do it!*

Paul laughed, chuckled, nodded and shook his head as he worked his way down the list, "This is so revealing! And what you're saying is so true! This one in particular made me smile." He tapped at one of the items in the 'Losers say' column. There is a guy who works in our office, and last year we bought him a T-shirt with his name on it and his favourite catch phrase in the middle of it. It was a spoof of boxers who have a nickname, like Ricky 'hitman' Hatton, the world champion from Manchester. His T-shirt read, 'Nic 'How do you expect me to find time to do that?' Robinson'! Because every time anybody asks him to do anything, it's like pressing the play button on a CD system. And, surprise, surprise, he is the one who gets the least done in an office of 50 people! He has become, so far as our office is concerned, one of life's victims, always overworked, overwhelmed and being picked on. But tell me, how would you change that if you were Nic?"

Maya replied instantly, "Nic must change the words he uses. He must change his self-talk. Instead of telling himself all the time he is overworked, why doesn't he say he's in demand, or something similar? By changing the words, we can change the meaning, and therefore the way we feel, which in turn begins to change the belief, and the behaviour will automatically follow!" Paul nodded his understanding. He continued, "So, instead of being overwhelmed, why doesn't he say he is coping, and instead of being picked on, why doesn't he say that he is one of the chosen few? Maya, the power of this is immense!"

Maya nodded in agreement, "You're not kidding. It lies at the heart of taking control. It's about people learning a whole new winner vocabulary and dumping the loser vocabulary. And, it's something we need to take control of, from the minute we wake up in the morning until we go to sleep at night. For instance, if you bump into someone you know in the corridor at work first thing in the morning, and ask them how they are, what are the typical responses you get?" Paul thought for a moment and answered

"Well, the responses vary from things like 'Believe me, you don't want to know!' to 'Not too bad', 'Can't complain' or 'I'm OK, thanks'."

Maya continued, "From those responses, what does that suggest is really going on in their minds? If someone says, 'Not too bad', they mean that they're not too good as well! Do you understand how incredibly powerful this self-talk thing is? This one is an absolute classic: 'Can't complain!' Think about it: what do they actually mean? What they mean is, 'Well I can't complain to you right now, but if you give me 4 hours of your time, I'll chew your ear off and tell you how bad things are'! Remember, the words people use all the time are windows into their soul and, in this instance, how much of a maelstrom of negativity are they suffering from, do you think?" Paul laughed out loud at this, but then felt saddened as he realised that this was all self-inflicted and, therefore, all so unnecessary and avoidable.

Maya elaborated further, "A lot of people fail to appreciate how much power and control they exercise in their lives as a direct result of the words they use. I attended a conference recently and the topic of self-talk was on the agenda. One delegate, called Simon, got very defensive about the words he used, and tried to brush off the importance of this. 'They are only words,' he protested, 'they're not that important. They don't mean anything'. A close associate of his almost exploded with exasperation at how blinkered people can be sometimes. He asked Simon a question that he already knew the answer to: 'If you meet anyone you know, or answer the phone to anyone you know, and they ask you how you are, what is your automatic response?' Simon looked a little uncomfortable and somewhat embarrassed, as he answered the question honestly. In a faint, mumbled voice, he said, 'Well, I say "I'm miserable, as usual!"' Simon justified this by explaining that he was only kidding, and that his first ever boss used to say it; he'd picked it up from him years ago and it had stuck.

"The facilitator went on to ask Simon how many times a day he was asked, 'How are you?', face to face and on the phone, and he worked out that it was a minimum of 150 times. The point was gently pushed, 'So, 150 times a day, you are telling yourself that you are "miserable as usual". It's not the best self-talk or programming in the world, Simon, is it? And, before you say you're only kidding one more time, do you know what everyone has observed about you?' Simon shook his head. 'The only thing that has been consistent in all of our descriptions of you, is that you're a miserable sod!' The colour drained from Simon's face as he realised the awesome truth. He was responsible for this, solely and entirely. He vowed that second to change his self-talk.

"We went on at the conference to have an excellent discussion about the fact that life is a matter of choice, and that the words chosen that dominate our thoughts determine how we feel, build our beliefs and determine our behaviour. We wondered, if we do have a choice, how would we want to be when anyone asks us. We all agreed that phrases, said with real feeling, such as 'I'm on top form!', 'I'm great, thanks', 'I'm terrific', 'I'm wonderful', were infinitely preferable to 'I'm not bad' or 'I'm fair to middling'. We all agreed to create a success vocabulary that builds only the beliefs we want, thereby channelling our full power to create the positive outcomes and behaviours we choose. Again, it's so simple, but it's not easy. Here are some of the favourite suggestions we came up with: we never 'get depressed' but we sometimes get 'calm before action'; nothing is 'terrible' but we encounter lots of 'challenges'; we don't make 'mistakes' but we have some tremendous 'learning experiences'; we are never 'lost', we're always 'searching'. Do you get this, Paul? I mean really get it?"

Paul was nonplussed at how simple this was. But he wasn't disappointed he hadn't realised it sooner, he was excited that he'd discovered it now. He didn't feel stupid for not understanding it before, but exhilarated that he now did. He didn't feel he'd wasted his whole life up to now, he couldn't wait to put it all into practice. He didn't just feel good about it all, he felt in control and unstoppable!

Maya drew the conversation to a close by saying, "I think we've done enough for tonight. We've covered a huge amount. Just one thing to finish with: the guy who vowed to change his self-talk on the conference, Simon the 'miserable as usual' one? Within weeks, he was getting comments from all his friends and colleagues about how he had changed so radically in such a short time. Some of them even confessed to him that they had been reluctant to speak to him because, after 10 minutes, they almost lost the will to live, he was so negative and miserable! And now, they said, they call him up just to get the 'feel good' factor he oozes! They wanted to know his secret!"

Maya suggested they stopped their discussion there for the night, and agreed to call Paul. They left together; Paul was buoyant.

Chapter Seventeen

Paul was amazed over the next few days as he listened intently to the self-talk of the people around him. His astonishment grew the more he learned to control his own self-talk. Now that he'd disciplined himself to replace positive words and phrases for the negative ones that had, over the years, become an automatic part of his vocabulary, he was in a constant state of euphoria. A cocktail of positive feelings intoxicated him. He felt calm, in control, powerful beyond measure, energetic, full of health, energy and vitality; he felt boundless; he felt a connectedness to all things.

He found the discipline needed to replace his traditional negative words and phrases with positive ones quite tough at first. However, after a little practice, he found it easier and easier to master. As the words and phrases he now used, or rather the meaning and feelings he associated with them, changed, so did the fabric of his very being. He learned that merely using positive words and phrases without meaning them or believing them made no changes at all. He also learned that the more intense and heart-felt the feelings he attached to the words and phrases, the more profound the change.

These dramatic and positive changes were commented on by everyone who met him. His feelings of boundlessness and connectedness radiated out through every aspect of his behaviour.

He saw, heard and felt the world in a different way. As he observed, he realised that at one time he would have been saddened and frustrated by the sea of negativity in which the human race had chosen to swim. Today, however, he was enthusiastic and determined to do all in his power, and whatever it took, to alter it, to change it for the better. He felt compassion and love for the whole of the human race in a way he had never previously experienced. He was having deep, powerful and positive feelings about himself and other people at a level he hadn't previously known existed. 'There may be 6.2 billion people on this planet,' he thought, 'but we're all one, we're all connected at this deeper level'.

He became more and more determined to change the cold sea of negativity to a warm sea of positivity. 'Once people realise that they have a choice,' he thought, 'who wouldn't choose the warm sea of positivity that benefits both the individual and the whole of humankind?'

The sheer size and scale of this task simply made Paul more resolute. If he started with his family and relatives, then his friends and people at work, within a short time scale the impact would be dramatic. He smiled to himself as he thought that this was the next logical step for humankind to take: 'We've had an agricultural revolution, an industrial revolution, a technological revolution, an electronic revolution, an information and knowledge revolution, now it's time for a thinking revolution! The thinking revolution would have a bigger and more positive impact on humanity than all other revolutions put together.'

It has to start with people the day they're born, and percolate into every facet of what they think, say and do. He laughed at himself, as he remembered that the first words his children learned to say were negative ones: 'No!', 'Naughty' and 'Don't!' He was intrigued to discover how many times he overheard one person telling another person how to do something, when the reality was they were actually telling them what not to do! He overheard a classic example in the sales office at work, where an experienced account manager was instructing a new member of the team how to handle a particular customer. The discussion went like this: 'Now, don't say such and such, and don't do this or that, and for goodness sake, never mention da, da, da'. 'All they were doing,' Paul thought, 'was making it more likely that what they didn't want to happen happened! It's ludicrous when you think about it.'

No wonder so many people's lives are made up of one series of struggles and disasters after another. So many people are lost, confused, miserable and sinking, all because they are using the wrong words, triggering the wrong pictures, creating the wrong feelings and emotions, building negative beliefs that are then presented back to them in the form of the world they live in.

'The world we live in,' he thought, 'in the physical realm, is nothing more than a giant hologram of the one we have chosen and created in our thought realm. Our physical reality is nothing more than a reflection of the multi-dimensional, multi-sensory one we have created with our thoughts in our minds.' He was definite about that.

'So, is the physical realm we choose for ourselves real?' Paul's mind struggled to find the answer. 'Surely it can't all be an illusion?' He decided, 'It's not an illusion, it's a creation! I've created mine. Jackie has created hers. And Maya has created hers.' Then it hit him. 'No, no, Maya hasn't created hers, she has recreated hers. That's what the guidance has been about!' He thought deeply, and came to a realisation: 'Of course, we accept the reality of our world as it is presented to us! Maya simply refused to accept the reality of her world the way it had been presented to her up to her recent transformation. She has rejected the old, negative reality and decided on a new and positive one of her own; a glorious, positive, technicolor, multi-sensory production of her own making, and now she's living it. Human beings really do become on the outside what they think about on the inside.' Now he understood what that meant at a deeper and more fundamental level. He felt his world tremble as he locked onto the simple truth: we really do create our own reality with our own thoughts. He decided to take control. The world trembled in anticipation.

When Paul opened his eyes and moved his arms, he realised that the water in his bath had almost gone cold. His thoughts had taken him to another dimension for nearly an hour, but to Paul it had been an eternity where there was no such a thing as time. It was a good job he had been alone in the house, so that his thinking could come to such a monumental conclusion without interruption. Just as he had dried himself off and put on his dressing gown, the phone rang. It was Maya. "Hello, stranger", he answered. Maya replied, "Stranger? What do you mean? It's only been 5 days since I last saw you?!"

"You know as well as I do," Paul said, "that I have journeyed for what seems an eternity and back in the last 5 days." Maya laughed and asked, "So you've had an awakening, then? It's a marvellous experience, isn't it? Did you feel the whole world tremble? That's what happens when you have such a seismic shift in your thinking and you accept the great universal truth that we create our own world with our own thoughts."

Paul commented, "I don't think the world trembled. I think the universe trembled! I think I shifted the centre of gravity of the entire universe when it hit me. My thoughts are now marshalled. I am in control. My thought world is changing and my real world is responding accordingly. I now realise how unstoppable I am, so watch out world! In fact, watch out universe!"

Maya spoke calmly down the phone , "Paul, you're not quite unstoppable yet! There are a couple more things you need to understand and embrace fully before you can turn the power up to maximum." Paul protested, "But surely I can't feel any more powerful and unstoppable than I do now?" Maya continued in a calm voice, "You are still in first gear and, before you can reach top gear and full revs, you have to face and overcome your biggest challenge. Every individual on this journey finds the next stage the biggest challenge. When can we meet, so that I can guide and navigate you through these potentially perilous waters?" Paul replied with eagerness: "Well, is tomorrow night OK for you? The Old Fox at 7 pm?" Maya said, "That will be fine, I'll see you then", and hung up.

Chapter Eighteen

When Maya saw Paul sitting at their usual table, her face lit up with a warm smile. "My word," she said "the power is really beginning to build in you! I can see why you were so insistent that you were already unstoppable when I spoke to you. All the forces in the universe are aligning themselves to flow through you and from you."

Paul quizzed Maya, "You mean you can see that?" Maya responded, "See it! Goodness Paul, you can feel it, and anybody in a 10 mile radius of you can see and feel it, too, if they just quiet their minds and tune in to you. However, for all the aligning and for all the force and power you now have, one major blockage still remains that could stifle and nullify your unlimited nature."

Paul said a little flippantly, "OK then, let's get this little devil exorcised!" Maya replied quite seriously, "A devil it is, little it is not!" Paul was humbled and waited patiently for her to take the lead.

Maya liked using diagrams to help Paul understand the key lessons in the journey towards total fulfilment, so she once again produced a piece of paper, "OK, here goes. There is the constituent part of our self-image or beliefs that is primarily responsible for our performance. It is called our self-esteem. You have heard that term before?" Paul nodded, and Maya continued, "And have you heard that you should do everything possible to maintain your self-esteem, for yourself and for others?" Again, Paul nodded.

Maya then asked, "If you have to do everything possible to maintain self-esteem for yourself and others, why is it so important do you think? What is self-esteem, that it is so important, that you have to do all in your power to maintain it? We know what self-esteem does: it is primarily responsible for regulating our performance, but what is it exactly?"

Paul struggled to answer, "I feel I know the answer implicitly, but I can't seem to find the words to explain it explicitly. Isn't it something to do with how we feel about ourselves?" "That's a good answer, Paul, it's pretty close. Self-esteem is actually the value that we place on ourselves; it's our feeling of self-worth." Maya drew on the paper again:

"One of the reasons that I, as your guide, am so tough on eliminating any kind of bad talking for yourself and for others, is because all kinds of studies have proved, over and over again, that any kind of bad talk reduces your self-esteem and proportionately reduces your performance. It erodes your confidence and the value you place on yourself by highlighting inadequacies, pitfalls, shortfalls and the like. If you want to understand this at the deepest level, you need to study the way top-performing teams operate and talk to each other. For instance, most people would agree that the British SAS are the top performers in the world when it comes to elite fighting forces, right?"

Paul nodded his head and said, "Without a doubt!" Maya continued, "So, do you know anything about the way these guys get trained, when they get selected to serve in the SAS?" Paul shook his head, "Well, no, not really. All I know is that it's tough."

Maya nodded, "That's a huge understatement! SAS training actually has two phases. In phase 1 new recruits are methodically and deliberately taken apart, both physically and mentally. Why do you think they do that? Why get the finest individuals in the armed services, and then pull them apart?" Paul answered confidently, "Well, I guess it is to expose all their fears and doubts and 'black holes'?"

Maya continued, "Yes, but again the question has to be asked: why would they do that? What are they trying to achieve? And the answer is that they are trying to strip them naked mentally, to get them down to the equivalent of bare rock. Once they've got them at rock bottom, with all their negatives exposed and then out of the way, then they can move on to phase 2. And guess what they do to them in phase 2?"

Again, Paul answered confidently, "Well, build them back up again, from a solid foundation." Maya said, "Exactly! That is exactly what they do. Now what do they build them back up to believe during phase 2?"

Paul replied instantly, "Well, they build them back up to believe that they are invincible, that they can do anything. They build them back up to believe they are so tough they can withstand anything; they are so bright they can outwit and outmanoeuvre the enemy in any circumstances; they are unstoppable whatever obstacles may get in the way."

Maya nodded approval, "Now, let me ask you something else: during phase 1 of this training, how much bad talking do you think goes on, especially by the trainers, the commanding officers and other people in authority?" Paul replied, "Well, I've seen what goes on. There was a television programme about it just last week, and I've read loads of articles about it. The bad talking barrage is almost non-stop: 'You useless thing, you', 'You think you're so tough, and what do we find on your first outing, eh? You're a wimp!', 'You are nothing!' and 'You're less than a dog's bottom of a nothing!' It's quite incredible." Maya asked, "And what impact do you think that has on the new recruits' self-esteem and confidence?" Paul replied, "Well, it would destroy them, of course."

Maya went on, "So, when the job is complete and their self-esteem has hit rock bottom, exposing the foundations, the rebuilding process begins. And as the recruits are built up to believe that they are invincible, how much bad talking goes on now, especially as they are preparing for a mission?" Paul's face, and an almost imperceptible shake of his head, told Maya that he knew the answer. "Yes, yes, that's right," she said, "none! Absolutely none! And, do you know what happens to anyone in the SAS who gets caught bad talking themselves or anyone else on the team? Paul shook his head this time and guessed, "I don't know. Do they have to go through phase 1 again?"

"No, no," Maya replied, "it's much more serious than that. They get thrown out! They get what they call RTUed, returned to unit. They get sent back to the unit from which they were originally recruited. It can take you 3 years to get into the SAS, and it can take you 3 seconds to get kicked out!

"What's interesting about this, is the reason why an organisation such as the SAS would be so strict and punitive about bad talking during phase 2 of their training, or when they are preparing and building up for a mission. Why do they have zero tolerance towards it?" Paul was puzzled for a moment, and then it dawned on him, "Well, surely it is because, during a dangerous mission, with all the unknowns and uncertainties and things that can go wrong, they need to be 100% focused and on top of their game, firing on all cylinders, in order to succeed." Maya nodded her agreement, and Paul continued, "Because if their performance is not 100% of what it should be, they could pay the ultimate price! They could pay with their lives, or the lives of their colleagues or hostages, or whoever they have been charged to take care of."

Maya resumed, "So, when people in the SAS have got their own or other people's lives on the line, and they, therefore, allow no bad talking, that tells us something important, doesn't it? They understand, probably better than most, how much power and focus can be lost, and what it could, potentially, cost. The key to all this is about building belief; total and absolute belief. You can put all the effort in the world into blowing up a car tyre, but if someone is round the other side driving nails in to it ..." Paul finished the sentence for her "... you will never be able to get it to do the job for which it was intended, in anything like the way it was intended!"

Maya continued, "When you ask anyone in the SAS how they manage to complete their mission impossibles and succeed against incredible odds, they will tell you their secret. They'll tell you that it's because they are the best! Purely and simply, the best. But their secret is not so much in what they say, as in how they say it. They say it like this," Maya picked up her glass, "See this? This is a glass, right? Fact!" Maya picked up the paper she had been drawing on, "This is a piece of paper, right? Fact!" She then pointed both hands at herself, and said, "See me? I'm the best, right? Fact! You see, they say I, and mean it, with total belief. Total and absolute belief, a powerful knowing, with the absence of any doubt: they simply are the best! Fact! That belief is so deeply ingrained and embedded in their minds, and is so constantly reinforced by themselves and everyone else around them, that there is no room for any doubt whatsoever. It's not a wish, not a hope, not hype; it's a total and absolute belief.

"Once that belief is locked in place, in fact, as you know, once any belief gets locked in place to that degree, all the forces in the universe are effectively instructed to come together to find and present to us the set of circumstances needed to turn that belief into a reality. As long as that belief remains firmly locked in place, extraordinary levels of commitment, determination, stamina, energy and creativity become the norm. You find that you get the lucky breaks. You get those strange coincidences that guide you towards an inevitable reality. This is truly metaphysical. It is, literally, beyond the physical.

"It works. In fact, in this instance, it goes beyond the belief that they, the SAS, are the best. They also believe that they've got the best of everything: the best selection procedures, the best equipment, the best training, the best intelligence and reconnaissance, the best back-up support and command systems, and the like. They believe they are the best, and that they've got the best, of everything!"

Paul was open mouthed as Maya continued, "Now for a really important question: is it 100% incontrovertibly true that the SAS are the best elite fighting force in the world, and that they've got the best of everything?" Paul answered quickly, "Well, most people would tell you that they are." Maya nodded, and said, "Yes, yes, I know that, but is it 100% true that they are?" Paul was slightly uncomfortable, "Well, I don't know. I'm no military expert". Maya continued, "That's exactly what I'm trying to get at. If you brought military experts in here from the USA, Israel, etc., they'd all make a really strong case that the USA Navy Seals are the best, that the Israeli Air Force, the red bereted paratroopers, the Golani are the best. Do you get my drift? They would probably bring charts and statistics and all kinds of proof to show that their elite fighting forces have the best selection procedures, the best equipment, the best training, etc. And they could probably prove it, on paper. But the important thing is this, does any of that so-called proof matter?" Paul shook his head, and Maya continued, "It doesn't matter one bit! Once again, what matters is not what's true, but what you believe to be true! It's belief that gets reflected into your life as a reality, not what's true!

"Another thing is that, when they say they're the best, they don't say it arrogantly. It's not a 'Oh, look at me, I'm the greatest thing since sliced bread' bragging approach. They just say it in a very matter of fact way. It's just a fact they're stating. You see, when people believe, really believe, when they know, they don't have to go out and shout about it." Maya pointed her hands to her heart, "You see, when you know, you don't go out you go in! You become centred and aligned. You go quiet, not loud. Because when you believe, when you know, you just know! So there is no need for bluster, or hype, or any form of bullshit or arrogance. You know your actions and the results will speak for you.

"If you do fall into the trap of going out and telling people how wonderful and gifted and talented you are, the feelings associated with those very words begin to steal the energy and dissipate the power! You effectively rob yourself of the creative energy and force that was working on your behalf. We must trust our actions to do the impressing, rather than use our words to do the expressing. There is an old saying that sums this up beautifully: 'Let other people blow your horn, the sound will travel 10 times further!'"

Paul laughed in response, thinking of all the people he knew who tried to big up every aspect of their lives with talk, but no belief, and ended up falling flat on their faces! "So, what you believe doesn't need to be true for all the forces in the universe to begin working for you, to present you with the circumstances to bring it all to fruition? You just need to believe it's true?"

Maya nodded, and Paul continued, "And it's not a good idea to show off to other people your intentions, either? Mmm, it kind of flies in the face of conventional thinking and practices, doesn't it?" Maya replied, "Well something needs to, doesn't it? How many people do you know live a life overflowing with true treasures, such as love, friendship, joy, success, happiness, health, wealth, compassion, energy, vitality and the like? Conventional thinking and practices are imprisoning us instead of liberating us. If we free up our thinking, we free up our lives. Our entire existence takes on new dimensions." Paul nodded in agreement. He knew she was right. He just knew.

Maya continued, "Let me give you some examples of how free thinking, or rather non-conventional thinking, affects actions and results. First is an experiment that is probably run hundreds of times every year in psychology departments in universities all over the world. They take, say, 100 students and gather them together in a room to sit an academic examination. The students complete the examination and are told to come back after lunch for the results. The examination papers are marked by experienced invigilators, and, of course, invigilators never lie. When the students return, however, the invigilators do lie, and tell the students who were in the top 50 that they were in the bottom 50, and that 'This examination topic and style does not suit your particular academic prowess!' The ones who were in fact in the bottom 50 are told that they were in the top 50, and that the examination topic and style 'suited you down to the ground'. They are then given another examination in the afternoon; same topic, same style. But this time the beliefs of the students have been altered by the invigilators telling them a false truth. The students complete the second examination and are asked to return in 2 hours for the results. And guess what?"

Paul was a little unsure, "Do the results get reversed? Were the ones who believed they were in the top 50, when in reality they were in the bottom 50, actually become the top 50? And vice versa?"

Maya responded, "That would be a miracle, wouldn't it! It's not quite as dramatic as that, but it is hugely significant. The students who were told they were in the top 50, when they were in the bottom 50, all performed better in the afternoon than they did in the morning. Not on average, but every single one of them performed better! And the students who believed they were in the bottom 50, when in reality they were in the top 50, all performed worse in the afternoon than they did in the morning! Every single one of them."

Paul picked up on this quickly, "So, this is another example of how people don't behave or perform in accordance with what is real or true, but in accordance with their perception or belief of what is real or true!" Maya said, "Exactly! What people perceive and believe becomes real."

She went on, "We, as human beings, cannot behave or perform on the outside in a long-term, automatic and free-flowing manner in a way that is different from the person we perceive ourselves to be on the inside. What is real and what is true is irrelevant, because our internal perceptions and our beliefs create our external realities. Our perceptions and beliefs create and rule our world! When we change them, our world changes. Our world is a reflection, a three-dimensional hologram, of our perceptions and beliefs, good and bad.

"The example I've just given you is known as a blind experiment, which means that the students did not know the truth, so they acted in accordance with the truth as they perceived it to be. There are millions of examples of this all around you, if you look for them. It is so subtle and sublime that sometimes what you don't 'know' to be true can work its way out into a reality as well. Let me explain."

"You'll need to," said Paul, "you've lost me a bit with that last statement"

Maya continued, "One day in 1939 a student called George Dantzig arrived late for a higher level statistics class at the University of California, Berkley. On the blackboard Professor Neyman, whose class it was, had written two problems. Dantzig assumed they were the homework assignment. Having copied them down, it took him a few days to complete the homework because the problems seemed a little harder than normal. What Dantzig hadn't realised was that the two problems had been presented in the part of the class he'd missed as two famous unsolvable problems in statistics that mathematicians since Einstein had been trying to solve without success! Dantzig didn't 'know' these problems couldn't be solved, and it just goes to show, when people are unfettered by any perceived limitation of what they can accomplish, how they can manage some extraordinary feats through their natural talent and hard work! It reinforces that Mark Twain comment about 'If you think you can, or if you think you can't, you're right!'"

Maya went on, "There are other, more powerful, examples. I heard of a professor of psychology at Harvard or Yale, Rosenthal was his name, who ran a series of experiments with students in high schools. One was at a school in southern California, where he experimented with 14-year-olds. Apparently, that age group has particularly bad problems because of raging hormones. Teachers all over the world say that they are the hardest age group to work with.

"This school in California was a large one, with about 110 teaching staff. Once he had the headteacher's co-operation, Rosenthal asked if he could borrow his office for a couple of hours in order to apply some strict selection criteria to the list of staff, and find the best three teachers for the experiment. Then Rosenthal arranged a meeting with the three chosen teachers and the headteacher, to tell them they had been selected to take part in a really exciting experiment. The teachers were told that the strict selection criteria had placed them head and shoulders above the other teaching staff and so, as the best three teachers in the school, they were to be given the best three classes of students. They were told that the basic tenet of the experiment was to put the best teachers with the best students and see what the results were. They were also told that the normal school policy of picking mixed ability classes at random had been overridden on this occasion, so that they had the best students in their classes. The teachers were to run the lessons and cover the curriculum as normal but abide by two rules for the duration of the experiment, which was to cover one academic year. The first rule was that the teachers could not tell the students they were the best 14-year-olds in the school. The students must not know that they had been handpicked or specially selected for this experiment. The second rule was that the teachers could not tell anyone else about the experiment, not their fellow teachers, their partners nor their friends. Absolutely no-one was to know, apart from the five of them in the headteacher's office that day. They all agreed. At the end of each term they would be asked to give the headteacher and Rosenthal an update on the progress they were making, so they could all review the results. There was agreement all around.

"The three teachers went about their work, and at the end of the first term duly reported their experiences and results. The three classes of students were a full 18% ahead of the other seven classes of students in that year group, across the whole range of subjects taught. The reports from each of the teachers were fabulous: 'These kids are great', 'There are no discipline problems', 'They all help each other out', 'We've got to push them out of the door at 2.30 p.m., they're all so keen!', 'It's great to have nobody in the class slowing everyone else down'. They all agreed that this had been the most fulfilling and enjoyable teaching term they'd ever had in their extensive school careers. The reports were exceptional. In fact, they wanted to make the results official after just one term, and announce to the world what they'd achieved by selecting the best teachers and the best students and putting them together! However, Rosenthal reiterated that the experiment was to run for the whole academic year before any announcements were made.

"The second term went just as well, if not better, than the first one, for the teachers and students alike. When they got together for the second review, the results had moved the three classes 39% ahead of the other seven classes. The reports from the teachers were spectacular, and everyone was delighted with the way the experiment was going. The students in the three classes were all, from an educational viewpoint, flying.

"At the end of the third term the results put these three classes of students 52% ahead of the other classes of 14 year olds. The teachers expounded the virtue of the experiment, not just because of the academic results produced, but also because of how it had made the teachers and students feel. They had never felt better, the team spirit was brilliant, and it was a rip-roaring success in every way imaginable. The teachers were keen to tell everyone why the results were so good. The staff room had been awash with rumour regarding the reasons why.

"Rosenthal explained that he would be more than happy to let everyone know what they had done, once he had enlightened the three teachers with more details about the experiment. This created some unease, because the teachers thought they knew exactly what the experiment had comprised. Rosenthal then revealed to them that the three classes they'd been teaching had been selected randomly in the normal way, the way that had been established in the school for about 20 years! The students in the three classes were, therefore, of the usual mixed ability. They'd been selected in the usual way, by matching school roll numbers with randomly generated numbers from a computer.

"The only difference, therefore, was that the teachers believed their classes had been specially populated with the school's best students. The three teachers were almost violent in their reactions to this revelation, and insisted that this could not be the case, because the students were so fantastic. There was something special about them, there could be no doubt, based on the experiences of the year and the results. Eventually they accepted, however, that the students were of the usual mixed ability and that the only thing special about them was that they believed them to be special.

"Despite this revelation, the teachers were all still, metaphorically, blinded. All three fought hard in their minds to justify and rationalise what had happened. They continued to argue that that there must be a more logical reason for the results: surely it couldn't be down to something as simple as belief. They then concluded that, if the children were not in fact specially selected, the great results must be because they were specially selected. Remember, they had been told they were selected because they were 'head and shoulders' above the others. They were therefore even more stunned when Rosenthal confessed that the strict selection criteria he had used for choosing the three of them was nothing more than writing the names of all the teaching staff on individual pieces of paper, folding them up and putting them in an empty waste paper bin, closing his eyes and picking out three. So the teachers and the students had been chosen at random!

"This is called a double-blind experiment, because neither the students nor the teachers knew the truth. But the critical thing here is this: what did the teachers believe?" Paul answered conclusively, "Well, they believed that they were the best and that they were teaching the best!"

Maya continued, "Correct! And, what was the truth or the reality?" Paul replied, "No" and "That they were an ordinary bunch of mixed ability students picked at random and that the teachers were picked at random as well" Maya emphasised the point by asking, "So, where did the extraordinary results come from? Did they come from the truth, or did they come from and reflect the belief?" Paul affirmed, "Well from the belief, of course. I now understand what you mean when you say the truth is irrelevant. Truth does not create our reality, our beliefs create our reality."

Maya now asked, "Have you heard the phrase 'I'll believe it when I see it'?" Paul nodded and said, "Surely everyone has heard that?" "Maybe," Maya said, "but our understanding now turns that on its head, and so it should. That phrase is a sceptic's viewpoint. What truly visionary people know is: 'When I **believe** it, I will see it'! The belief comes first, the reality comes second, and the reality always follows the belief. It's a dynamite discovery, isn't it?"

"Maya, it's brilliant. It explains so much. And I want to know how to build these beliefs, so that I can create a brand new reality for me and, eventually, the rest of the world." Maya laughed at his enthusiasm and he remarked, "How could anyone *not* be enthusiastic about this? It's truly the stuff of life; it's what humans have been searching for since time immemorial, isn't it? This can set humankind free to build a new world order, to create a heaven on Earth."

Maya conceded the point, "That is undoubtedly the case. We just need enough people, with what we can call right thinking, for a peaceful and joyful revolution to take place throughout the world. One of the problems is that thinking isn't taught in schools or universities. However, coming back to what you were saying a minute ago, you don't need to know how to build beliefs to create a new reality for yourself. You know that already. You know how beliefs get built. You just need a little guidance on how to take control of what you're building. But before you can do that, you need to understand the two laws that drive all the processes in the universe that make all we've been talking about happen. It doesn't happen by accident you know! Beliefs manifesting themselves into reality, irrespective of what the truth might be, follow laws. Everything in this universe is governed by laws, natural laws, and beliefs becoming reality for every individual is no different. The first law is the law of attraction, and this is a process that instructs and aligns all the forces in the universe to come together and turn beliefs into realities." She handed Paul another piece of paper and written on it was:

Law of Attraction

We draw towards us the people, relationships (personal and business), friends, houses, cars, jobs, responsibilities, results etc... that we feel WORTHY of receiving. ☺

Paul read it thoroughly, twice, and then said, "Mmm, that seems to make sense. I think I understand it, but I want to be 100% sure. I don't want to miss anything out about this." Maya replied, "Believe me, you definitely don't want to miss anything out about this. This is vital to understanding how we communicate directly with the intelligent, creative energy that holds all the forces in the universe together, that can work through you, around you and from you. These natural forces will give you, or help you find, the circumstances and resources needed to fulfil every right and proper desire you may have. They never let you down.

"The law of attraction is, effectively, a process; what this means is that, in our minds, we have the equivalent of both a transmitter and a receiver. Depending on the range of the bandwidth that we transmit, that is what tends to be reflected back into our lives. In other words, what turns up in our lives, or what we receive, is determined by the range that we transmit in the first place! The range of the bandwidth that we transmit is directly related to what we, as individuals, feel worthy of receiving. It's determined by the value we place on ourselves and our heart-felt feeling of worthiness. So nothing, and I mean nothing, will remain a permanent and automatic part of our lives, unless we feel worthy of receiving it. Now, at one end of the bandwidth the consequences of the law of attraction are easy to understand. Let me give you an example."

Paul readied himself for another revelation, as Maya continued, "If something enters their life that is way below what they feel worthy of receiving, what do you think most people do with it?" After a few moments of thought, Paul answered, "I guess they would push it away, push it out of their lives. They'd reject it, wouldn't they?"

Maya responded, "That is exactly what they'd do. For instance, imagine someone hijacked you, took all your money and credit cards, drove you to London and told you that you no longer lived in your house, but had a new home, a cardboard box in a cardboard city. As you know, that is where many of the homeless and down and outs live, in cardboard boxes in certain areas of London. I suspect the prospect of that situation is way below anything you've ever felt worthy of receiving in your life, even in your worst nightmare!"

Paul replied, "You bet!" Maya went on, "So, knowing this is way below anything you've felt worthy of receiving, when you get pushed out of the car and find yourself at the cardboard city, how long would you stay there? A week or two? Just to see what it would be like living in conditions like that?" Paul shook his head hard and stated, "No chance!" Maya pushed the point further, "Well, maybe a day or two? An hour or two? No? A minute or two?" Paul exclaimed, "Maya, I'd be out of there in a nanosecond! My feet wouldn't touch the ground! I'd have no money, no nothing, but I'd be walking straight out of there!" Maya suggested, "And, chances are, at the first phone box, you'd call the operator and make a reverse charge call to me or one of your other friends, to come and pick you up and get you out of there, right?" Paul nodded, "Absolutely. Or I'd find another way out of there, that's for sure!"

Maya continued, "Now, if something entered your life that was way too good for what you feel worthy of receiving, what do you think you'd do with that?" With a solemn expression, Paul said, "Well, you'd push that away as well! You'd reject that too!" Maya replied, "Precisely! Even though it might be the very thing you've wanted most in your life, a promotion, a certain amount of money, a car, a house, a group of friends, if you don't feel worthy of receiving whatever it is, you would, somehow, push it away and lose it!"

Paul nodded confidently, "You are absolutely right. It happens all the time! I can think of an example straight away, of a colleague of mine at work. I've known him for years, and he has a real inferiority complex when it comes to women. He's not particularly tall or good looking, but he has got a heart of gold and a terrific sense of humour, and all the women he meets love him. He is a tremendous character. However, he cannot imagine how any of them can find him attractive and want a serious relationship with him. After a string of disastrous liaisons, he started dating a woman who'd just joined the company.

"It was clear to everyone that this girl loved him to bits, but he just couldn't accept it. She was drop-dead gorgeous, had a fabulous personality and was kind, considerate and understanding. She was everything any man could wish for, and she only had eyes for him! Yet every time I met him he would slip into the conversation statements like 'She is way too good for me' and 'I don't know what she sees in me'. Anyway, the relationship developed and they announced their engagement, much to everyone's relief and joy. But at their engagement party he was still telling everyone who'd listen to him that 'She is too good for me' and 'I don't know what she sees in me'. More than 12 months later, they got married and on their wedding day he was still saying the same things. He even announced in his speech that he'd married her for better or worse: he couldn't have done any better, and she couldn't have done any worse!

"A few years later, he got in with a bad crowd at work and started staying out late. He drifted into staying out all night, up to no good. Eventually, his wife caught him in the arms of another woman and kicked him out. Apparently, her parting words were 'I don't know what I ever saw in you, I'm way too good for you, never darken my door again!' He's been a mess ever since, because he knows he blew it, and blew it big style. The problem here, from what you've just explained, is that his self-worth was so low he couldn't accept that such a beautiful, lovable woman could ever be an automatic and permanent part of his life!"

Maya nodded, 'That's a really good illustration of the law of attraction. I wonder if he had any idea why he did what he did, and how it was linked to his feeling of worthiness? I doubt it. Most people have no idea that their own heart-felt feeling of what they are worthy of receiving is invariably reflected back into their lives."

Maya then looked Paul straight in the eye and asked, "Tell me honestly, truly, deeply and passionately, what you feel worthy of receiving in your life? Do you feel worthy of receiving the finest things that life has to offer? Do you feel worthy of receiving the true, true treasures of life, such as friendship, love, joy, wealth, happiness, success, health, vitality, energy, compassion, even material things if that's what's important to you? Do you feel worthy of receiving all these things at the very highest levels?"

Paul looked away from Maya, and his head shook almost imperceptibly, "No, not really", he replied almost wearily. He realised now that the real reason why all those wonderful things had evaded him all his life was that he just simply didn't feel worthy of receiving them in the first place, not really, not deep down. He'd like to have all those things, of course he would, but he didn't feel really worthy. At least not yet.

"You see, Paul," Maya continued, "for beliefs to turn into realities, you have to know in your heart of hearts that you are worthy of receiving them. Otherwise they can not qualify as beliefs; they register in your mind as a wish, a hope, but not as a heart-felt worthiness and belief. You've got to believe that you are worthy of receiving them, because if you don't, all the forces in the universe cannot join and work together properly to bring it to your life on a permanent and automatic basis. That is the essence of this natural law.

"We are in constant communication with the field of creation, the source energy, that holds all the forces of the universe together. This field of creation is intelligent. It permeates and connects everything, animate and inanimate. It is through this field of creation that the atoms in a diamond or rock know what positions to hold. It is how a tomato seed knows it's a tomato and not a rose. This intelligent field of creation responds positively and unerringly to human emotion and feeling. It responds to the non-verbal language we use all the time to communicate with it. That non-verbal language is our heart-felt emotions and feelings. When our thoughts and emotions are combined in heart-felt feelings to produce a belief, we effectively issue an instruction into the field of creation that awakens all the forces in the universe in response. They, in turn, find and present to us the circumstances and resources to transform those heart-felt, belief-driven feelings into a physical reality in our lives."

Paul was open mouthed as Maya continued, "This field of creation is also like a blueprint where all possibilities already exist. All the joy, happiness, peace, success and health already exist in this field of creation, as do all the despair, fear, suffering and illness. We choose what we receive from the blueprint in the physical realm by what goes on inside us in our thought realm. We claim the future of all possibilities through the feelings we have. The part of the blueprint we choose is determined by our feelings. We must feel within ourselves what we choose to experience in our world. This allows us to be in control and fully participate in our world, choosing the future we desire.

"That is the law of attraction. It's a universal law and, as I've said to you before, if a law is universal it means it's everywhere, and if it's everywhere it means that there's nowhere where it isn't. This means that it applies to everything and everyone. No matter how small, no matter how big, and no matter who or what you are. OK?"

Paul nodded, "Yes, yes, got it!"

Maya expanded the point, "The big problem with most people is that they've been conditioned to believe in their unworthiness. It's not altogether clear where this comes from in our society. Is it in our education systems, our religious teachings or in our social environment generally? But even if we're not altogether sure about the why, we can be sure that most people have been conditioned to believe that it is almost evil, sinful, wicked or just plain nasty to think well enough of themselves that they are worthy of receiving the finest things in life, the true, true treasures we have talked about."

Paul agreed wholeheartedly, "Well, that is certainly the case for me. It had never entered my mind that all the abundance that this universe has to offer is as much for me as anyone else on the planet, that all the true treasures are there and available to me. The highest levels of friendship and love, and power, wealth, health, happiness, success, energy, compassion, material possessions, all there and available for me and anyone else who chooses them. I never thought that! I've always chosen something in the middle, something a bit more than my Mum and Dad had, a bit more than my brother and my sister, a bit more than the guy I started work with in my company 20 years ago! All that stuff is OK. But, believing that I am worthy of receiving the finest things in life? No, I've never believed that's for me!"

Maya was sympathetic, "I understand where you are coming from." Paul went on, "My parents used to remind me at least once a week not to get ideas above my station. This was usually after I had visited my cousins and auntie and uncle who lived in a house three times the size of ours! At school, you'll remember how we used to get treated by the teachers when we told them what we wanted to be and do when we grew up. They mostly ridiculed us and made comments about how children from this school don't end up doing things like that, about how unrealistic we all were. Even at church, the general theme is that this life is all about struggle, and pain and poverty, and that our reward will be in the next life! All the treasures we seek will be available to us in abundance there, not here!"

Maya guided Paul further, "The important realisation for every individual on the planet is that the only qualification anyone needs to have as much of anything and everything this universe has to offer is simply to be alive. No other qualification is needed; you don't need to be of any particular family, race or creed. All the abundance in the universe is available to us all. The power and the force of the natural laws is no respecter of persons. However, how much shows up in our lives is determined by the extent to which we feel worthy of receiving it. It's a simple as that. So, if you want more in your life, more happiness, more success, more health and wealth, joy and power, you have to begin by knowing, through your heart-felt feelings, that you are worth it.

"Once you open yourself up to that, and it is almost a physical sensation when you do, you will begin to sense the whole universe, and all the forces in it, align themselves to bring into your life your every right and proper desire. You become omnipotent, you become unstoppable."

She continued, "Whatever weakens your sense of worth or value, or the tenderness of your conscience, or reduces your desire for the true treasures in life, simply obscures and obstructs your connection with the field of creation and all the forces it holds together. This responsive field of creation doesn't make judgements about your worthiness; only human beings do that. When we judge ourselves poorly, all the awesome power and forces in the universe that are available to us get diverted elsewhere." Paul now knew exactly what Maya meant. He silently vowed to never judge himself harshly again.

Maya returned to the lesson, "Now, the law of attraction, as I've said, is a process, but there is another law you need to understand, and become an expert practitioner in, in order to make the law of attraction work in a way that will frighten you in terms of the extent of your personal power. This is the law of indirect activity. I'm going to explain it to you a bit backwards, by describing the law of direct activity first. I'm doing this because the law of direct activity never works, whereas the law of indirect activity never fails. You need to understand clearly the difference between the two.

"Have you ever met anyone and, within a few minutes of talking to them, been so taken with them that you wanted to impress them in return?" Paul nodded, "Yes, quite a few times actually." Maya continued, "How do most people set about the task? What do they talk about?" Paul replied, "Well, it will be all about themselves and their accomplishments and where they've been, what they've done and what they've got." Maya answered, "Yes, of course it would. Now, if the person they are trying to impress isn't impressed enough, what might they be tempted to do?" Paul giggled and replied, "Well they might be tempted to exaggerate a little, to 'gild the lily' as my mother would say." Maya nodded, "Yes that's exactly what people do! And if the person is still not impressed enough, what might they be tempted to do then?"

Paul laughed louder than before, "Well, they might well be tempted to lie." Maya nodded and said, "Sadly, all too many people would. If this is what most people do to impress someone else, and believe me that is exactly what they'd do, where is the conversation going?"

Paul answered, "It's going nowhere!" But Maya shook her head, "No, Paul, no: it is definitely going somewhere! There is only one place this is headed, but it's not nowhere!" Paul looked confused and Maya continued, "The conversation, and resulting relationship, is going to crash and burn as surely as night follows day. Eventually, the person trying to impress is going to push it too far, get caught out by exaggerating or lying, and lose the very thing they were trying to get in the first place, i.e. to make a good impression." Paul nodded his understanding.

Maya explained, "This is an example of direct activity. As I said before, direct activity never works, whereas indirect activity never fails. So, what do you think indirect activity suggests you should do to really impress another person? Think of the words 'indirect activity'."

Paul thought long and hard before answering, "I guess you should listen to them; be interested in them?" Maya replied, "They're very good answers, but the law of indirect activity is very precise. If you listen to people, you will come across to them as being a good listener. And if you show interest in people, you will come across to them as being interesting. However, the fastest, most genuine and sincere way to be impressive to another human being …" Paul finished off the sentence, "Oh, I get it! You have to be really genuinely and sincerely impressed with them."

Maya smiled at Paul, "Yes, you've got it. The people you're trying to be impressive to may not be at your dizzy levels of achievement, but if you look hard enough there is always something going on in their life that you can be genuinely impressed with. It may be something that you first did 20 years ago, that you can do with your eyes closed, but to them, at that moment in their lives, it may well be a massive achievement, and therefore something to be impressed by. Get your own ego out of the way, throw yourself into their world, and understand their motivation for doing whatever it is, the challenges they've had to overcome, the joys of overcoming them and the celebrations they'll have when it's complete. Take yourself out of the situation; it's not about you, it's about them! It's not about matching their accomplishments, or competing against them, or anything like that. This is at the heart of building a good relationship with any other human being at any level. This even sorts out the problem of the generation gap", Maya's tone was slightly mischievous.

Paul asked, "What do you mean by that? If we could sort out the generation gap, that would change the world positively for most parents and their children!" Maya continued, "A couple of days ago, I was with an acquaintance, Harry, when his brother and eldest nephew turned up. I'd never met either of them before. The nephew, David, had just turned 17 and started driving lessons, so within a few minutes we were talking about learning how to drive. Harry told David how easy he'd found it, that he'd learned to drive in a week and passed his driving test the first time. He went on to say that one time he had driven to London in 2 hours 30 minutes, and how he could drive to anywhere in the UK with his eyes shut! He went on and on about how easy it was, how brilliant he was then, how even more brilliant he is now. He never asked his nephew one question about his experiences of learning to drive. Was David impressed? No. Did his uncle's credibility go up in his estimation? No. The whole interchange was regarded by the 17 year old with utter derision.

"Harry eventually ran out of steam and began talking to his brother about something else. I quietly asked David about how many driving lessons he'd had, how he was finding them, what bits came easy to him and what bits needed more concentration and effort. He explained that he knew it would take some time but, if he practised hard enough, it would all become second nature to him. He even confessed he'd been practising on a chair in the dining room with a place mat for a steering wheel. I told him I'd done the very same thing and we both laughed! I asked enough questions to become genuinely impressed with this young man's approach to learning how to drive, and he knew it. I was attentive, supportive, encouraging. I was genuine and sincere. David proceeded to tell me about other things going on in his life, at his sixth-form college, with his girlfriend, his favourite football team, everything! He also told me that he thought his uncle was the biggest jerk on the planet!

"When I left, Harry said that I would have to come again when his nephew was visiting, because he had never heard him talk so much in all the years he'd known him! And when I saw him a few days later, he told me that David thought I was the most genuine, sincere and impressive adult he'd ever met! But I hadn't said a word to David about myself! He didn't know anything about me apart from my name."

Paul had a query at this point, "But couldn't this come across as being patronising or insincere?" Maya replied, "Only if you did it, or meant it, in a patronising or insincere way. You can't use this technique to be manipulative or to con people. Not really. Human beings are much more sensitive creatures than that. You'd be able to tell if someone was patronising, insincere or manipulative. The laws of attraction and indirect activity are very precise and accurate. What you give out, is what you get back. Like attracts like."

Maya continued, "Let's just see whether you've learned the principle and practice here. Tell me, what is the fastest, most genuine and sincere way to get people to respect you?" Paul answered promptly, "You've got to respect them!" Maya congratulated him, "You've learnt quickly, haven't you? The number of people who don't understand the law of indirect activity and how it works, and the dynamic impact it has on people's lives through their relationships with others, simply staggers me.

"I visited another acquaintance of mine, Gill, a few weeks ago on business at her office. She told me she had taken over a new team 6 months ago and that she was having terrible trouble with them. They were apparently not showing her any respect whatsoever in the workplace, and output was beginning to suffer because of it. She asked if I could have an informal chat with a few of them to see what the problem was. I agreed and suggested to the staff we have lunch together once business was concluded. Over lunch I asked some questions about their department, the processes they followed, the way they operated and what things got in the way of outstanding performance.

"I was shocked at the ferocity of their answers. They told me that they all worked every hour God sends, went to the ends of the

Earth, to achieve the production targets. Despite all kinds of hurdles, in the 6 months that Gill had been in charge they had never missed a production target. Not once! Even though on occasions they'd only managed it by working through the night. They then went on to tell me that not once had Gill called them together as a team, or spoken to them individually, to say what a great job they'd done and thank them for their hard work. They'd all decided that Gill was the most disrespectful boss they'd ever worked for, and they were all really unhappy and wanted her to leave.

"Later that afternoon, Gill asked me what I'd found out over lunch. I prefaced what I had to tell her by saying she would not like my answer. 'I'm a big girl', she said, 'I can take it!' So I told her straight; the depth of feeling from the team warranted nothing less. Afterwards, I asked her what had happened to her lately, because when we first started our business relationship, some 3 or 4 years ago, she was renowned for the support, encouragement and respect she gave to all her team members.

"Gill reflected silently on what she'd heard and then said, 'Thanks for that. I needed a reminder on how building a winning team really works. I've lost sight of the basics. Just leave it with me for 3 or 4 weeks and come back and see the changes'. I was there yesterday, and you wouldn't believe how the atmosphere, the morale, the attitude and performance had improved. Everyone in the place was transformed. So, guess what Gill had done?" Paul suggested, "She had started giving out loads of respect, recognition and the like?" Maya replied, "Correct! She'd started giving out respect and recognition by the spadeful, but genuinely and sincerely, and she was receiving it back by the bucketful! When it comes to the law of indirect activity, what you hoard you lose and what you share multiplies.

"If you want something in your life, you've got to be willing to give it first! If you want to be surrounded by positive, enthusiastic, dedicated, hard-working people, the fastest way to achieve it is to be all those things yourself first. You create a kind of force field that guides and directs people towards you. My favourite poem in the whole world is four lines long, and sums this lesson up beautifully." Maya handed Paul a piece of paper. Written on it was:

> *I went out to find a friend*
> *And couldn't find one there*
> *I went out to be friend*
> *And friends were everywhere!*

"Paul, the one thing I have learned, over the last 6 months, is that the universe is not only wonderfully abundant, but also magnificently responsive. Wonderfully abundant, because everything you could possibly want or need in life, all the true treasures, are all around us in plenty. Magnificently responsive, because what you get back is only a reflection of what you give out in the first place! The law of indirect activity is precise and accurate. It's as if what shows up in our lives is a reflection of some massive magnifying mirror of what is going on in our souls! It all starts and ends with us, with what feelings we have about ourselves, other people, and the world we live in.

"The law of indirect activity is a technique that makes the law of attraction, as a process, work. To help you understand this fully, I have a suggestion. Next time you meet a few people that you don't know very well, or that you don't know at all, treat them as if they were the most important people you've ever met in your life. You may need to think about how exactly you'll go about doing that. However, I suspect it will involve you being courteous, respectful, witty, interested, fascinated, helpful, etc. Give out all these things to these people in a genuine, sincere and honest way. Try it and, when you do, call me straight away and let me know what you get back". Paul nodded, "OK!"

Paul knew exactly what he would get back, but Maya continued, "Be prepared to be shocked at the results. Be prepared to be shocked by the realisation that all the things that most people long to get from relationships, they've actually had them all along! They just never give them out and, therefore, they never get them back! The universe, and all the forces in it, is set up in a way that makes sure that every individual's heart-felt beliefs will always be reflected back into their world. This is what the intelligent field of creation wants for each and every person. In order to access all the abundance, the only requirement for each person is the enlightenment you have been through in recent months and the odd technique or two that I've shared with you, and then it's all yours. All of it. Is it easy? Heck no! But is it simple? Yes!"

Paul responded, "Over these last few weeks, I have experienced a complete transformation on the inside. I've gone from my old basic feelings, those of fear, ignorance, doubt, shortfalls, shame, guilt and unworthiness, to the most precious and awesome feeling of self-worth, knowing that nothing is too good for me. I feel like the sun has just emerged after an eclipse. But I now know that I've got to do the shining! No-one will do it for me. I've got to do the radiating! No-one will do it for me. But, hey, how much shining and radiating have I got?" He paused for a moment before he answered his own question, "Enough to light up and energise the whole world!" he said triumphantly.

He continued, "Joy, happiness, success, health, wealth, friendship, love, compassion, ecstasy and the like, are not confined to heaven and the hereafter, as most people mistakenly believe, are they?" Maya shook her head, "No, they're here, they're all around us! People just need to guided and they can all have their heaven, right here on Earth, just like you will Paul, and just like I will." Paul resumed, "It's all so clear, it's all so simple! Why don't more people know about this? Why?" Maya replied, "There is a growing band of people who are following this guidance. The world is ready to make this path wide and clear, thanks to a thinking revolution. It's ready to change.

"Believe me, this is the best place to be. You just need a few more lessons and then you will be fully prepared to have every right and proper desire come true; intention and attention will fuse together as one. As someone once said, 'You cannot travel within and stand still without'."

Maya drew an end to their meeting and said she would be in touch for Paul's next step down the path of total enlightenment. And she reminded him to phone her when he had applied the 'most important person in the world' approach to talking to new people.

Chapter Nineteen

The next few days were the best Paul had ever had in his life. He now believed, truly believed, that he rightly deserved the finest things that life had to offer him. He now knew that this was his rightful heritage and the reason he was on this Earth. The positive transformation had already begun.

He also believed that every other person on the planet deserved the same, and that they had been given the same opportunity and means to access the true treasures in life for them. But he could see and hear why most people never get close to enjoying the finest things in life, or the true treasures; their sun is constantly in either total or partial eclipse. It isn't the moon that blocks out their light and power, it's their fears, their doubts, guilt, shame and their belief in their unworthiness. He could see it, hear it and feel it in the way people looked, spoke and felt about themselves.

Paul had learned to see right into people's souls! What a sorry sight; how little of the field of creation's power and energy was being used, and yet it was available to everyone. So what was it then that determined how much of this infinite force was being used in a lifetime? It didn't take him long to work out that it was the heart-felt beliefs and feelings at the very core of people's beings that determined it. We've all been given the same and, through our beliefs and feelings, as he'd heard before, some choose greatness and some choose mediocrity. Some choose heaven on Earth and some choose hell on Earth.

He realised that what we end up experiencing and achieving in life all starts and ends with the individual, and the way each individual communes with the field of creation through their heart-felt feelings and beliefs. He was reminded of this as he recalled a couple of statements that he'd never really understood before. Paul knew that we, as human beings, can't succeed on our own; we need other people to help us on our way. He also knew that, because of the law of indirect activity, the way we feel about ourselves tends to be reflected back to us in the way other people feel about us, hence the statement 'Love thy neighbour as thyself'. The revelation hit him that the biggest problem in society today is that this statement is already true! We do love our neighbours just as much as we love ourselves, and that isn't very much at all! We have to start the process by loving ourselves, totally, utterly and unconditionally. 'Wow!' Paul thought, 'now that is a toughie, but we reduce or stop the flow of the universal spirit and energy if we don't'.

'How can we give other people our best, genuinely and sincerely, when we don't want the best for ourselves?' He corrected his thinking on this point. 'It's not that we don't want the best for ourselves, it's that we don't feel worthy of receiving the best for ourselves. Our wanting the best for ourselves is overridden by our belief that we don't deserve the best for ourselves. This type of thinking cuts us off from the infinite, creative force that fills the universe, and renders us virtually powerless.

'Our wanting, therefore, is shallow; it's nothing more than empty, vague wishes, hollow hopes with no substance. We think that what we want is not for the likes of us, not really! The starting point for receiving all the true treasures that life has to offer is loving yourself enough to know that you deserve it all. That's a big one,' Paul thought, 'but without that powerful knowing, the ability to use the forces that bring forth the true treasures will always be muted or reduced.'

Another statement began to make sense after he heard a radio programme by chance the day after he'd last met Maya. It was a programme discussing how the meanings of words had changed over the years. The programme started the discussion using the word gay as an example, and finished with the word charity. The presenter explained that the word charity had only meant almsgiving, i.e. giving to the poor, in the last 200 years or so. Prior to that, charity had had a very different meaning. A lot of confusion therefore arises when statements that have been around for hundreds of years contain words that have changed their meaning. The example given was 'Charity begins at home'. Most people today think that this statement means 'Look after yourself first', which, if you think about it, is not very charitable at all! However, 'Charity begins at home' was coined as a phrase when the word charity meant 'something beyond love'. Charity is derived from the Latin 'caritas' and one of the derivatives of the word is 'carus' as in 'caress'. Paul was taken aback when he realised how big this statement really is. Starting with yourself, with loving yourself enough to know that the true, true treasures in life are all yours for the taking and sharing, is one of the major keys to the kingdom people seek. Why had he not known the real meaning of these statements before now?!

The profoundness of these two statements was constantly reinforced in his mind as he worked hard to build his belief in his worthiness, as he learned to love himself unconditionally. The two statements became the corner stones of his thinking and doing, doubly so as he practised the law of indirect activity as Maya had suggested.

The results from treating people like they were the most important people he'd ever met in his life were stunning. He'd first tried it with a young man who worked at the local petrol station; even though he'd seen him many times before he'd never made conversation with him. Paul commented to him that he was always very cheery, no matter what time of day or night he was working, and asked him how he managed to be like that with the thousands of people he must see every day. The young man responded by going into raptures about his approach to work, about wanting to brighten everybody's day, and how he loved doing the very best he could for everyone, etc. The conversation ended with the young man saying that he wished all his customers were like Paul, and that there was a special promotion on the following week so he would make sure he kept a voucher for him.

Paul also tried the technique with his neighbour, Tony, who had moved next door 2 years previously. Apart from the usual polite pleasantries, Paul had made no real effort to get to know Tony, and over the last few months relations had become strained while Tony was having an extension built. They happened to arrive home from work at the same time one evening. Paul waved and said "hello", and walked towards the fence that separated the two houses. "Hi, Tony, I've been meaning to have a word with you for ages." Tony's hackles visibly rose, obviously expecting some kind of complaint about the building work, but Paul continued with, "I just wanted to say how fantastic your extension is looking! It's going to be fabulous when it's finished, isn't it? I'm jealous of you: we've been talking about having an extension for years, but we've never done anything about it. We're not sure that we'd be able to cope with the upheaval".

Tony relaxed instantly. He smiled, laughed and joked. He reassured Paul that he could cope with the upheaval. "It seems a lot worse than it is. Come round and have a look. Bring your wife with you, and we can have a drink and a chat; it's about time we got to know each other better". It was amazing. After that they arranged to go out for dinner as a foursome the following Saturday. Then Tony told him that the company he worked for was about to change its supplier for the services Paul's company provided, and he was happy to introduce him to his purchasing manager! Amazing!

In just a few days, his team at work had begun to hit productivity levels that had previously seemed impossible. Surely it wasn't just because he'd made a point of saying to them what a privilege it was for him to be head of such a winning and capable team. But then he concluded that it must be a major factor, because nothing else had changed. There were no new systems or processes in place.

Four of the five people he'd practised the law of indirect activity on had responded brilliantly. He asked Maya on the phone why it hadn't worked with all five, and she explained to him that nothing works every time. About 20% of people are so damaged, so hurt and perplexed, that they have great difficulty wanting to become undamaged, unhurt and unperplexed. At least not at first. Maya advised Paul not to be put off by the minority but to keep offering friendship, love and respect, and they may get to the point where they accept it eventually.

During the same phone call, Paul and Maya agreed to meet again at The Old Fox. Paul arrived first and ordered drinks for himself and Maya. While he waited, he observed how many people's lives were clearly in an eclipse of some kind. He thought deeply about what it would do for everyone if the self-imposed obstacles that obscure and block the infinite universal power and energy were removed. The more he thought about it, the more he felt himself glow. He felt radiant. It reminded him of how Maya always looked and felt.

His deep thinking produced a truly inspiring vision that made him shudder with excitement. This vision, to him in that moment, was at the very core of his being; it was real. He felt strange.

Maya's voiced startled him from his thoughts, "So, are you ready for the penultimate piece of the jigsaw, the one that will show you how to achieve everything you could want in life?" Paul took a moment to compose himself before answering, "I think I've been ready for it all my life!"

Maya commented, "I doubt that, Paul. You are being guided in a planned, step-by-step way. If I'd explained this next stage when we first met, you'd have thought I was talking complete rubbish. You are ready now though. Your journey is almost complete."

Paul prepared himself for another awesome revelation. He knew Maya was going to alter his world for the better again.

Chapter Twenty

Maya began, "We need to look at one of the most misunderstood aspects of human behaviour: motivation. So, what is the traditional way of motivating people?" Paul thought for a while and then answered, "Well it's a carrot, isn't it? Some kind of reward or incentive?" Maya nodded, and said, "That's certainly part of it." Before she could finish, Paul jumped in with, "Oh, and if that doesn't work, the stick usually comes out!" Maya laughed and enquired, "Does it work?" Paul responded, "From experience, it does work, but only in the short term. And sometimes you've got to keep offering more and more carrots or use more and more stick, just to stay in the same place!"

Maya continued, "The carrot and stick technique works brilliantly when it is used properly, with a true understanding of motivation." She pulled out a piece of paper and began to draw. "To understand what motivation is all about, we have to visit our three friends again." She drew the now familiar model of the outer conscious, the inner subconscious and the deeper subconscious, and made some additions.

"There are a number of ways of illustrating this, and this is my favourite. You know the process here. We perceive with the outer conscious element of our mind. We then store the information in the neurone cells that form the inner subconscious element of our mind. This information we store becomes the beliefs we have about ourselves, about other people and about the world we live in. Our deeper subconscious, in order to maintain the wonderful thing that we call sanity, acts as a servomechanism or check and balance system, to always find the circumstances and resources to deliver what we believe into our real world, whether it's good for us or not, and whether it's true or not." Maya's recapping of the process reinforced the simplicity of it all for Paul, and he was pleased at how much of it he'd remembered. It was reassuring to hear it again, said in such a succinct and authoritative way.

"Now," Maya continued, "the deeper subconscious has got two other subfunctions that are responsible for the maintenance of sanity. The first of these is to solve and resolve conflicts, as and when they arise." Maya pointed to the words on the paper. "I'll explain what a conflict is in a moment. The second subfunction is to give us the drive and energy to complete tasks and goals." Again, she tapped the paper in the appropriate place:

"If you stop thinking of yourself as a human being for a moment, and consider yourself to be some kind of guided missile, what you've been doing all your life up until now, although not consciously, is programming in here," she tapped at the beliefs box, "the directions you choose in life and the co-ordinates of where you want to eventually end up. What you have over here," she pointed at the two subfunctions of the deeper subconscious, "courtesy of your natural ability to solve and resolve conflicts, is your equivalent of an on-board guidance system. This is, effectively, your on-board computer, unlimited in its capacity to find ways to get you from anywhere you find yourself, to anywhere you want to get to.

"The other thing you've got, because of your drive and energy to complete tasks and goals, is a virtually unlimited fuel tank. This drive and energy is pretty miraculous and unlimited! Think about it! We, as human beings, can go for days and days on a couple of glasses of water, an apple and an orange!

"However, these two functions, solving and resolving, and drive and energy, or effectively our creativity and stamina to take action, are only stimulated to the highest degree when we are in conflict, and we, as human beings, are in conflict all the time. Being in conflict is a natural human condition. And creativity and stamina are the foundations of motivation. Based on what is on this piece of paper, can you hazard a guess about when we, as human beings, are in conflict?"

Paul thought for a moment before answering, "Is it when we find ourselves behaving in a way that doesn't match the way we should be behaving according to our self-image and beliefs?" Maya nodded, "That's a really good answer, and is a large part of the actual answer, but it's not the whole answer. We find ourselves in conflict when what we perceive is going on in our real world," she tapped the word 'Perceive' before moving to 'Behaviour' on the diagram, "doesn't match the way we know it should be in our thought world," she tapped the 'Beliefs' box. Maya then wrote in the words 'Real world' and 'Thought world' to clarify the picture and deepen Paul's understanding:

MOTIVATION

PERCEIVE

OUTER CONSCIOUS

BEHAVIOUR (Real world)

Information storage

INNER SUBCONSCIOUS (Thought world)

Picture of Reality
BELIEFS
Self Image

DEEPER SUBCONSCIOUS

1) Maintains SANITY

2) Solves and resolve CONFLICTS as and when they arise.

3) Drive and energy to complete tasks and goals.

"When our picture inside our mind, of the way things should be, doesn't match what we perceive on the outside, what things are actually like, we find ourselves in a conflict. That's when all our creativity, all our drive and energy, kick in to find the set of circumstances and the resources to make the external perception and internal picture match. But, which of the two is always the dominant one, the external perception or the internal picture?"

Paul came to a sudden realisation, "Why, the internal picture is the dominant one, surely?!" Maya smiled broadly and nodded, "That's correct, and the degree of clarity, belief and desire associated with the internal picture determines how much creativity, drive and energy is released to find and attract the set of circumstances and resources in order for it to materialise, or manifest itself, in the real world. If the internal picture is only accompanied by an empty wish or a vague hope, the limitless forces in the universe that are available to us will not be alerted sufficiently to respond appropriately and make it manifest in our real world."

Paul was finding this a bit difficult to follow, so Maya expanded, "Let me give you some examples of how this process works, and then I'll show you how to turn on the full power, so you can have every right and proper desire in your life. Let's start with a very safe example to illustrate its simplicity.

"This morning, when you got out of bed and wandered into the bathroom, when you switched the light on and had a good look at yourself in the mirror, you would have been in conflict." Paul looked puzzled and Maya went on, "What I mean is this. You probably have a pretty clear picture in your mind of what you need to look like before you leave your house in the morning for work: showered, shaved, well groomed, smart, presentable, yes?" Paul nodded, "Yes." "So, this morning, when you first walked into the bathroom, what kind of image was staring back at you out of the mirror?" Paul exclaimed, "Well, I think it was something in between 'death warmed up' and 'the creature from the swamp!'" Maya laughed, "So your internal picture and your external perception didn't match, right?" Paul nodded and she continued, "You know that our deeper subconscious handles the automatic functions on behalf of our bodies, so did you have little yellow 'post-it' notes all over the bathroom reminding you to 'have a shower, have a shave, have a shirt ready to put on', etc?" Paul responded, "Well, of course I didn't. All that stuff is completely automatic to me!" Maya said, "Exactly! However, it is only automatic to you because of this process. Your self-image, or picture of what you look like when you leave the house in the morning, is so crystal clear and so strong that your deeper subconscious takes over and finds the set of circumstances and resources required to turn it into a reality." Paul nodded in agreement, "Yes, definitely yes! I guess that explains how sometimes, if I've stayed up late and had a bit too much to drink the night before, I still end up looking pretty presentable in the morning, even though I can hardly remember getting ready?" Maya nodded this time, "Indeed! Consciously, you are not really with it, but subconsciously, with the inner and deeper subconscious working together, you get sorted out."

Maya expanded the point, "Our deeper subconscious is infinitely flexible, co-operative and powerful when it comes to delivering any internal picture. For instance, has your alarm clock ever not gone off, for whatever reason?" Paul replied, "Oh yes!" "So when this happens, and rather than, say, your normal hour to get ready for work in, you've only got 20 minutes, you now have a double conflict: not only do you look like 'death warmed up' but you only have 20 minutes to sort yourself out in. In this instance, what do your creativity and drive and energy do? Do they accept the situation, carry on at the normal speed and decide to turn up for work half an hour or so late?" Paul protested, "You've got to be joking! People rely on me being there not just on time, but ahead of time!" Maya pushed further, "So, what happens to your behaviour?" Paul responded, "It moves up a couple of gears. I end up rushing around like a blue-arsed fly and", he hesitated for a moment and Maya finished the sentence for him, "and somehow you make up the time, or at least most of it." Paul nodded, "You're right. But doesn't everyone do that?"

Maya continued, "No, not really, the reason being not everyone has your strong sense of purpose at work, or responsibility for being on time and not letting others down. Your desire whips your creativity, and energy, into overdrive. Some people would just roll over, go back to sleep and phone in later with an excuse." Paul could relate to that. One of the challenges he'd been given at work was to reduce absenteeism. He was beginning to understand why it was so high but, as yet, he hadn't figured out a solution to it.

Maya explained, "Any mismatch between the way things are perceived to be on the outside, in the real world, and the way we know things should be on the inside, according to our picture of reality and self-image, will cause our deeper subconscious, with all its creativity and drive and energy, to turn the internal thought picture into an external physical reality. And, so long as that internal thought picture is held strong and clear, nothing can stand in the way of our deeper subconscious finding the set of circumstances and resources to manifest it!"

Maya elaborated, "I'll give you some more examples to illustrate this major point in understanding motivation, but a word of warning: any conflict is automatically solved or resolved by our deeper subconscious. There are two types of conflict, and our deeper subconscious throws all of its infinite creativity, drive and energy equally behind both type, in order to solve or resolve them.

"The first type is created when something like this happens: you announce to your team at work that you've learned the secrets of motivation and, as a result, you are now increasing productivity targets by 25%. By announcing the productivity increase you want in this very superficial way, it will only register at the outer conscious level with the team members. In other words, it will make absolutely no impact on their belief structure and their self-image. In fact, their current belief about their performance is probably something like 'Our performance is as good as it can be, we're doing everything possible now'. So what you've actually done is create a negative external conflict."

Paul frowned, not quite understanding this. Maya explained further, "By merely announcing that a 25% increase in productivity is required, it only registers at the outer conscious level with the team. It is completely at odds with, and different from, their internal belief that their current performance is as good as it can be, and, therefore, a massive negative external conflict is created. The two pictures do not match, and which is always the dominant picture?" Paul answered, "Well, the internal picture, of course." Maya went on, "Exactly! So, if that picture is that 'we're doing all we can now' and that 'no extra productivity is possible', what do you think will happen to make their internal and external pictures match?" Comprehension dawned for Paul, "All their energy would be used to find the circumstances, evidence and resources to prove that a

25% increase in productivity can't be done!" Maya asked, "Does that sound familiar?" Paul spluttered, "Sound familiar? That's all I ever seem to get with my team sometimes. I try to persuade them that the changes and improvements needed can be achieved, but all they seem to do is find evidence that proves it can't be done! So the much-needed changes take forever to implement or, even worse, the improvement project gets abandoned! It costs our company millions every year!"

Maya continued calmly, "It costs every organisation a lot of time, money and heartache in terms of underperformance and damaged relationships. The main reason is that most managers in most organisations don't understand real motivation. They don't know how to get people to willingly and voluntarily change their behaviour, so they resort to coercion, bullying and threats. Simply making announcements to people about what new behaviours are required, in a manner that only registers at the superficial outer conscious level and creates negative external conflicts, has no place in high-performance organisations.

"We must learn to communicate with ourselves and others in a way that impacts directly and speedily on our beliefs." Maya pointed to the 'Information storage' arrow on the diagram she had drawn. "We need to be able to deliberately change the input in the most positive and dynamic way, a way that allows brand new and improved pictures and beliefs to be imprinted on the inner subconscious self-image. The imprinting should be not only of what these new behaviours look like, but also what they feel like. This needs to be done in a way that creates a new, solid and certain belief in the inner subconscious. This belief, once locked in place with feeling, is the forerunner of its own outward manifestation.

"Once a new belief is locked into our self-image, it creates the second type of conflict, a positive internal conflict, where again the internal and external pictures don't match. But in this instance, for the new and improved internal picture to be externalised in reality, positive action is required. So now all our unlimited creativity, drive and energy is focused and directed towards finding the set of circumstances and resources to transform the belief held in the thought realm into a reality in the physical realm! But let me reiterate what I've said before. This won't work for us if it's just a vague hope or an empty wish-type belief. For all our resources and those in the universe to be made available and ensure manifestation, the belief has to be total and absolute! The belief needs to be a powerful knowing; there needs to be a total absence of doubt. In our minds, the object of our desire needs to have already happened. It needs to already be ours!"

Paul interjected, "Is this what some successful people mean when they say the secret of their success is that they 'start with the end in mind'?" Maya nodded, "That is precisely what they mean. They know the outcome before they start. The degree to which this works for people, in terms of delivering whatever they want in life, is directly related to the degree of desire and certainty that is attached to the particular beliefs beforehand. People need to begin, as you've just said, with the end in mind, and revel in the heart-felt feelings that will be associated with the desired outcomes once they are achieved. Once those feelings are projected outwards into the field of creation, they then marshal all the forces in the universe to flow through you and from you, to turn your desires into realities. When, in your mind, you know how good the outcomes feel, ahead of time, and you hold onto those feelings, then you become unstoppable. You will have used this process in your life already, but you will have used it by accident, not by design, and all you, or anyone else, need to make this work for you is your imagination and the courage to take action."

Paul listened attentively as Maya elaborated, "I'm almost certain that some of the most successful things you've ever achieved in your life actually came about through this process. Think of the times when you knew, you just 100% knew in your mind, that you were going to achieve a particular thing. You didn't know necessarily how you were going to achieve it. You just knew that it was already yours. In your mind, it was a done deal. In your mind, it already existed. Am I right?"

Paul was stunned, "I've done that a number of times. I knew I was going to be a parent governor at the school my children go to! I knew before the first interview that I was going to get the job I've now been doing for 15 years!" Paul's excitement then turned to melancholy, "And, I knew I was going to get stressed and ill because of my job. Oh, boy! We really can, and do, change our worlds with our thinking and believing."

Maya said, "Remember in one of our first meetings, I said to you that, whatever we believe with feeling, becomes a self-fulfilling prophecy in our lives? Do you also remember in a later meeting, I said that human beings become on the outside what they think about on the inside, whether it is good for them or not? Does this understanding of motivation make all that much clearer now?"

Paul gave a bemused nod. He was reeling with this new revelation, its power and, more importantly, its significance. He summarised what he had heard as best he could, "What you are saying is, that real motivation, or rather the motivation to achieve every right and proper desire we might choose, is all about deliberately throwing our mental system out of order. In our mind, we need to create a total and absolute belief that what we desire, we already have. We then need to use our imagination so that we *know* our goals and objectives already exist, and that we can, internally, feel the feelings and the positive sensations of how good it is to have achieved them." Maya nodded and Paul went on, "Am I right in thinking that the goals and objectives could be about anything: a quality, a characteristic, health, happiness, wealth, success, energy, relationship, absolutely anything?" Maya nodded again. "So I guess there are no limits to this, except for the limits we have in our own minds, in terms of how much we can turn our desires into total and absolute beliefs?"

Maya nodded proudly, "You've got a really good grasp of this!" The only thing you need, to have anything that you want in life, without limit, is imagination. You just need to vividly and realistically imagine what you want to effectively hard-wire it into the depths of your inner subconscious belief structure. It needs to be done in a way that drives those feelings into the subatomic structure of your entire body, into the very fabric of your being. It needs to permeate your DNA, and this means that, in your mind, it already exists at the deepest and most certain level. This feeling of certainty changes the chemistry of your body, and opens up a direct channel of communication with the infinite and intelligent field of creation that connects all things. This means that the forces in the universe are set in motion to find the set of circumstances and resources to turn your desired outcomes into realities. The forces connect you with a higher intelligence, where all possibilities already exist. The river of potentialities keeps you afloat and guides you to the achievement of goals. You become omnipotent, unstoppable, unlimited. You become as much divine as you are human. Your creativity, drive and energy become turbo-charged. They are on full power, all the time, to make real any desired objective and goal. They only stop when your objectives and goals are achieved, or when your inner belief is lost."

Maya then changed tack, "Let me give you some more examples to illustrate this process. Do you ever have problems getting your children out of bed in the morning?" Paul nodded, "Most of the time, actually. They're funny, you know. They accuse us of putting them to bed at night when they're wide awake, and then dragging them out of bed in the morning when they're fast asleep! So yes, we have problems." Maya went on, "But I can almost guarantee that there is one morning in the year when you don't have any problems getting them out of bed!" Paul laughed, "You bet! Christmas Day! They're up really, really early in the morning that day."

Maya asked him, "Based on what you have discovered tonight, what do you think is behind their excitement being such that they're up every hour through the night asking if Santa's been? What pictures and feelings associated with Christmas Day do you think they have, over time, programmed and hard-wired into their minds?"

Paul replied, "Well, they know it is going to be the best day of the year, by miles! Their picture is of getting up early, staying up late, getting lots of presents, adults playing with them, getting a big meal, having loads of visitors!" Maya continued, "That's right, and if 'Father Christmas' gives them the brand new bike they asked for, how many times do you think they've played on that bike in their minds before they've ever clapped eyes on it?"

Paul laughed, "Thousands, if not millions, of times!" Maya nodded and said, "So how real is the anticipated pleasure of what this day will bring them?" He replied, "It's as real as anything that is already in their minds, I guess." "You guess right," Maya confirmed, "in their minds they've relived this whole day a million times, and been around the world a gazillion times on their new bikes, before it's happened in reality. The picture is so clear and real for them, at the inner subconscious level, that the whole day is already a fabulous one, in their minds!

"That's why the problem most parents have is not getting children out of bed on Christmas Day, but getting them into bed, and staying in bed, on Christmas Eve! The children have created a positive internal conflict in their minds. The internal picture, which to them is real, is so much fun and enjoyment for all concerned, that they can hardly wait to actually experience their thoughts in reality. Their excitement stimulates their creativity, drive and energy towards getting the whole thing started as soon as possible, even if that is 3 o'clock in the morning!" Paul laughed, "You're so right".

Maya then became very serious, "As someone said to me the other day, can you imagine getting so good at this for yourself, and eventually for other people, that you, and everyone else around you, can start looking forward to each and every day just as a child looks forward to Christmas Day? And why not? Once motivation, and the achievements that come from it, are really understood and practised properly, every day becomes an adventure. People need to realise that success and achievement are firstly an inside job. Combine this knowledge with the fact that life is a matter of choice and not chance, and knowing that all the forces in the universe will, on demand, manifest our desires in the real world, why would anyone not want to take control?

"Let's talk about you now. Wouldn't you want each and every day to be part of a wonderful adventure, an adventure for which you have written the script? And wouldn't you want that not just for yourself, but for everyone else as well?" Paul nodded and Maya continued, "This whole process allows you to do just that. You can make it a wonderful adventure, or you can make it really mundane. Now you realise how much choice you have, and the unlimited power and resources you have at your beck and call, what would you want your life to be?" Paul replied, "That's a no-brainer: a wonderful adventure, of course! Bring it on."

Maya went on, "Always remember, there is no force, power or set of circumstances on the outside of us greater than the force, power and set of resources available to us on the inside. And the 10 most important words strung together in the English language: 'if it is to be, it is up to me'."

Paul interjected, "I remember those statements from our earlier meetings, and now they mean so much more to me. This is all so amazing! This discovery could change the world for the better, when people begin to understand how simple and powerful the process is! But why doesn't everyone already know about all this? Is it new? Is it some kind of new breakthrough?"

Maya smiled and shook her head, "This discovery is not new at all. This whole philosophy on how to take control in life is as old as the hills. It's worth reiterating here what we've said before: we are not discovering new areas of how the mind works, we are rediscovering the most ancient. It appears that, as our civilisation has developed, this process has been unlearned! It defies logic, rational and scientific explanation, but it's been largely abandoned. It also appears that its simplicity has worked against it." Paul looked confused and Maya explained, "This whole process is so incredibly simple that many people cannot believe it is effective. Many people seem to want to make the whole process of controlling what happens in our lives way too complicated. They also want some sort of proof of the existence of the infinite creative and intelligent force, but as yet that's not possible. But they don't need this proof; all they need to do is try it and see for themselves the incredible results it brings, or recall what they have already achieved and realise that this process has been driving their success.

"This unerring, natural process is about taking control by deliberately throwing our mental system out of sync to create positive internal conflicts. It's about programming into our minds new and improved pictures, feelings, beliefs, goals, objectives, visions, whatever you want to call them. However, as we said earlier, the programming needs to be done in a way such that, as far as your inner subconscious mind is concerned, your goals and objectives already exist. There can be no halfway measures.

"You are already living, eating, breathing and feeling your desires in a multi-sensory manner in your mind. Once locked in, their external manifestation becomes inevitable, a certainty! It's as simple and uncomplicated as that." Paul nodded and said, "One of my favourite books says the same thing. Jonathan Livingston Seagull: 'To fly as fast as thought, to anywhere that is, you must begin by knowing that you've already arrived'. Now I know what that means!"

Maya continued, "Lots of people have described this process in the past. Remember Helen Keller, the blind and deaf lady? She summed this up beautifully when she said 'The greatest tragedy to befall a person is to have sight but lack vision'. It is so true: poor eyes limit a person's sight, but poor vision limits their deeds! That's a pretty good description of the process from a deaf and blind lady, don't you think?! She knew a thing or two about this stuff!" Paul responded enthusiastically, "You're not kidding! That degree of insight and understanding shows wisdom beyond measure. It's incredible! I guess she knew more about this than most, because she couldn't see on the outside. She could obviously see on the inside; not just see, but feel! She learned that what you see on the inside invariably shows itself on the outside. Wow! This is just amazing."

Maya went on, "Someone else said 'There is nothing that inspires and motivates people like a vision to accomplish something special'. The something special can be an aspiration, a goal or an objective; one that arouses the most powerful, positive and evocative feelings of how good it is going to be when it is actually achieved. This statement was actually made in relation to the vision of the United States of America putting a man on the moon. Alan Shepard was the first American to go into space. That was on 5th May 1961. Twenty days later, President John F. Kennedy addressed Congress and in his speech said 'I believe that this nation should commit itself to achieving the goal, before this decade is out, of landing a man on the moon and returning him safely to Earth'. Talk about using words to paint pictures and create incredible feelings and emotions around an evocative vision. This example is a classic. And what a challenging, stretching vision it was! It took root in the hearts and minds of every American. Yet when Kennedy said those words, did he, or anyone else, have any idea how they were going to do it?"

Paul was slightly puzzled, but answered, "Of course they didn't know how they were going to do it! In fact, if I remember correctly, Alan Shepard didn't even go into space in a rocket powerful enough to get him into orbit. Wasn't John Glenn the first American to orbit the Earth in space?" Maya nodded, "Yes he was. Do you know the real magic of understanding the process of motivation?" Paul braced himself for the answer. "You don't need to know *how* you're going to achieve your goal, all you have to do is to choose and decide what you *want*! Your deeper subconscious will give you the how." Maya tapped the piece of paper again, pointing at the 'Solves and resolves' and the 'Drive and energy' roles that the deeper subconscious fulfils. "Why do you think we have such colossal capacity in our minds and only use a tiny portion of it? What other purpose could there be for it to be so big, except to make all our desires, goals, objectives and visions come true?

"The problem we have with using our capacity and potential to the full is threefold." Maya counted them on her fingers, "One, we don't understand the processes. Therefore two: we don't understand how much in control and how powerful we are. Therefore three: we let most of our incredible resources go to waste by concentrating on resolving negative external conflicts. Because of this lack of understanding, it doesn't take much more than a blink of an eye to seemingly prove that some visionary, like Kennedy, is stark, staring mad, and that any particular vision or worthy goal, whatever it may be, can't be done!

"The limitless resources we have available to us only get used to the full when we have positive internal conflicts to resolve. When we have goals, objectives, visions, magnificent obsessions, hard-wired into our belief structure for us to strive towards and achieve, it's only then that all the forces in the universe are commanded to join together to flow through us and from us, to help us find the resources to turn them into realities.

"If the goals, objectives and visions are evocative enough, and are embedded in enough people's minds, whole teams, departments, organisations, countries even, can be involved in creating the momentum for transformation. Kennedy didn't just motivate a few scientists to turn the moon landing vision into a reality. He engaged the whole nation who, at the end of the day, had to finance the space programme. Again, evocative, powerful words were used to imprint the vision. In the same speech to Congress on the 25th May 1961, he said, 'It will not be one man going to the moon. If we make this judgment affirmatively, it will be an entire nation, for all of us must work hard to put him there'.

"This vision, and the feelings associated with its completion, channelled the creativity, drive and energy of an entire nation. In fact, it transcended national borders and the entire western world got caught up in achieving this goal. And, as we have said, when Kennedy said those words they had no idea how they would achieve it; they didn't even have a rocket powerful enough to get a man into orbit, let alone to the moon and back! But, that didn't matter one little bit, did it? Not when you understand what motivation and achievement are all about. Once that picture, or vision, is locked in place, the result is inevitable. All the creativity, drive and energy needed were summoned from that day forth, to find the set of circumstances to make it come about.

"The outer conscious mind gives an order to the inner subconscious mind about what it wants and desires and, once that is locked into place, together with the certainty of the outcome, the deeper subconscious simply obeys and delivers it. It'll deliver the means of inventing and building Mercury rockets, Gemini rockets, Apollo rockets, lunar landing modules, anything required to make it happen. Will it be easy? No! Will it be inevitable? Yes! As long as you hold onto the vision, with absolute certainty of the vision being accomplished!

Maya continued, "Will the realisation of a vision be a smooth, easy and trouble-free experience? Not a chance! There will be setbacks, frustrations, wasted effort and lots of blind alleys to go down but, as long as the vision is held firm in the inner subconscious mind, and you keep trying all the different ways of fulfilling the vision that your deeper subconscious mind presents to you, you will get there in the end. It's inevitable!

"Having the right attitude towards the setbacks, frustrations, wasted effort and going down lots of blind alleys helps. Too many people give up on a vision or goal too easily, after encountering just a few obstacles. If they take the attitude of 'what has this setback taught me?' and look for the lesson, learn from it and try again with their newly realised knowledge, most people would achieve a thousand times more things in their lives. Remember Thomas Edison and all his failed experiments? If people in the past hadn't had a positive and productive attitude towards setbacks, and the ability to fuel the courage of their conviction with the desire to see things through, we'd still be reading by candlelight and riding on horseback to get anywhere! Thank goodness for visionary people!"

Paul was awestruck by what Maya was telling him, and she continued, "I think that actually putting a man on the moon and bringing him back alive is our greatest technological achievement to date. If humankind, with the right mindset, desire and motivation, can achieve that, by using our minds properly we can achieve virtually anything. Another quote is 'Whatever the mind of man can conceive and believe, it can achieve!' How utterly true! Another magical part of this process is that not only will our minds deliver our greatest achievements, it will also save us from the depths of despair.

"One of the best examples to illustrate this comes from one of humankind's greatest tragedies: The Holocaust of World War Two, when 6 million Jews were exterminated by the Nazis. Viktor Frankl, an Austrian Jew, managed to survive years of incarceration in four different concentration camps, two of which were death camps. He was a prisoner in both Auschwitz and Dachau. When the concentration camps were liberated, people were amazed to learn what Frankl had survived: the starvation, the beatings, the disease, the gas chambers, the firing squads. He gave a speech to explain how he'd managed to survive while so many others had perished. Listen to these words, just listen: 'What kept me alive was you. Others gave up hope, but I dreamed. I dreamed that one day I would be here telling you how I, Viktor Frankl, survived the Nazi concentration camps. I've never been here before, I've never seen any of you before, and I've never given this speech before, but in my dreams I have stood before you and said these words a thousand times.'"

There were tears in Paul's eyes, as he realised the power and intensity of what Frankl described. Maya paused for a moment before asking, "Paul, what was Viktor Frankl doing here?" She continued, saying exactly what Paul was thinking, "He did not leave this situation to chance! He preordained his destiny! He developed a vision, an unshakable vision, of surviving this ordeal, a vision where he was giving a speech explaining how he had managed to survive, and by repetition, repetition, repetition, he had hard-wired that vision into his inner subconscious. He managed to do it in a way that meant, in his mind's eye, it had already happened; he'd given the speech to the liberating soldiers; he'd felt how good it was to explain this, and what it was like to still be alive! In his mind he had been there a thousand times, a million, maybe.

"The inhumanity he had suffered was awful, but he had a vision. He knew that by holding onto the vision with something beyond hope, with absolute belief, faith and expectancy, it would be fulfilled. He knew, he 100% knew, that the instruction he had programmed into his inner subconscious already existed in the field of creation, where all possibilities live simultaneously in space and time. It was up to him to claim the destiny he had chosen. He knew that the choice he made would be obeyed and delivered by his deeper subconscious.

"He used the words of Nietzsche to help him through the ordeal, 'He who has a why to live, can bear almost any how'. His survival is a testimony to the power of belief and the natural law of the universe. It also reminds me of the unlimited, mysterious resources available to us to deliver us from all kinds of evil. We need to believe, that's all. But believe at a level beyond hope. To believe at a level of total certainty, to simply know and feel in our mind that it is done, that it has already happened, no matter what the it is."

Paul was still awestruck but asked, "I understand what you are saying and believe it totally, but surely it can't be that easy?" Maya answered, "No-one is suggesting that these key factors in understanding how goals, objectives and visions get delivered into the real world is easy. Simple, yes, but easy, no! It is quite difficult for us, as human beings, to stay focused on our goals, objectives and visions. There is a lot of noise coming at us from all angles at the outer conscious level." She referred to the process and the diagram again and reiterated how external perceptions get stored in the inner subconscious, "There's television noise, radio noise, newspaper noise, friends' opinions noise, colleagues' noise, bosses' noise, partners' noise, all bombarding the pictures we have on the inside that make up our goals, objectives and visions. The more direct hits the pictures get, the less clear they become, which makes it more difficult for our deeper subconscious to have full access to the forces of infinite intelligence. The unlimited power to which we can have direct access is scattered and defused by our lack of clarity and focus on our heart-felt desires.

"These outside influences, the random, haphazard, unchosen thoughts and opinions of others that conflict with and cloud our goals, therefore often come to dominate our minds. We need to be strong and resolute in our thinking, once we have decided what our goals and objectives are in life. The degree of desire we attach to our goals will determine how focused we are, and the depth of belief will determine how quickly they will become realities in our lives. All you need to do to have anything you want in life, is firstly decide what you want, secondly ensure the desire is there in sufficient amounts, and thirdly know it's already yours because you've imagined how terrific it looks and feels for you and all concerned to have it. Fourthly, you need to take appropriate action. Once the first three things are locked in place, then it is on its way to you; it's inevitable; the outcome is a certainty; providing you take the appropriate action!"

Paul wrestled to come to terms with what Maya was saying, "But surely you need skills, talents, qualifications, contracts, money and loads of other things to achieve any right and proper desire in life? What if you don't have any of those things? How can you achieve anything you want in life then?" Maya smiled, remembering that she'd had similar difficulties understanding how this part of the process works, "Paul, the only thing you really need is faith; faith in yourself as an integral part of an intelligent, abundant, responsive universe; faith in yourself as a creator, with access to unlimited resources, skills, gifts, talents, just waiting to be unleashed, once they are channelled and directed properly. You don't need any particular skill or ability to be successful at anything. You just need to want to do it enough! Desire, vision and faith are the dynamic and inexhaustible fuels that ignite our passion to overcome challenges and keep us going through the difficult times, which will appear, on the road to success. The effort required will vary depending on the vision, but it will always be an effort. There are no hard and fast rules in terms of being successful, there are only hard ones. But when the effort is fuelled by the absolute certainty of the outcome, most people are more than willing to pay the price in terms of the learning needed, the sacrifices required, the discipline to be shown. What would you attempt to do if you knew you couldn't fail?

"The reality is you can't fail, not when your belief and faith are absolute. The desire, vision and faith together give real focus, unshakeable focus; the externally generated noise becomes irrelevant. In fact, with such focus, you don't hear, see or feel the noise anymore. When you're on such a mission, you rise above it all; you operate at your highest level. This is when you're unstoppable. The ladder of success isn't crowded at the top.

"Just to finish for tonight, there is one other reason why people don't achieve anything and everything they want in life: the world is full of dream-stealers." Paul once again looked puzzled, and Maya continued to explain, "You may not like this particular bit, but the world is full of dream-stealers and some of the biggest dream-stealers are the people who are closest to you! Here's an example. You tell the person you regard as your very, very best friend, that someone really rich is going to buy you your dream car. There are no strings attached to this act of generosity, they are doing it simply because they think you are a great guy. OK?" Paul nodded.

"Let's say your dream car is a Mercedes SLK; £38,500 worth of joy. Your very best friend would say that they are thrilled for you, because they know how much you love that make and model of car. They want to come with you to the showroom when you pick it up for delivery, just to see the look on your face. They want to be the first to have a drive in it with you, to see the smile on your face and the wind in your hair!

"Now let me tell you what 99.99% of the people in your life would actually say: you don't want one of them! Overpriced German crap! You could get two brand new cars for that price, and have some money left over for a new kitchen and a deposit for a holiday!" Paul agreed strongly, " You're right! You're so right! Most people would say something like that." Maya continued, "But you must understand that these people are not, for the most part, doing their dream-stealing deliberately. It's just the way they've been conditioned, to give an opinion, to give their thoughts. Unwittingly, in the process they rip your dream from your mind, tear it into a thousand pieces and effectively flush it down the toilet!"

Paul could think of many instances in his life when dream-stealers had succeeded in destroying his dreams. They had stolen his dreams because he did not have the courage of his convictions to hold onto them! Every time he told anyone what his dreams were, they would explain and prove that it couldn't be done, or it would be too much effort, or not worthwhile. He also realised that when he was successful he had simply made up his mind to do something, got on with it, not told anyone and, hey presto, in double-quick time, he'd actually achieved it!

He excitedly explained his thinking to Maya, and then realised that she already knew he had used the law of motivation and achievement. He had already mastered this technique by accident! He couldn't wait to begin to use it by design and realise his destiny to the full. He told Maya how keen he was to take control. She was just as keen.

Maya added, "You've got pretty much all you need now to succeed at anything. You just need to understand how to direct and channel your unlimited powers properly, and for that you need a goal-setting master class! You first need a week or so to reflect on how the law of motivation and achievement drives all success, and then you'll be ready for that last step. Just remember that motivation is about deliberately throwing your mental system out of order, and visualising, imagining and feeling the desired outcome in your mind, as if it has already happened. This belief, ahead of time, marshals all the forces and resources available to you in the universe, to find the set of circumstances to make the belief come true in the real world. Used properly, it will never let you down. Never!"

Paul was truly inspired by his new-found knowledge. Maya continued, "As I've already said, don't think that we have discovered new aspects of how the mind works; ancient traditions knew about this. But they didn't concern themselves on finding, measuring and understanding how these forces worked, or where they came from; they just concerned themselves with how to use them.

"All spiritual traditions recognise this; it's eloquently summed up in the Bible: 'Whatever you ask for in prayer, believe you have received it, and it will be yours'. However, there is another dimension to motivation that is truly mind-blowing, and not for the faint-hearted. It is not an obligatory part of your journey. But, if you want to understand motivation at the deepest level, I can show you it." Paul was enthusiastic about learning everything he could about this life-changing subject. Maya told him, "Sleep well and deeply tonight with your new-found knowledge and, tomorrow lunch time, meet me for half an hour in the park near your office. I will explain it all to you then, OK?" Paul agreed and they left The Old Fox together.

Chapter Twenty-one

Paul had been in the park, sitting on his favourite bench, for about 5 minutes when Maya arrived. He had been experimenting with feeling the infinite forces of the universe pulling this way and that, in response to his thinking. He realised he was now 'at one with the world'. He'd heard that expression before and had always thought it was a load of hippy nonsense. With his new-found knowledge he now knew it could be true.

Maya sat next to Paul and, after the briefest of chit-chats about how beautiful the weather was, she looked across the park and said "Just sit here with your eyes closed and listen to my words. It will help with your understanding. Listen with every fibre of your being. Don't just listen; hear and feel the words too. Hear what the words have to tell you". Paul closed his eyes and Maya began.

"Last night, you began to get to grips with the basics of the laws that drive motivation and achievement, and to understand that, for our unlimited creativity, drive and energy to be stimulated to the highest degree, we have to deliberately throw our mental system out of order. This is accomplished by imprinting brand new beliefs in our inner subconscious, through visualising and imagining them as if they've already happened. You also know that, for us to access all the creative and intelligent forces in the universe that will unerringly turn these beliefs into reality, they have to be much more than hollow wishes and vague hopes. Only belief, total and absolute belief, ahead of time, together with the heart-felt feelings that their realisation will bring, will make the outcome inevitable.

As with any belief, newly chosen ones will only get created and hard-wired into our inner subconscious through a combination of the repetition, repetition, repetition and repetition of disciplined thinking, together with a burning desire for its outcome. You need the belief to already be in your possession so much that it hurts. You will understand how this works fully when you've been through the goal-setting master class we'll do at our next session. You'll then be able to write your goals down, imprint them and stay completely focused on them. And then you'll be ready to begin living the joyous existence you deserve. How does that sound?!"

Eyes still closed, Paul beamed, "It sounds brilliant, but it looks and feels even better!" They both laughed out loud because he had clearly demonstrated his ability to convert the words he was hearing into visualisation and imagery.

Maya continued, "Being totally focused on how it feels to already possess what we truly want is a key aspect of achieving it. However, we need to understand that all thoughts have power. Someone once said, 'Every thought you think is contributing its share to the ultimate result of your life'. In other words, it's no use being focused while we are in the process of hard-wiring new goals and beliefs into our minds, if the rest of the time our thoughts are, literally, all over the place. That would just result in the creativity and energy that makes up our life force being diffused. Every thought, every single thought, uses some of our life force. That is the way the infinite and intelligent universal forces available to us operate. So, to use all our unlimited resources to the full, you can't afford the luxury of any unfocused, negative thought, and I mean none!"

Paul instinctively knew that what Maya was saying was true. How many times had he had his dreams stolen by his own negative thoughts?! He told Maya this, and added: "Negative thoughts, on the surface, are seemingly so harmless, aren't they? I can recall so many occasions when all my enthusiasm and passion to achieve something wonderful was ruined with a single negative thought like 'You'll never be able to do that' or 'Who the heck do you think you are to deserve that in your life?' And woosh! The life force needed to bring it about is gone, diverted and stolen by the negative thought."

Maya went on, "That is why taking control of your thinking at the outer conscious level is so crucial. If you don't control your conscious thinking, you can give up all too easily on your dreams. This means none of your unlimited life force is used to think up ways of achieving your dream, with the result that your dreams evaporate into nothing. Someone once said 'When you cease to dream, you cease to live'.

"Victor Frankl, the concentration camp survivor who I mentioned last night, tells us that the highest mortality rates he witnessed in the camp were during the first week of 1945. The reason for this was that, towards the end of 1944, everyone knew that the Nazis would be defeated and that the liberation of those people in the concentration camps was only a matter of time. However, most prisoners had convinced themselves that it would be Christmas 1944, or New Year 1945 at the latest. They'd set their heart on the fact there'd be a Christmas or New Year armistice. When the camps were not liberated by early New Year 1945, many prisoners' hopes and beliefs regarding their liberation were shattered. With belief gone, deadly diseases moved in and did their work on their weak and feeble bodies. Frankl tells of seeing many people losing the will to live right in front of his eyes."

Paul responded, "This is literally life and death stuff, isn't it?" Maya continued, "The greatest work that anyone can undertake is to harness the mind and direct the unlimited power at its disposal towards achieving constructive, joyous and glorious things to the benefit of humankind. Those who do not know how to develop and control their minds, or refuse to, are lost souls. They are set adrift from experiencing the highest levels of joy, happiness, success, health and all the abundance that life has to offer. They are left searching and seeking fulfilment externally, and always find themselves falling short. They are also, unknowingly, slipping further and further away from finding true fulfilment. The reality is that true fulfilment starts on the inside and works its way out! Because people don't control all their thoughts, the world is crowded with the fearful who struggle in blind, visionless despair. Yet still they search and seek in vain, externally! If only people had not been brainwashed into the negative thinking that builds fears and the seeds of failure from infancy, the whole universe, and all the glory in it, could and would be theirs. The world is ready for a thinking revolution, don't you agree?" Paul nodded; his eyes were still tight shut as Maya explained further.

"The level of control of thought required in the mind is significant, but it is not beyond the capability of anyone, with a little practice. A simple discipline begins the process: any negative thought must be removed immediately and replaced with a positive one to reinforce the desired picture. This is called laser thinking. It whips the deeper subconscious and all the forces available to it into line, to focus and direct all its powers of concentration to find the set of circumstances needed to turn the desired outcome into reality. Thomas Carlyle, a famous Scottish mathematician and philosopher, once proved that if you walk from one side of a park to the other and stay there for a while, you will have shifted the centre of gravity of the entire universe! You might think 'Not little old me, because I only weight 150 lbs' but, while it might have been an imperceptible shift, Carlyle proved it is mathematically true. Our thinking is just the same: unfocused, undisciplined and negative thoughts shift the direction our lives begin to take. Oh yes, it may be imperceptible at first but, if there are enough negative thoughts around a particular area, they take control and, rather than achieving the glory that is ours to be had by channelling and directing our thoughts on our goals and desired outcomes, most people end up going around in circles, and ever decreasing ones at that!

"Albert Schweitter, a famous explorer, once said 'The tragedy of life is not that we die, it's what dies inside a man while he lives'! What do you think he meant by that?"

Paul realised the answer quickly, "He's describing that, while our minds should grow sharper and keener with use as we get older, because most people don't understand the power and control they have, they lose faith in themselves as omnipotent achievers. It's describing how the inner subconscious self-image shrinks rather than expands; our beliefs become infested with negatives rather than positives; we achieve less rather than more, and eventually give up trying at all."

Maya nodded in agreement and added, "He is also describing the fundamental breakdown of control where we let the negative and destructive images we perceive in the world rule our thoughts, so that our thoughts are ruling us rather than us ruling our thoughts. There are two realms in this universe: there is a thought realm and a physical realm. Nothing has ever shown up in the physical realm without it starting in the thought realm first. Victor Hugo once wrote 'An invasion of armies can be resisted but not an idea whose time has come'. In other words, physical entities can be resisted but not thoughts, visions and ideas. I'll give you some examples. Abraham Lincoln had a good idea, he thought slavery in America should be abolished. What a promise eh, Paul? However, he paid a price. He plunged his country into a civil war and was assassinated. But even if you kill the man, you can't kill the idea. Nelson Mandela is another example. He thought apartheid was evil and wicked and should be abolished. Did he have an easy time of it? I think not! He was locked up for 27 years. Again, you may lock the man up but you can't destroy the idea. Both men had vision fuelled with an unquestionable desire and, through seemingly impossible circumstances, found the resources to turn the vision into a reality."

"Thoughts and ideas rule the world", Paul said with the biggest smile of his life.

Maya continued, "How did this park come into being, Paul, or your office building around the corner? Someone once commented 'The only difference between a thought and a physical reality is a certain amount of time and physical activity'. Look at the example of Leonardo De Vinci, who invented a helicopter 400 years before it could technically be built. Within those 400 years there were many inventions needed before helicopters could take to the air."

Still with his eyes closed, Paul said, "I can see it, I can see and feel the whole process, it's all so clear and obvious. Every thought must become part of our purpose, the purpose we choose for ourselves. It's so brilliantly clear now. We command our inner subconscious mind to be completely focused on how good the end result looks and feels, and the outcome is inevitable. The outer conscious mind becomes aligned to it, and relaxes. Then the full power of the deeper subconscious mind is released to find the solutions and resources to make what we desire real."

Maya replied, "That's incredibly insightful Paul. However, it's more mysterious than that. The deeper subconscious mind does not just find the answers, it receives the answers too! You must know that what you are seeking in this universe is also seeking you. Have you ever been talking one evening on a feelings and emotions level about some good friends you've lost touch with, and the phone rings and it's them?" Paul nodded.

Maya continued, "We have powers we don't understand. When we learn to totally control our thinking, and the three individual elements of our minds become one through the absolute certainty of the outcome, our reach becomes endless. The feelings generated by such total belief create a connectedness with all the forces and intelligences in the universe. The deeper subconscious is the element of our mind that links the physical realm to the field of creation and universal intelligence. This is the realm where all knowledge exists, and it is open for us all to draw upon, for the total fulfilment of heart-felt desires.

"The intensity of the desire and belief always carries with it the power of its fulfilment. It is a power that transcends the physical realm. It's in this field of creation and universal intelligence, where all possibilities, all eventualities, all outcomes already exist. There's enough power and resources here for everyone to have anything and everything they need, want and desire. There's no need to compete. There's enough for everyone. We just need to choose the outcomes we want and desire. By tapping into the field of creation and universal intelligence, any circumstances and resources required to materialise any desired outcome will present themselves, without fail.

"True inspiration, literally being in-spirit, comes from this, as do flashes of genius and what people who don't understand this may call coincidences, as does intuition and even luck! Once you learn to control your thinking, you will become the luckiest person alive, where nothing can be denied you, nothing that is a right and proper desire. Planting the desired outcome or belief in your mind is like the seed, the seed that carries with it the power to bring forth and fulfil the perfect product of its existence!

"Do you remember we talked about the phrase 'I'll believe it when I see it'?" Paul nodded and Maya continued, "That's the sceptic's view. The truly visionary and inspirational view is exactly the opposite. When you believe it, you will see it! The belief comes first and the reality comes second. We've known this from time immemorial, we've just forgotten it it recent times. Now we're learning it again, and the world is ready for a thinking revolution. It will make the world a much better place to live in. Its positive impact will be greater than anything we've ever witnessed when it sweeps the world.

"We don't need to understand how the powers we have work, we just need to know that they work! Let other people study the roots if they want to, while we pick the fruit! This makes for a life worth living.

"But be careful with this. Remember, when you believe it, you will see it; I can guarantee this. The belief, however, operates at two levels. Firstly, you must believe that all the forces in the universe are at your command through the non-verbal language of heart-felt feelings, and secondly you must have the faith to know that the desired outcome already exists and, therefore, its manifestation is inevitable. Nothing short of total belief and total faith will work. As we've said before, a vague hope, or an empty wish, will not make it work. Once these two elements, total faith and total belief, are locked onto any right and proper desire, everything that holds us back, every impossibility, insurmountable barrier, every wall, will crumble as the intensity of feeling drives the whole process of turning desired outcomes into realities.

"John Macdonald wrote a book called *Message of a Master*, published in 1929. In it he describes this process beautifully and eloquently: 'Any picture firmly held in any mind in any form is bound to come forth, that is the great unchanging Universal Law that when we co-operate with it intelligently makes us absolute masters of all conditions and situations in our lives'. Can you see and feel that Paul? 'Masters of all the conditions and situations in our lives', not slaves to, but masters of."

Paul was radiant; with his eyes still closed he was able to absorb all Maya had said with no external distraction. He could picture how the process works. The cosmic energy that made up the 60 trillion cells that were his body and soul was now ready to be unleashed. It was wonderful. It was bliss. He now knew that nothing was impossible for him. Nothing.

He reflected, "When we intensify the desire and stop the negative thoughts and quieten our mind, our deeper subconscious not only has access to the full powers and resources contained within our own minds, but there is also a direct connection with the universal mind; the mind where all possibilities already exist and where all knowledge, past, present and future, is held. It all becomes available to us." Paul felt his body tingle from head to toe as he felt a new force begin to flow through him, as a revelation entered his mind. Maya could sense it, as he said, "So, what you're saying here is that we, as human beings, with the right mind training, can manifest all the possibilities that already exist. So that means, if we choose to, we can become perfect?"

Maya was impressed with Paul's clarity of thought, "Providing you can give me a crystal-clear picture of what being perfect looks and feels like, the answer is yes. Why do you ask me that?" Paul replied, "I'm not sure that I could give you a crystal-clear picture, but some of my friends who are of a religious persuasion could. I'm now beginning to see a higher meaning to the outer conscious, inner subconscious and deeper subconscious mind model you have shown me."

Maya was ecstatic that Paul had opened himself up so quickly and effectively to the new force, or spirit, that was beginning to flow through him. The main reason for her heart-felt joy was that no one can be given it, this spirit; it's already there. Each individual must simply find it, accept it and work with it. It's everywhere at once, across space and time. You just need to let it into your very being, into your heart and mind, in order to enliven your soul.

Paul continued, "My Christian friends tell me that we are created in God's image, so the vision they are imprinting into their inner subconscious is that of being perfect, like God, the Father. They also tell me that Jesus Christ was God's conscious representation here on Earth. So, at the outer conscious level, the behaviour represents the Son. And, of course, the power source in the Bible is a divine force that is called the Holy Spirit. This flows from and through the deeper subconscious." In his mind's eye, Paul could clearly visualise the piece of paper Maya used last night, with new words printed on the top:

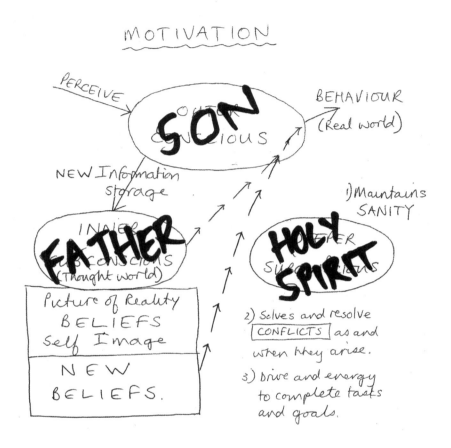

He exclaimed, "It's the trinity! It's the three in one that every spiritual work ever written describes and is built upon. Christianity, Islam, Buddhism, Hinduism, Sikhism, Judaism. Every spiritual tradition has the same base. The desired outcomes are the same for all faiths; a world full of joy, peace of mind, happiness, success, health, abundance of any kind. Only the characters and stories differ, but the base is identical."

Calm came over Paul, as all fears and doubts evaporated. Maya said, "You can open your eyes now, Paul." As he adjusted to the light, he saw a very different world from when he'd closed them.

He saw a world of energy being channelled and directed through each individual's thoughts. He saw each person as the fruits of the seeds they had, themselves, planted. The Maya he saw, of course, was a fertile garden of glory. Most other people he saw were weedy and barren. "The forces at our disposal do not respect people, their position, their status, just their thoughts", he concluded.

"What do you see?" Maya asked. Paul replied, "I see that you are your thoughts. They are you. All matter that you see is just spirit or energy, and the spirit and energy are directed by the mind. The body and the real world are the material expression of the mind; the inner subconscious mind in itself has no power. However, once thoughts are locked into the inner subconscious mind as beliefs, they effectively serve to instruct the deeper subconscious mind to use its unlimited power and energy to transform them into the reality they are destined to be. The inner subconscious mind simply instructs and the deeper subconscious mind, which is servile, simply obeys! One becomes the vision, the other the means of provision. Whether the vision is glorious or barren, joyous or fearful, happy or sad, rich or poor, the deeper subconscious simply obeys! Wow! Used properly, we, as human beings, could literally work miracles, could we not?"

Maya nodded, "Indeed we could, and we have done so in the past, and we still do today. It takes training and discipline to get to that level and, should you choose to, I can show you how to walk with the gods. As we've discussed before, we are as much divine as we are human. There is no mystery to working miracles or to walking with the gods. It just needs a little practice! Very few people have ever perfected it, yet it's as simple as breathing, eating and walking. Every spiritual work ever written tells us how to do this, yet, for some reason, it's usually in unclear and confusing terms. This is especially true of the work of most clerics who are supposed to be custodians of the truth and who live by it! The Bible is full of references to us being as much divine as we are human. In the

Gospel according to John, it says 'Jesus answered them, "Is it not written in your law, I said, ye are Gods?"' and 'You can do all that I have done, and even greater things'. It's in there; it's in them all. It's just difficult to explain how it all works and what to do in terms people can understand. When people realise that all the abundance in the universe is here for them to enjoy for eternity, their journey has begun. When they understand and master how to control all the forces of the universe available to them, nothing, absolutely nothing, will be impossible for them and the journey will never end.

Maya continued, "It's about visualising and imagining the outcome we want of the future, building the desire for it, holding it firm in our mind and heart, cultivating it, working for it, enjoying the journey. This is the process by which all things are produced. No one religious group has the monopoly on this process, because it is a universal process. It is open and available to all. The fact that you don't go to church, or you didn't go to church last Sunday, doesn't disqualify you, but the thought of it does! Banish all doubts, all fears; focus and believe and the universal process will produce. It is irrevocable.

"The prophet Habakkuk in the Old Testament in the Bible sums the process up beautifully and indicates that there is another lesson you need to complete, in order to be in control and fulfilled. Maya handed Paul a piece of paper and read the words to him without looking at it. She explained that the first part described a conflict and the second part was an instruction:

> *How long Lord, am I to cry for help while you will not listen;*
> *To cry 'oppression!' in your ear and you will not save?*
> *Why do you set injustice before me?*
> *Why do you look on where there is tyranny?*
> *Outrage and violence this is all to see,*
> *All is contention, and discord flourishes.*

Maya paused, and asked Paul, "Has anything changed much in the world since this was written?" Paul shook his head, "Nothing in the slightest." Maya continued, "This was the Lord's reply. Remember, if you are of a religious persuasion, this is the big guy, this is the boss talking:

> The Lord answered and said,
> 'Write the vision down,
> Inscribe it on tablets to be easily read,
> Since the vision is for its own time only:
> Eager for its own fulfilment, it does not deceive;
> If it comes slowly, wait,
> For come it will, without fail.'

"You don't get much clearer than that! The big challenge you now face is spending some time deciding what the desired outcomes for your life are. What is your destiny? What do you want for you, for your family, your friends, your career, for humanity? You'll need the help and guidance that the goal-setting master class offers, in order to be ready to take control and have any amount of happiness, success, health, wealth, joy, material possessions, relationships and the like."

Paul blurted out, "So, when can we do the master class?" Maya spoke softly, "At our next meeting. However, are you OK with what we've discussed today?" Paul gushed, "It has been a true revelation and explained so many things I sort of knew about, but never really understood, before. But there is one thing I don't yet understand: if this knowledge is in all the spiritual traditions and is now known to you, and me, why doesn't everyone know about it?"

Maya said, "I wish I knew the answer to that one. It's a combination of things; people unwittingly complicate things that are incredibly simple. Some people refuse to admit the whole process is so straightforward.

"Some people seem to need more complex techniques and processes. People don't believe in their unlimited nature. People don't know how the process works. People want to keep the secret to themselves. People want instant results and, therefore, try to change their behaviour. They don't understand that thinking is planting, doing is harvesting, and that thoughts are things. People allow the planting of the glorious to be choked by the weeds of doubts and fears and inadequacies. There's a whole variety of reasons. But all that anybody needs to do to prove how effective this is, is to try it for themselves! Follow the process and the techniques and, voilà, there it is. The object planted in the mind becomes the subject in the real world. It's very Zen!

"Again, understanding and believing in the process and having the faith to use it, and quietening the negative thoughts, is all that anybody needs to be able to master it and to have any amount of the true, true treasures in life. Then they've actually got to get on and do it. People only need to practise this for themselves to find how powerful it is. Mathew 7:7 sums up the opportunity:

> *Ask and it will be given to you,*
> *Seek and you will find,*
> *Knock and the door will be opened to you.*
> *For everyone who asks receives,*
> *He who seeks, finds,*
> *And to him who knocks the door will be opened.*

"The biggest problem is that, even though people don't understand the process, they know that the true treasures of life are not very far away. In fact, they're just on the other side of the door. So, they push and push and push against the door, then kick it; they punch and try to force it to open. They break their backs, break their hearts, break their souls trying to push the door open. What they don't realise is that they just need to take a step back and pull the door open! The door to happiness, joy, love, friendship, health, abundance, success, vitality, energy, etc., opens inwards! Success is an inside job! We need to change the future we want on the inside first, in our minds, and let it work its way out into our real world. Trying to change on the outside doesn't work, because we are dominated by our internal pictures. That is the universal process. It's a universal law. As we've said before, but it's worth repeating, you cannot break the law, but millions have broken themselves against the law, trying to achieve what they want in life by doing it the wrong way round. The result is misery, poverty, depression, ill health, despair, jealousy and envy."

All the problems Paul had ever had in achieving anything had just been summed up in about 20 seconds! He added triumphantly, "So, with the power of thinking, comes the power to think oneself into and out of any condition in life." Maya responded, "I couldn't have put it better myself. However, real thinking develops a mental maturity that puts you up there with the best of them. There is a methodology that requires discipline and patience but, after a little practice, it will become second nature to you. It's like learning to play a musical instrument. It's awkward and clumsy at first, but you soon get to the point of not having to search desperately for the next note. The result of the practice is truly amazing. Instead of our minds being clogged, tired and candle-powered, they become truly alive and alert to everything; nuclear-powered, and worried about nothing. There is a calmness, control and certainty of the outcome that is serene and joyful beyond measure. At higher levels, some people commune with the spirits. But it takes a lot of practice to get there!"

Paul laughed because it sounded so real yet so ridiculous, at the same time. 'Who am I to be able to commune with the spirits', he thought. Maya knew what he had thought, and said, "You need to quieten the negative thoughts." Paul nodded and she continued, "And we need to show you how to write goals and create visions and begin the process of fulfilling your destiny." Paul responded,

"Oh yes! Please! As soon as we can! Part of my destiny, however, has to be to share this with the rest of humanity. How good a world would it be then?" Maya said quietly, "A lot like heaven on Earth?" Paul nodded.

Maya finished with, "I'll call you soon when you've had time to take on board today's lesson. You are now only one step away from all the glory this universe has to offer. I'll see you soon." She walked towards the park gates and disappeared behind the trees and the railings. Paul reflected for a while before returning to work feeling ecstatic!

Chapter Twenty-two

Paul now saw the world very differently. He saw people for the first time in his life as what they really were, outcrops of the unlimited universal energy force, individual in expression and united in spirit. He was saddened to see the way that people chose to express their unlimited nature because of the mental straightjacket that was their thoughts. He was also exhilarated at the prospect of sharing the insights and guidance he'd received from Maya with as many people as he could. He knew so many people who were like him before Maya began to guide him, well meaning, hard working, wanting to do the best for themselves, their families, neighbours, friends, work colleagues and the like, who were not only lost but buckling, physically and mentally, under the strain.

He thought about what the world would be like if everyone could think, feel and behave in this new way. A warmth and radiance filled his entire body, and he felt that anyone who was within a 200 mile radius of him would feel it too and, as a result, become a little more energised. He also realised that this new way of thinking, together with the power, control and glory that went with it, was the next logical step in the development of the human race. As Maya and he had discussed, it was an agricultural revolution that had changed the human world first, followed by an industrial revolution, then a technological revolution, recently an information and knowledge revolution, and now it was time for a thinking and spiritual awareness revolution, a non-national, non-religious, non-denominational thinking spiritual awareness revolution! It would unite all people on Earth with the beliefs they have in common, not the differences. 'It really would be heaven,' he thought, 'heaven on Earth!' Something clicked inside his mind, 'Why not?' he thought, 'A new era for humankind.' He had started his journey to heaven on Earth. This thinking revolution was the key to joy, happiness, wealth, health and success for everyone, but they must begin working together rather than separately. Different people would contribute to the journey in their own way; Paul had noticed that some people had huge amounts of energy and connectedness and others little. He wondered why that was.

The feelings these thoughts were producing were indescribable. He felt like the strongest man on Earth, the fittest man on Earth, the most creative man on Earth, the most intelligent man on Earth. 'All this power and unstoppable ability', he thought, 'wow!' He realised that, like a rocket, he was now fully primed, but he had nowhere to go. He knew what he wanted to achieve in general terms, with success and happiness and the like, but he had no crystal-clear picture of what his major desires, outcomes and goals were in life.

Just then his phone rang. It was Maya, "Hi, Paul, how've you been since we met?" Paul replied immediately, "Mesmerised, totally mesmerised. I see the whole world totally differently. Everything and everyone is an individual expression of a swirling mass of cosmic energy, whether it's locked away in a solid form of particles, as in the rocks that make up the mountains, or in more fluid forms of cosmic energy that possess reproductive intelligence, such as plants, trees and animals. It's all one, big, universal energy force, individual in expression and united in spirit. And then there is the highest and most sophisticated level of expression: humans, put in our dominant position by our consciousness, yet thwarted in our ability to dominate in terms of achievement by our thoughts! Our failure to dominate is because we are unaware of our position within the whole swirling cosmic dance that is the universe. If we were aware, we would dominate all aspects of our life with health, happiness, success, love, friendship, energy and vitality. Our awareness has been dulled, dulled to the point that we are unaware of the forces that flow around and though everything in our world. It's so sad, but a terrific challenge at the same time." He informed Maya that one of his goals was to enlighten as much of the world as he could to the benefits of this thinking revolution, and that it would be a peaceful, non-violent, high-impact revolution.

Maya responded, "I'm glad you see it this way, the world is ready for this now, but don't forget that it isn't new. In fact, this type of thinking and knowing is ancient. As we have said before, we are not finding new ways of thinking here; we are rediscovering the most ancient. We are learning to reconnect with what lies at the very core of our being, the part of our essence that is connected with the universal energy source, our spirit.

"Having been separated from, and lost the awareness of, our very being, we've been cut off from the infinite creative potential that is contained in our spirit. The result: pain and struggle. By taking control of our thinking, we can reconnect with our true being, and be! Be, and have, anything, any right and proper desire, without limit. Reconnecting with our ability to plant our intent for the future firmly into the field of creation, with the certain and absolute knowledge that it will manifest itself, will liberate us! However, we need to learn and master techniques that will awaken our being. This allows us to harness our spirit and channel and direct all our creativity and energy to enable us to achieve unlimited levels of joy, love, happiness, peace, success, etc. So, when do you want to meet to go through the goal-setting master class?"

Paul replied, "I am available anytime that you are. The sooner the better, as far as I'm concerned. What about meeting at The Old Fox straight after work, say 6 o'clock?" Maya agreed, "I'll see you then."

Chapter Twenty-three

Maya was already there when Paul arrived, and she greeted him with, "Hi, Paul, you are looking terrific! I don't think I've ever seen you looking so fit, healthy and relaxed." Paul responded, "Why, thank you, my friend, I don't think I've ever felt better! I'm yet another different person from the one you last saw. You seem to do this to me every time we meet! Some major metamorphosis takes place afterwards." Maya smiled, "So long as you and everyone around you feels better for it, that's great!"

Pleasantries over, Maya began, "You now know the fundamentals of how all the processes work for you to achieve every right and proper desire in life. Now you need to understand how to decide what those desires are, and how to imprint them properly onto your mind, so that they can be translated into their physical equivalent in the shortest time frame."

Paul nodded enthusiastically, "Yes indeed, I feel elated and frustrated at the same time, because I know, I really know, that I can achieve anything, but I don't know what the anything actually is!"

Maya continued, "That's not unusual, and there are right and wrong ways of making sure it all works for you without fail, so let's investigate it some more. I saw some statistics recently that suggest only 3% of people have goals or objectives in life and actually write them down. My own experience tells me that in reality it's nothing like as high as that. In fact, if my own research is anything to go by, the actual percentage is less than one half of 1%! The same statistics suggest that some 10% of people have goals but don't write them down. I think that 10% figure is about right. The statistics then show that the people who have goals and write them down achieve 50 to 100 times more in their lives than the people who have goals and don't write them down! Any ideas why that is the case?"

Paul thought for a moment, "Well, knowing what I now know, it must be something to do with focus. Writing goals down allows an individual to create a crystal-clear focus." Maya nodded, "That's a large part of it. The other part is that actually writing goals down shows a great degree of commitment. The term 'committing' your goals to paper is not used lightly because, once written, it is impossible to alter them or fudge the outcome. This means that all our inexhaustible energy and creativity can be channelled to finding the circumstances and resources to make the goal into a reality. And, depending upon the intensity of the desire behind it, the realisation of the goal becomes inevitable over time; the greater the desire, the shorter the time scale to realisation. OK?" Paul nodded his understanding.

Maya went on, "Let's say that the 3% and 10% figures are correct. What do you think happens to the other 87% of people?" Paul answered promptly, "Well, they do what I've seen them all doing since we last met. They wander through life aimlessly, going nowhere, achieving little or nothing, not using their resources for anything much." Maya agreed, "Yes, that's right. Most people just drift through life. They go wherever the winds and the tides take them because, firstly, they don't know how much power they've got locked away inside them and, secondly, they think that life is a matter of chance and not one of choice. So the limitless power they have is not channelled or controlled. Most people are like rudderless ships!

"The whole philosophy behind goal-setting is to turn people from being wandering generalities into being meaningful specifics. This results in all our creativity, energy, drive, etc., being focused and directed, rather than being scattered and diffused. This creates something that I've mentioned before, laser thinking, which is a beautiful term, don't you think?" Paul's expression suggested that he was unsure how beautiful the term was to him.

Maya continued, "Let me explain why it is such a beautiful term. Do you know what a laser beam is?" Paul nodded, gesturing with his hands whilst answering, "It's, er, concentrated light isn't it? In fact, isn't the word laser a mnemonic? I think it stands for 'light, amplified, stimulated, emission of radiation'."

Maya nodded, "That's correct, and it's really interesting what happens when you concentrate light energy, or any form of energy come to that. Some of the most fulfilling days I have are when I do voluntary work at our local primary school. Just recently, I did a day with a class of 10-year-olds, and we had some fun trying to explain this goal-setting concept and how it works and can be applied.

"Even with the *Star Wars* films and the introduction of light sabres, the 10-year-olds had difficulty understanding the concept of a laser beam. They couldn't understand how highly concentrated light could be so powerful that it could cut through 10 metre thick bars of steel like a knife would cut through butter.

"Think about it this way," Maya held her arms out below the light fixture that was above the table at which they were sitting, "I've now got an armful of light, right?" Paul nodded. "Pretty harmless stuff, wouldn't you say?" Paul nodded again. "In order to get the children to understand the concept of a laser beam and connect it with goal setting, I asked one of them to bring a magnifying glass from the table at the back of the class to me, because I was sitting in bright sunshine. I then asked the child to show me the back of her right hand.

"Positioning it in the sunlight to get the focal point as bright as possible on the back of the child's hand, I deliberately moved the magnifying glass so that it didn't stay in one place for long. Even on the hottest, sunniest day with the biggest magnifying glass one can hold, what do you think happens?" Paul answered confidently, "Nothing will happen, the focused and magnified light will have no time to have any impact at all if you keep on moving it around the back of the hand."

Maya agreed, "That's right! The impact is only felt when you leave the focal point of the concentrated light on one spot. Obviously I didn't leave it on the back of the child's hand long enough to burn her, but I did leave it just long enough for her to feel the heat building up, to illustrate the point. I then asked the children to imagine the same light 10 thousand times more concentrated: then you've got a laser beam. Their faces lit up when their understanding became complete. I used this idea to illustrate the point that any energy that is concentrated can become a powerful and unstoppable force.

"The whole universe is a swirling mass of energy engaged in a cosmic dance. Some energy is not vibrating at a sufficient frequency for it to exist in the form of waves, so it appears as particles. But even particles are pure energy. Split the smallest particle, an atom, and a whole city can be destroyed. Just above particles, in the energy spectrum, is sound. Concentrate sound, and you can blow down the walls of Jericho. Just above sound, in the energy spectrum, is light. Concentrate and focus light, and you have laser beams capable of cutting through 10 metres of steel. Above light are X-rays and gamma rays, concentrate these and galaxies are created. Any form of energy, concentrated and focused enough, will turn into an unstoppable force. Right at the very top of the energy spectrum is something called etheric energy. This is the energy that fuels our minds, our thinking energy. This is where infinite intelligence lives and where the universal spirit that connects everything resides.

"The process of setting goals and writing them down allows total concentration and focus of our etheric energy, which, when used properly, makes us unstoppable! That is why having crystal-clear goals is so important in achieving every right and proper desire in life. It focuses our thinking, energy and creativity by marshalling all the forces in the universe, and the infinite intelligence they contain, to not only flow from us, but also through us. As I've indicated before, this is what it means to be inspired, being in spirit. Truly inspired people achieve great things."

Paul was enthused, "I've heard a lot of people say that it's important to have goals, but up until now I've never really understood why, in terms of the infinite resources they open up to us. I always thought people who set goals are just greedy, ambitious, get-ahead kind of people, who don't mind who or what they trample on in order to get what they want."

Maya explained further, "Don't get me wrong. There are plenty of people who set goals who are exactly like that. But that's not what setting and achieving goals is all about. Most people who strive for money, possessions, power, recognition, status and so on, are trapped in the compulsive pursuit of some ego-gratification. Even if they attain all their self-centred goals, the emotional hole they are trying to fill re-emerges and proves to be bottomless.

"You can't get enough of what you don't need! These self-centred goals are used to cover a deep-rooted sense of lack or incompleteness. Being 'me'-centred cuts you off from the force, being 'other people'-centred opens it up for you." Paul now understood why some people had huge connectedness and others didn't!

Maya went on, "True goals come from the very centre of our being, not from the periphery of our ego. They are selfless, not selfish. The old adage, 'If you help enough people get what they want in life, they'll help you get anything you want in life', which we've mentioned before, is quite apposite here.

"The most dynamic and fulfilling goals are always set for the individual's 'highest good and the highest good of all concerned'.

A good tip to remember when setting and achieving goals is that the real joy, the real delight, is not in what you get but in what you become in the process. Again we've hinted at these things before; having a million pounds in the bank may be your goal, but what you become in the process in order to achieve it is the true treasure. Becoming a parent may be some people's goal, but what they become in the process, by being the best mother or father they can be, is the true treasure. These statements are in 'context' now.

"All that said, we need to decide what we want out of life and choose the future we want. Then, and only then, can we begin to focus our unlimited creativity and energy towards the delivery of these goals and objectives. There are five questions that need to be answered before goals can be chosen and written properly. These will probably be the toughest questions you've ever asked yourself. They need to be asked sincerely and they've got to be answered honestly and 'in the now'." Paul looked puzzled, and Maya explained, "As we've said before, your goals and objectives, which will emerge from answering these questions, cannot be vague wishes or faint hopes for the future. They need to be sharply defined and crystal clear in nature, because you're going to imprint them into the very core of your being. You will plant the intent into your mind, into the field of creation, via your feelings in such a way that it serves as an instruction to be transformed into its physical equivalent. Therefore, in your mind's eye, the desired outcomes have already got to have happened. In other words, they already exist 'in the now'. It's an instruction for the future; it's not one that's in the future!

"The answers to these questions mustn't be tainted with any doubts that they may not happen, or any feelings of not being worthy that come from your past conditioning and experiences. Again, it must have already happened or exist 'in the now', completely devoid of any shadow of doubt, no matter how pale. Your inner subconscious can't accept any goals tainted with doubt or any hint of your unworthiness to receive them. Operating at this level, at the level of universal and infinite intelligence in our minds, all possibilities already exist. You need to know that all the desired outcomes are already yours. You're now just going to claim them!

"The questions to answer sincerely are these", Maya handed over a piece of paper where the questions were neatly spaced out. She read the questions out to Paul as he himself read them, adding a few comments to help him understand them. She began by saying, "Most people have incredible difficulty answering these questions honestly and 'in the now' because they don't know that all possibilities already exist. Therefore they don't realise that they've got complete freedom of choice. This means they are restricted with their thinking, and often regard an exercise like this as nothing more than wishful thinking, rather than life planning. So, to question number 1: **what do you want to be?** 'In the now'? Honestly, truly, deeply, passionately? Do you want to be a millionaire? Do you? Really? Because there's a lot of crap that goes with being a millionaire. The envy and jealousy it attracts from others goes with the territory: comments from others, such as 'rich bast***', 'lucky bast***', 'selfish bast***', go with it. It matters not a jot how you've worked to get your money, how generous you are with it, or what worthy and valuable services you provided the world with in order to accumulate it!

"Don't misunderstand me here, though. There's nothing wrong or inappropriate about having money as a goal. You've just got to be careful, as many people think that having more of it will bring an end to their problems. The reality often is that it's just the beginning of them! Most people don't realise that having more money just makes you more of what you already are. It merely serves to amplify the person you are. If you're a miserable, selfish and paranoid person, having more money will make you more miserable, more selfish and more paranoid! If you're a wonderful, benevolent and generous person, having more money will make you more wonderful, more benevolent and more generous. If you're slightly dependant on drink or drugs to get your highs in life, having more money will just make you more dependant on them. Why do you think it is that rock stars and film stars work for years for next to nothing to become rich and famous and then, in a relatively short period of time after making it, end up killing themselves from overdoses?" Paul's mind raced with example after example of what Maya was talking about.

Maya continued, "So, what do you want to be? Respected and admired by everyone? A brilliant parent? Physically fit?

"Question 2: **what do you want to do?** Do you want to own and run your own successful business? Do you? Really? Deep down inside, people know that for that promise to come true there is a high price to pay in terms of the long hours, days, weeks, months and years of hard work needed to succeed. Many people would love all the advantages of running a successful business, but few are willing to put in the effort. That's why most new businesses fail. So what do you want to do? Really?

"Question 3: **what do you want to see?** Do you want to see the pyramids at Giza? The Great Wall of China? An MBA hanging on your office wall? Your ninetieth birthday? What do you want to see? Really?

"Question 4: **what do you want to have?** A four-bedroom detached house in the best part of town? A brilliant marriage? A Harley Davidson? A Porsche? People offering you terrific jobs all the time?

"Question 5: as you are preparing to get all this abundance out of life, all the things you want, **what are you going to give back?** What are you going to share? Are you going to work with the scouts in your local community? Work for free at a hospice at weekends? Raise money for Children in Need every year, or give 10% of everything you earn to charity? What do you want to share?

"Once you've answered these questions, the question at the bottom of the page becomes the most important one to answer: **are these really your goals?** Or are they to please or impress someone else? The instruction regarding this is a very simple one: if anything you choose to be, do, see, have and share is not your goal, throw it in the bin. Throw it away, because it is highly unlikely to manifest itself in your life. The reason for this is that it's almost impossible for you to be able to generate the right amount of desire, focus and feelings around it, if it's not yours. For that to happen, it has got to be your goal. As we've said before, you need to want to have the desired thing so much that it hurts!

"This will probably take you a little while to complete, and I suggest you begin with putting between 5 and 10 goals under each of the headings. Then you'll need to establish which ones are most important to you, which of your goals carries the greatest value to you personally. The ones you choose are the ones to start with. Again, this is because the ones you prioritise as most important are the goals that carry the greatest value to you and will generate the strongest feelings and the biggest desire.

"It may not be easy to prioritise your values, so I'll help you with this. The kind of values that people hold dear in their lives include things like loyalty, integrity, financial security, health, safety, family and so on. Many people have a dilemma establishing which values are most important in their lives. This is because it's different for different people, and it's different for the same people at different points in their lives. I've found that playing around with a few 'what if's' helps me prioritise the most important values in my life.

"If the chairman of your company calls you to a one-on-one meeting and praises you for your hard work and contribution to the success of the company, and says he wants you to join the Board of Directors on three times your current salary, how would you feel about that?" Paul replied, "I'd be bowled over, really chuffed, and I'd tell him that I'd be the most loyal, dedicated and hard-working director the company has ever had."

"Now, what if the chairman says to you that, before you make the decision to accept the position or otherwise, he needs to explain to you the only condition attached to his offer. During the board meetings you would be attending, when any decision goes to a vote, you would always vote the same way as he did; you would never, ever deviate. He asks if he has made himself clear and if you now want the job. Depending on the decision you've just made in your mind, you now know which is the most important to you in terms of values such as loyalty, integrity and financial security.

"I'm not being judgmental here, just establishing what values you hold most dear. If you say to yourself that you admire the chairman enormously, and that you trust his judgement implicitly and are happy to vote the way he does always, then loyalty might be the most important value to you. If you think that, while the chairman is usually sound in his decisions and that you normally agree with him, but your respect for yourself is such that you've got to vote the way you think is right, it may tell you that integrity is the most important value you have. If you think what the heck does it matter, the money would come in really useful for so many things that you want in your life, for yourself and others, it may tell you that financial security is the most important value to you. Do you understand what I'm trying to do here?"

Paul nodded, "It's perfectly clear. But this is not going to be an easy task, is it? To determine my most important values in life will require a lot of thought. I probably know what my values are implicitly, but not explicitly. I've never really sat down and thought about them, and I don't know many people who have. Coincidently, we had an interesting discussion at my daughter's parents' evening a few weeks ago on this very subject. The headteacher is delighted with Sally's progress, but there have been a few incidents that have affected her and everyone else in the school, things like name-calling and some low level bullying. We were discussing where children get their values from in this day and age. It's not church anymore, nor school. The parents have the responsibility. However, many parents try to instil in their children values that they don't exhibit in their own lives. Children tend to do what they see, not what they're told! We came to the sad conclusion that the television is probably the biggest influence when it comes to establishing values for our children. How frightening a thought is that?!"

Maya agreed, "There's a values-based thinking revolution on its way! It's the only thing that will fill the emptiness most people feel in their lives. Material possessions don't fulfil people, they leave them feeling emptier than ever. Clear-cut values anchor us to the really important things in our lives. They will also help us prioritise our goals and objectives, because we'd want to begin the process of having everything we want in life by deciding what's most important and valuable to us, wouldn't we? Here's one more 'what if' and then we can move on.

"Most people would put being healthy and keeping safe and secure in their top 10 values, yes?" Paul nodded and Maya went on, "And somewhere close to the top of the list would be family and financial security. Now, let's imagine we are in Kuala Lumpur and we're inside the Petronas Towers, which at 1483 feet are the tallest buildings in the world today. We're about two-thirds of the way up, and I'm in one tower and you are in the other. We've erected an 18-inch thick steel tungsten reinforced girder to connect both towers. There's no wind, there is no bend in this girder and there is no safety net! I've got a suitcase with £100,000 in it, and it's got your name on it. All you need to do to claim the money is to walk across the girder from the tower you are in to the tower I am in, and the money is yours! Are you coming?"

Just the thought of walking the girder made Paul go ashen, "You know I have a mortal fear of heights. There is no way that I'm coming!" Maya smiled and added, "OK then, let's up the stakes somewhat. It's now not £100,000, it's a half a million pounds

314

sterling, and it's all yours if you walk across the girder and collect it from me." Paul's face hardened, "Nope! I'm still not coming!" Maya continued, "OK! This is my last offer. It's now 2 million pounds. Are you coming now?" "Maya, you know that no amount of money would get me to walk across that girder." Maya concluded, "So, you can see that your health and safety and well being are more important and valuable to you than any amount of money." Paul replied emphatically, "Yes!"

Maya had a little twinkle in her eye as she altered the stakes again, "Now, let's change the situation slightly. I'm not this wonderfully benevolent person trying to give you money beyond your wildest dreams for simply walking across the girder. I'm a psychopath who has got two of your children by the hair and I'm screaming at you to walk across the girder because, if you don't, I'm going to let them go! Are you coming now?" In a nanosecond Paul had answered, "I'm there already!"

Maya eyed Paul very carefully, "You see, in this new 'what if' scenario, you may have come to realise that your family means more to you than anything else in your life. Establishing your real values will guide you regarding where to start with writing down the goals you want to achieve. You then need to fuel them with enough emotion to create a feeling that is so strong all the forces in the universe will automatically respond to create, in the real world, its physical equivalent. The outcome becomes inevitable.

"Planting such intent, fuelled by desire, into the field of creation, with the total belief that it already exists, communes with universal intelligence and makes it respond. This process needs to be emphasised; it makes the outcome inevitable. This is because it is inevitable! It's inevitable because your heart-felt belief that what you desire already exists motivates you to tirelessly find the resources and circumstances to make it come about. The future that we desire has been preordained. It's just waiting for our conscious perception of linear time to catch up with it. Once that seed of intent is planted, with the feeling of certainty and, more importantly, the deep imagining of what the desired outcome will be like when it has happened, that seed has now been germinated and the desired outcome is on its way.

"The depth of feeling, together with the frequency of implanting it in the inner subconscious, will determine how long the desired outcome will take to materialise from the unseen world to the seen world. As we've discussed, there are two realms in this universe: the unseen thought realm, and the seen physical realm. Not one thing has ever shown up in the physical realm without starting in the thought realm first. All we see began with an awakening in the unseen field of creation where the universal intelligence that connects everything resides.

"Because of our high level of consciousness, we constantly commune and are in dialogue with the universal intelligence through our thoughts, emotions and feelings. The language is non-verbal. We are connected to the forces of creation by the language of our hearts: feelings! Every moment we are projecting our feelings into the field of consciousness, into the field of creation that holds the infinite intelligence. Those feelings are reflected back into our lives with unerring accuracy. Remember, at this quantum level, all possibilities already exist, all the success, happiness, health, wealth, peace, etc., that you could ever want is already here, as is all the pain, unhappiness, despair and illness. What shows up in our lives is merely a three-dimensional reflection of the feelings we are projecting into this quantum field of creation.

"The process of omnipotence, therefore," Maya continued, "is as simple as it is powerful. A thought or desired outcome that, in and of itself, has very little power, sets the direction. This thought then needs to be fuelled with positive emotion, believing that the desired outcome is already in your possession. That's the feeling you need to generate, one that is felt in every fibre of your body, one so powerful that it changes the chemistry of your body and awakens the quantum field of creation. This depth of feeling positively changes the energy field surrounding your body. Deep, heart-felt feelings create a huge energy field that connects you with all the forces in the universe! These deep, heart-felt feelings are effectively the non-verbal language with which you send instructions to the infinite intelligence regarding what you choose to experience in your world. Infinite intelligence simply responds positively and obeys.

"You claim what you want for your future by first becoming the very thing that you want in your mind via your thoughts, in your body via your emotions, and in your heart via your feelings! It has to be emphasised that it is not good enough to ask for, wish for or hope for healing, success and happiness. In the field of the creative universal power that surrounds you, you're already healed, you're already successful, you're already happy! By asking for healing, you're acknowledging that you don't have it. The field of creative consciousness that surrounds us, is part of us and that we all live in, is subtle, sublime and responsive. You may think this is just a matter of semantics, but it isn't. This is the stuff of life, and for you to have your every right and proper desire, you need to appreciate the subtleties."

Paul was open-mouthed as he took in the profoundness of the message and the mechanisms associated with successful goal setting. He spluttered, "But, but, every moment of every day is filled with thoughts, emotions and feelings. What kind of messages or instructions are we actually sending out into the field of creative consciousness? What you're saying is that this constant stream of thoughts, emotions and feelings creates impulses that just get reflected back into our lives as their physical equivalents, positive or negative. So, whatever we give out in spades we get back in buckets. That's the way of the world.

"Everything is so clear now. Before we joined up again, my life was a mess because all my thoughts, emotions and feelings revolved around fear, sadness and anger at not being in control. As you've guided me to replace them with joy, love, appreciation, gratitude and eager anticipation, and because I now know I'm in total control, my life has been transformed. I'm living proof that this works!"

Maya smiled at Paul, "Everyone who has ever walked on the planet is living proof that it works, it's just that most never make the kind of thinking breakthrough that you've made. You are in a good place now to appreciate the contrast. It's like the difference between night and day, and it's fabulous to see it.

"For you to truly master this you need to learn to get the directional thoughts right first in the form of well-written goals. These are then used to trigger the crystal-clear pictures that create the right emotions and feelings. This means that, once your well-written goals are repeatedly read and internalised into the inner subconscious mind, the right message or instruction can be projected into the creative field around you. This means all the forces in the universe can begin to respond immediately by bringing into your world all the circumstances required to achieve any goal. Well-written goals can be called affirmations, but they can also be called 'ThEmFees' because the word reminds us of the process: **Th**oughts/**Em**otions/**Fee**lings. If you use the word ThEmFee too, you'll find it reinforces what you're doing when you're writing affirmations and imprinting them. There are some rules to follow that will guarantee all your goals will be achieved or exceeded in the shortest possible timescale. Many people have been involved in developing these tried and tested rules."

Paul took out a notepad and pen, looked at Maya very seriously, and said "It sounds like I'd better not miss or misunderstand any of what you are about to say."

Paul took a moment to reflect while Maya went to the bar to get them a couple more drinks.

Chapter Twenty-four

Maya smiled and confirmed, "The first pointer to follow is not so much a rule as a piece of good advice. Make each ThEmFee affirmation just one sentence long. Any ideas why that is important?" Paul answered, "Well, I imagine it's all about creating clarity. By making your ThEmFees succinct, it helps generate a crystal-clear picture in the mind. Isn't there an army saying, 'An army will march for a sentence, but not a paragraph'? If you use too many words the picture can become a little blurred."

Maya responded, "You're right. You do understand the process, don't you! However, don't get too hung up if you need to describe your goal in two sentences. Just avoid the paragraphs!" Paul smiled, "Message received."

"The first rule, as such," Maya continued, "is to make your ThEmFee affirmations personal. They'll look and sound like this: 'I am …', 'I have …', 'I find it fun and easy being …' There are a number of reasons for this rule, the primary one being that you're putting yourself, in your imagination, in a situation where you have already accomplished the goal. So, you need to be centre stage, with it all happening around you. If, for instance, one of your goals is to own a villa in the south of France, you need to see and feel yourself on the terrace in the evening, with the sun going down, a drink in your hand and loads of friends enjoying your hospitality on a balmy evening. It's about being there in your mind, thereby planting an intent for the future into the field of creation. Can you understand this? Paul, Paul, can you understand this?"

Paul was startled out of his reverie, "Oh, sorry, Maya. I was on the terrace in the villa in the south of France. I was there! It felt terrific!" Maya confirmed, "If that's what you want, and you follow the rules for imprinting, the intention you have planted in your mind and sent out via your feelings into the universal creative field will become an extension to your reality, in time, as certainly as night follows day.

"It's also important to understand that you can't write ThEmFee affirmations for other people and expect them to happen. For instance, writing a ThEmFee affirmation about your children always treating others with love and respect will not work. You can write a ThEmFee affirmation that says, 'because of the way I treat my children, they always treat others with love and respect'. That will work when repeatedly imprinted in your mind and sent out into the creative field of the universe. The reason for this is that it describes something that you're doing, in the way you treat your children, to make the desired behaviour come about in them." Paul nodded, "Right, I see that. So, if I wanted my sales team at work to hit their targets month in and month out, I'd have to describe something I'm going to do to make it happen, yes?" Maya shouted, "Yes!" Paul continued, "So, rather than writing 'my sales team always exceed their monthly sales targets', I'd need to write something like, 'because of my inspirational leadership, my sales team always exceed their monthly sales objectives', is that right?" Maya nodded and smiled, "Yup, you seem to have nailed rule number 1!"

"Now, rule number 2, you have to make your ThEmFee affirmations positive. This is going to sound blindingly obvious, but it's crucial you understand this because it's one of the most common mistakes people make when writing their goals down. The key is to write down what you want, not what you don't want. Saying and writing down what you don't want will paint the wrong picture in your mind and, therefore, the wrong message or instruction will be sent into the creative field. Don't write, 'I no longer get frightened to death when I have a plane journey to go on' or ' I no longer blow up at the kids when they are having their mad half hour'. The very words you use only end up helping you paint the picture of what you don't want, i.e. being frightened or 'blowing up' at the kids. Is that clear?"

Paul nodded, "It seems perfectly clear; thinking about it for just a second or two, it makes absolute sense."

"Good!" Maya said before continuing, "The key is to describe what it is like now you have achieved what you want. Just describe what it looks like, now it's done. For instance, 'I remain calm, brave and ever so slightly excited when I've a plane journey to go on' or 'I remain calm and relaxed when the kids are having their mad half hour'. You can't stop the kids having their mad half hour, but you can stop yourself having an apoplectic fit every time they do!" Paul smiled as the penny dropped, "So, instead of writing, 'I no longer smoke', I'd write something like, 'Now I am enjoying the good life because of my 100% day-to-day healthy thoughts and actions, the feeling is exhilarating.'"

"Yes, something like that," Maya replied, "It's so simple, yet not so easy! We are all so used to describing what we don't want! It just takes a little practice but you'll get the hang of it pretty quickly.

"The third rule for writing goals or ThEmFee affirmations is to make them present tense. Many people insist when writing goals to put a timescale on them by which they're to be achieved. That can actually slow down the process, as strange as it may seem. Let me give you an example about a friend of mine, who had no real ambitions about accumulating money. The main reason for that was because he had seen what it had done to so many people he knew. His conditioning was that money made people selfish, greedy and materialistic. He'd seen previously nice people become quite nasty, arrogant and self-centred as they accumulated more money. What made it worse for him was the observation that, the more money these people accumulated, the worse they got!

"One day, my friend met a staggeringly rich person. He turned out to be the most benevolent, charitable, generous, wonderfully friendly, trustworthy individual he had ever met. It changed his perspective on life, and on rich people in particular, in an instant. He realised that being a nice person and being rich weren't mutually exclusive, and that you could actually be both at the same time! He was 33 years old when he met this rich, yet wonderful, human being. So he decided that he would continue to be himself, namely a really nice guy, but also accumulate a fair amount of money. He figured that with more money he could be an even nicer guy, more generous, more charitable, helping more people and the like. So, he decided to write a ThEmFee affirmation about money: 'Now I'm 50 years old, and I've got a million pounds in the bank, I really enjoy the good it helps me do for the benefit of humankind'. Now that is a really brilliant other person-focused ThEmFee affirmation. It isn't a 'me'-focused one, the benefits are for other people.

"The big problem with the way it is written is that it isn't in the present tense. The 'now I'm 50 years old' is 17 years away! My friend believed in the power of the mind more than anyone I know, and he had to confess that he'd done his imprinting routine religiously for weeks, months and years, yet nothing positive had happened to his financial status! In fact, he'd run his own business, which used to tick over financially, but then an economic downturn caused the business to struggle and he had to write a personal cheque to pay the salaries. He was broke, and the company was broke. This was 4 years after he'd written his affirmation and he'd been imprinting it ThEmFee-style perfectly. So, what was wrong? Why did he end up 4 years later with less money than when he started? Why did he end up further away from his '£1m in the bank' goal?

"Without understanding the importance of following the rules surrounding writing goals, it is easy to think and believe the process of attracting into your life what you desire most doesn't work. Well, it definitely doesn't work if you don't follow the rules!

"Your deeper subconscious will unite with infinite intelligence, without delay, to begin the process of finding the circumstances and situations to make your desire come true with immediate effect. So, to write a ThEmFee affirmation in a way that means it's only due to be completed in 17 years time will place it on the back burner and other, more urgent, affirmations will be given priority. The amazing end to this story is that when my friend discovered and applied the present tense rule, changing his affirmation from 'now I'm 50 years old and I've got a million pounds in the bank …' to 'now I've got a million pounds in the bank …' things in his business life began to change almost overnight. New contracts were won, existing customers, who were delighted with the results he'd helped them achieve, recommended other customers. The business went ballistic, even though the economic downturn was still biting hard! Within 2 years, his million pounds was in the bank and he had acquired assets in the business and elsewhere that made him a multi-millionaire.

"He had such fun too," Maya continued, "helping underprivileged children in particular, setting up educational foundation overseas visits, and the like. The money was put to fabulous use. However, the key here is that his goal had initially eluded him because he had not written his affirmation properly. He had future tensed it, rather than present tensed it." Paul frowned and asked, "But he would have achieved his original goal, wouldn't he? To have a million pounds in the bank by the time he was 50 years old?" Maya nodded, "Oh yes, he would, but why delay its achievement? By making his affirmation present tense, it made all the forces in the universe conspire to make it come about all the quicker. The good work the money allowed him to do was extended by about 12 years!" Paul nodded, "Yes, OK. I've got that one nailed as well. What's rule number 4?"

"Rule number 4 is a bit of a round-up of the previous three, but with a particular emphasis," Maya continued, "Rule 4 is to ensure that your ThEmFee affirmations actually indicate achievement. What is meant by this is that, in your mind, the desired objective must already exist. It's not to be a hope or a wish; it's got to already be here. We've covered this extensively in our discussions already, but it's worth reiterating. So, be careful not to write affirmations using phrases like 'I can be', 'I want to be', 'I wish I was', 'I try to be'. They simply will not work."

Maya continued, "They won't work because ThEmFee affirmations written using these words are already true. I know it's a matter of semantics again, but it's critical in order for goal setting to work that we understand the importance of the words we use and, more importantly, their meaning. 'I can be a warm and loving father', for instance, is already true. 'I want to be the managing director of my company' is the same, it's already true. You can almost hear your collective subconscious saying back to you, 'Yes, I know you want to be, and have wanted to be for ages, but the fact that it's already true means there is nothing for us to do. Next! Do you have anything stretching for us to deliver for you?'"

Paul nodded his understanding, and then started shaking his head before speaking, "Blimey, is it any wonder that I have achieved so little in my life to date? All my goals and objectives have been nothing but wishes and hopes at the most superficial level. Hoping for a promotion, wishing for a great standard of living! What have I been playing at?" Maya said, "Don't beat yourself up over this. Rejoice that you now know the way to achieve every right and proper desire that you want. As we've already mentioned, by wishing or hoping for something, you are actually acknowledging you don't already have it, so you're sending completely the wrong message into the field of creation. It cannot deliver what you, yourself, acknowledge doesn't already exist.

"By indicating achievement laced with heart-felt feelings and knowing the pleasure and good your goal will bring to you and all concerned, the message you convey into the field of creation becomes the instruction that marshals all the forces in the universe to conspire to find the circumstances and resources to turn it into a reality. It's that simple."

Paul was as excited as he'd ever been in his entire life, yet strangely calm. He chuckled to himself about how he felt. Who wouldn't feel excited and calm at the same time, if they knew that all the power, might and glory in the universe was at their disposal? His demeanour indicated to Maya that she could continue.

"Rule number 5," Maya said, "is to have no comparisons. What's meant by this is that you're trying to be as good as you can be, in any area of life you choose, and no-one knows how good that can be yet, not even you, because you're only just scratching the surface. The problem is that sometimes you can determine what you want by comparing yourself to others. For instance, 'If I could be in the same position as Joe Bloggs at work, I'd be really happy' or 'If I could live in a house like that, my family would be really proud of me'. Comparisons like that can be really restrictive.

"A friend told me about a job he had applied for. After the first two interviews, he went home and told his wife, 'If I could ever be half as good and professional as the man who just interviewed me, I'd be the happiest man alive!' He was just about to set his sights on being half as good as the person who had interviewed him, when the serious flaw in his thinking dawned on him! He then decided to be as good and professional as only he could be, and to not hide his light under someone else's shadow.

"He got the job. After being trained and putting his training into practice, within 12 months he was 10 times the person who'd interviewed him! Twelve months after that, he was running the company."

Paul nodded his understanding again, "Oh, I've been guilty of doing lots of comparisons in my life. OK, what's next?"

Many continued, "Rule number 6 is to make sure you use action words when writing your ThEmFee affirmations because they create better visualisation and pictures in the mind. A movie is better than a snapshot or photograph. Rule number 7 is that you also need to use excitement words when writing your ThEmFee affirmations. This is because a feely is better than a movie. The non-verbal language with which we commune with all the forces of creation is with feelings, heart-felt feelings. Turning your imagination up to full power, not only to see the outcome that you desire but also to feel how good it is now you've got it, is key to its achievement. The more clearly you can see it, the more intensely you can feel it, the more quickly and surely it will materialise.

"As we have said before, there are two realms in this universe: the thought realm and the physical realm. Nothing shows up in the physical realm without it appearing in the thought realm first, nothing! The conduit or pipeline that links the thought realm with the physical realm is powered by the clarity of the visual image and the intensity of the feelings associated with having the desired outcome already existing in your mind. It is the development of this powerful knowing or total belief in your mind, through pictures and feelings, ahead of time, that turns thoughts into things. You already know that the desired outcome exists, maybe at a different level of existence to the one you are experiencing just now on the mortal plane, but its existence, in your mind, is not in doubt. In fact, when there is a total absence of doubt in your mind, it's done! The depth of feeling generated means that the future is now decided, the outcome inevitable. Our claim is being processed and all the forces of creation are working in unison, in ways we don't need to understand, to find the circumstances to make real its physical equivalent.

"With the right level of clarity of picture and depth of feeling, the outcome is always certain. The importance of this can't be over-emphasised. The outcome is assured, providing the input, from a clarity and depth point of view, is right. You don't need to concern yourself about where the desired outcome will come from. Just be certain that it's on its way. Develop an attitude of expectancy. It's the best feeling in the world. Be careful not to be too judgmental regarding where the circumstances and resources to manifest the future may come from. Keep your radar on 360°."

Paul was transfixed, "This is so fantastic, yet so true! The most successful things I've ever achieved in my life to date have come about because I knew, I just knew, that they would. I didn't know how, I just knew they would. I've definitely used this by accident in the past, and now I can use it deliberately and on purpose! How good is that?"

Maya nodded with understanding, "We've all used this in the past, by accident. The next rule is number 8, and it involves developing accuracy when writing ThEmFee affirmations. The temptation is to be a little vague and write things like, 'I enjoy earning more money this year than last year' and 'now I weigh less, I really enjoy the feeling it gives me'. In both instances, one pound will make it a reality; one pound sterling more in earnings and one pound less in weight. However, the likelihood is that the desired outcome was more specific in both instances. So the rule here is a very simple one, describe it accurately. 'Now I am earning more than £100,000 per year, I really enjoy having no money worries' and 'it's fun and easy weighing 120 lbs'.

Paul nodded his understanding impatiently. It was clear to Maya that he was chomping at the bit and raring to get going. However, she continued in a very enthusiastic yet measured and methodical way, "I know you're keen to begin writing your ThEmFee affirmations, but it's vital that you follow the rules. I don't want you to fall at the last hurdle. I have to make sure there is no misunderstanding in your mind whatsoever, otherwise the 'out-picturing' of your desires may be severely delayed or delayed indefinitely. It's important that you get everything out of this that I have to give advice-wise. So many people rush through this bit and mess it up!" Paul nodded, less impatiently this time.

"Rule number 9", Maya continued, "is to create some balance in the areas of your life where you choose to focus and write your ThEmFee affirmations. Be careful not to focus on just one area of your life, such as work. When the full powers that are at your disposal are called into action, you can become so focused and obsessed in just one area that you lose sight of the other things in your life. So it is always a good idea to write two ThEmFee affirmations together that reflect opposite sides of your life. Write one about work and one about your home life. Write one about your education and one about your leisure activities, one about your health and one about your work in the community, one about enterprise and one about your spiritual life. It is also a good idea to be balanced by emphasising the benefit that others will gain from you achieving your desired outcome. This way you are making the world a better place for you and everyone in it. A group of good balanced ThEmFee affirmations will, by definition, be 'other people'-centred rather than 'me'- or 'self'-centred. This is another key that unlocks the door and connects us directly to the higher intelligence that contains all the creative forces in the universe. With a little practice, this 'other people'-focus can make affirmations turn into their physical equivalent almost instantaneously. Being 'other people'-centred flings open the doors to the true, true treasures in life.

"So, rather than writing 'now I'm sales director of my company, I find the status it gives me most satisfying' say something like 'now I'm sales director of the company, the double-digit growth we enjoy year-on-year creates a fabulously positive environment in which all the team work tirelessly to delight our customers, who in turn freely refer others'. Some of the ones we discussed earlier can be more 'other people'-centred. For instance, rather than writing 'now I earn over £100,000 per year, I really enjoy having no money worries' write 'now I am earning over £100,000 per year, I really enjoy the lifestyle I can give my family'. And rather than writing 'it's fun and easy weighing 120 lbs' write 'now I weigh 120 lbs, my increased energy levels and stamina mean I complete all my tasks at work, home, in the community and at play with a smile on my face that lights up everyone's life with whom I come into contact'.

"You see, a service attitude to others really does open up creative forces that are denied to people with a me-, myself-, I-attitude. This allows us to not only pick the low-hanging fruit but also the sweetest, most nutritional, fruit at the top of the tree! Everything in the tree of life is there for us to have, when we get the emphasis away from me and towards others. As we've said previously, you can have anything you want in your life, if you help enough people get what they want in their lives."

Paul was deeply affected by the insight, knowledge and wisdom Maya was delivering, "This is so exhilarating, so profound, so exciting. I can't wait to get writing!"

Maya replied, "Only one more rule and then you'll be ready! Rule number 10 is to make your ThEmFee affirmations realistic. There is a great deal of confusion around what realistic means when setting and writing goals, but it is incredibly simple. All you need to do is remember the word WYSIWYG and remember the processes we've learned together over the last few weeks."

Paul looked puzzled, "WYSIWYG?" he questioned, "What on earth is that?"

Maya smiled and said, "What You See Is What You Get: WYSIWYG! So, when you've written your ThEmFee affirmation, just read it through to remember it, and then close your eyes and ask yourself the following questions: 'Can I see it? Feel it? Touch it? Do I actually already have it in my mind? Has it entered my soul? Has it taken root in my DNA and my subatomic structure?' If the answers are unquestioning yeses then it's on its way into your life. All the creative forces of the universe have been ordered to conspire to work together to bring your affirmation to you as a sparkling reality. The language you've used is the non-verbal language of heart-felt feelings, heart-felt feelings where, in your mind, the desired objective already exists. Its future outcome has been preordained, the result is now inevitable. Expect it.

"If, for whatever reason, you can't see it, feel it and touch it in your mind, you may need to revisit your ThEmFee affirmation and break it down into smaller affirmations; ones that you can see, feel and touch with total certainty in your mind. For instance, I was told about someone who needed two hips replaced. However, she was overweight and the doctors would not operate until she had lost 3 stone (42 lbs). Without this weight loss, the operation would be a waste of time. She tried everything but couldn't lose the weight. Eventually, she confessed to herself and her ThEmFee affirmation writing guide that she couldn't see herself weighing 3 stone less, let alone feel what it would be like. This meant that the connection with the forces of creation hadn't been established so, not surprisingly, nothing changed! Her ThEmFee guide asked her what she could see and feel. The answer was that she could see and feel a weight loss of no more than 7 lbs. Therein was the answer! She couldn't see 42 lbs but could see and feel 7 lbs. Her ThEmFee guide showed her how to see and feel a 7 lb weight loss, six times! She broke her affirmation down into bite-size pieces that she could see and feel. She got to the point of doing cartwheels along the beach in Greece when she was on holiday whereas a few years before she could hardly walk! This works, Paul.

"You're now ready to take some time to determine the ThEmFee affirmations with which you will begin your new life-by-design

Maya handed over the "goal-setting masterclass guidelines for you to follow."

Goal-setting

master class

guidelines

for you to follow

"Laser Thinking" in Action

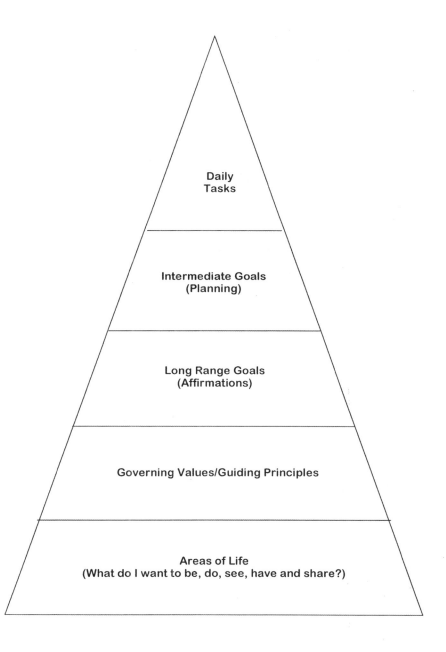

Goals

Ask yourself these questions and answer them honestly.

What do I want to be?

A millionaire?

Physically fit?

Respected and admired by everyone?

A brilliant parent?

What do I want to do?

Retire in Five years time with £10M in the bank and move to Canada?

Run a successful business with 20 branches, making £15M profit per year?

Only work Two days per week because the business runs successfully and profitably when I'm not there?

Run a marathon?

What do I want to see?

The Great Wall of China?

My great, great, great grandchildren?

My 90th birthday?

My M.B.A hanging on my office wall?

What do I want to have?

A six-bedroom detached house in the best part of town?

A Harley Davidson?

A brilliant marriage?

People offering me terrific jobs all the time?

What do I want to share?

Work with scouts?

Work for free in the hospice at the weekends?

Raise money for "Children in Need" every year?

Give 10% of everything I earn to charity?

Are these really my goals?? (or are they to please/impress someone else?)

Goals

Ask yourself these questions and answer them honestly.

What do I want to be?

....

....

....

....

What do I want to do?

....

....

....

....

....

....

What do I want to see?

....

....

....

....

What do I want to have?

....

....

....

....

What do I want to share?

....

....

....

....

Are these really my goals?? (or are they to please/impress someone else?)

Areas of life

(For governing values and guiding principles)

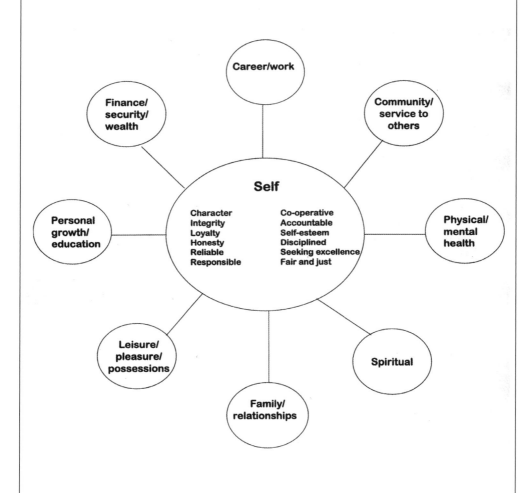

Sample Governing Values and Guiding Principles

Select your top five values and place them in order of priority.
(This list is not exhaustive. Please include any of your own values.)

I am financially secure

I am successful at work

I am physically fit

I grow intellectually

I am a 100 percenter

I am honest and reliable

I am a brilliant parent

I encourage fairness and justice

I have integrity

I am innovative

I am self-sufficient

I am proactive

I am respected by everyone

I have fun

I love life

I am generous

I develop other people

I have a positive attitude

I am an inspirational leader

I am organised

I am a team player

I am a brilliant partner

I am loyal and hardworking

I enjoy learning

I am trustworthy

I am open minded

I anticipate and embrace change

I am a true professional

I enjoy the admiration and
friendship of others

I care for and spend time with
my family

This next section includes two pages
for each individual affirmation.

Page 1: 'Turning values into goals' is to help you
get out of your head and onto paper what your
goal means to you.

The defining statements reflect what
this goal looks and feels like for you.

Page 2: 'Turning goals into affirmations and daily
plans' is to help you turn your goal into a well-
written ThEmFee affirmation, following the rules
explained.

The 'Intermediate goals' is to break
your ThEmFee affirmation down
into a plan, and the daily/weekly
tasks required to make it come about.

(Example page)

Turning Values into Goals

Area of life:	Value:	Defining statements:
Health	I am physically fit	• I have the energy and stamina to complete all my tasks at work, home and play
		• My exercise and diet habits allow me to maintain a weight consistent with my height, build and age
		• All my thoughts and actions create healthiness within me
		• My exercise programme and way of eating cause me to have deep, peaceful and exhausted sleeps every night

Turning Values into Goals

Area of life:	Value:	Defining statements:

Turning Goals into Affirmations and Daily Plans

Area of life:	Health

Value:	I am physically fit

ThEmFee affirmation

I find it fun and easy maintaining a weight consistent with good health for someone of my height, build and age and enjoy having limitless energy.

Timescales	Intermediate goals (planning) (daily tasks)
10th January	Complete a physical health check with my doctor to ascertain current condition and seek advice on suitable forms of exercise, timescales etc.
10th January	Obtain free "personal fitness profile and guidance" from local health club.
15th January	Choose the aerobic exercise(s) I enjoy most and that suit my lifestyle.
20th January	Choose the 'way of eating' that best suits my lifestyle and guarantees my weight will be consistent with my height, build and age.
25th January	My exercise plan is now completed, which starts gradually (10 minutes a day) and builds up to that required to maintain my ideal fitness level.
25th January	I have joined the health club/bought the equipment I need to complete my long-range goal.
Ongoing	I enjoy charting my progress and congratulating myself.

Turning Goals into Affirmations and Daily Plans

Area of life:
....

Value:
....

....

ThEmFee affirmation

Timescales   **Intermediate goals (Planning) (Daily tasks)**

Turning Values into Goals

Area of life:	Value:	Defining statements:
Work	I am an excellent professional and enjoy working with our clients.	• I am gracious in my dealings with others
		• I am creative and unafraid to contribute
		• I strive to deliver more than promised
		• I prepare before-hand for meeting and projects

Turning Values into Goals

Area of life:	Value:	Defining statements:

Turning Goals into Affirmations and Daily Plans

Area of life:　　　　Work

Value:　　　　I am an excellent professional and enjoy
working with our clients.

ThEmFee affirmation

Now my professional image and levels of customer service are truly
excellent with my five major accounts, the working relationship and
business gained is at record levels.

Timescales	Intermediate goals (Planning) (Daily tasks)
Ongoing	Be on time with every order
Ongoing	Return every call within 30 minutes if I am in the office, or within 24 hours if I am out of the office
10th August	Have a strategy meeting with all five clients. Be totally prepared for each meeting with a great presentation.
15th August	Prepare an updated and professional product binder for each client.

Turning Goals into Affirmations and Daily Plans

Area of life:

Value:

ThEmFee affirmation

Timescales	Intermediate goals (Planning) (Daily tasks)

Turning Values into Goals

Area of life:	Value:	Defining statements:
Self	I am organised	• I am easily able to find things in my office and home
		• I have organised my office
		• I am organised at home. I feel great because I have cleaned up the house and keep it clean and organised

Turning Values into Goals

Area of life:	Value:	Defining statements:

Turning Goals into Affirmations and Daily Plans

Area of life: Self

Value: I am organised.

ThEmFee affirmation

I am able to find everything I need when I need it.

Timescales	Intermediate goals (Planning) (Daily tasks)
Ongoing	Delegate with deadlines.
5th July	All the papers are off my desk.
10th July	All my phone numbers have been entered into one place.
15th July	All my books are up to date and in order.
25th July	Bills and key papers are in order and are filed correctly.
28th July	Clean attic.
30th July	Create pending file.

Turning Goals into Affirmations and Daily Plans

Area of life:

....

Value:

....

ThEmFee affirmation

Timescales	**Intermediate goals (Planning) (Daily tasks)**

Turning Values into Goals

Area of life:	Value:	Defining statements:
Self	I enjoy the admiration and friendship of others	• It is important for my self-respect and emotional security to have the friendship and admiration of the people I respect
		• I respect people who utilise common sense and are deliberate in their actions and thoughts
		• To earn people's friendship and respect, I strive to offer understanding and honest counsel. I will be patient and fair. I will build on their strengths and disregard their weaknesses.
		• To gain control over the life/work balance and fully enjoy both aspects of my life

Turning Values into Goals

Area of life:	Value:	Defining statements:

Turning Goals into Affirmations and Daily Plans

Area of life: Self

Value: I enjoy the admiration and friendship of others.

ThEmFee affirmation

Now I have my life/work balance under control, I really enjoy holidaying with Anne and the children each year.

Timescales	Intermediate goals (Planning) (Daily tasks)
1st July	Have a family meeting to update family members on my plans.
5th July	Call my travel agent to put together hotel recommendations.
9th July	Review package from travel agent and formulate questions.
15th July	Call my boss and clear my work schedule for the holiday days.
25th July	Call travel agent and book our flights, hotels, tours, etc.
2nd September	Go on that cruise, shop till I drop, gain 7 pounds from great food and take lots of pictures of Kelly, Nancy and Anne that I will cherish for the rest of my life!

Turning Goals into Affirmations and Daily Plans

Area of life:

Value:

ThEmFee affirmation

Timescales	**Intermediate goals (Planning) (Daily tasks)**

Turning Values into Goals

Area of life:	Value:	Defining statements:
Finance	I am financially independent	• I save money regularly
		• I pay my bills on time
		• I track my expenses using my Day Planner
		• I stick to a monthly budget
		• I put money aside regularly for my children's education
		• I have a plan to ensure financial security and act on it
		• I am not an impulse buyer

Turning Values into Goals

Area of life:	Value:	Defining statements:

(Example page)

Turning Goals into Affirmations and Daily Plans

Area of life: Finance

Value: I am financially independent.

ThEmFee affirmation

Actioning the plan that makes me financially secure now and for the rest of my life, including retirement, gives me and my family an incredible sense of well-being.

Timescales	Intermediate goals (Planning) (Daily tasks)
1st July	Analyse current budget and make necessary adjustments.
5th July	Evaluate value of property owned.
9th July	Determine possible expenditures for home repair in the next three years.
15th July	Select financial consultant.
25th July	Read three books regarding financial planning.
3rd August	Attend money management seminar.

Turning Goals into Affirmations and Daily Plans

Area of life:
....

Value:
....

ThEmFee affirmation

Timescales   **Intermediate goals (Planning) (Daily tasks)**

Sample ThEmFee Affirmations

1. I am full of resolution and absolute assurance of the best possible outcome of everything I do. I am, therefore, free of worry.

2. My mind is constantly tuned with the positive, it is bright, cheerful, enthusiastic and full of good positive thoughts and ideas.

3. I enjoy the tremendous results that come from 'doing my affirmations' and always thinking positively.

4. All my thoughts create healthiness within me.

5. I willingly, and without fail, take care of the duties, responsibilities and obligations I have set for myself.

6. I am able to relax easily and comfortably in my body and my mind, I am always calm, confident and self-assured.

7. I receive brilliant feedback because of the 100% customer satisfaction we achieve and enjoy praising the team who make it happen every day.

8. Because of my inspirational leadership the whole team really enjoy turning goals and objectives into reality.

9. I do only those things which are best for me and, therefore, create the best within myself, attract the best within myself, attract the best in others and I always find the best in the world around me.

10. I automatically think in a decisive and determined way that always produces an outcome for my highest good and the highest good of all concerned.

11. I like who I am and always feel good about myself.

12. I like and respect myself, the way I feel, the way I think and the way I do things for myself and others.

Sample ThEmFee Affirmations

13. I am full of life, energy, enthusiasm and creativity, I enjoy being me and other people like to be around me.

14. I smile a lot because I am warm, sincere, honest and genuine, all these things are me and they radiate outwards and touch other people positively.

15. My constant encouragement ensures we have great pride in maintaining our number 1 position in our industry.

16. Everyone I talk to wants to buy from me, if not now … eventually.

17. My mind is full of bright ideas, it is quick, alert, clever and fun, I always think good thoughts and people are excited and comfortable at being around me.

18. I am interested by many things and fascinated by other people, the more I work to understand and respect them, the more confident I feel about who I am.

19. I allow other people to accept their responsibilities for themselves and enjoy seeing them grow because I do not try to accept their responsibility for them.

20. I alone am responsible for who I am, what I do and what I tell myself about me, other people have contributed, but no one else other then me is responsible for it.

21. I deserve to make the sales I create because success in selling starts with believing in myself as a capable, productive and skilful individual.

22. Being sincere and honest allows customers to quickly like and trust me in a way that puts me on top of their list of people they regularly buy from.

23. Customers only say 'no' to me when they mean 'not yet' and it always triggers me into action to ask more questions to understand their precise needs so they can say "yes".

24. It's fun and easy being organised so I can quickly find anything I need.

ThEmFee Affirmations

1. I find it fun and easy maintaining a weight consistent with good health for someone of my height, build and age, and enjoy having limitless energy.

2. Now my professional image and levels of customer service are truly excellent with my five major accounts, the working relationship and business gained is at record levels.

3. I am able to find everything I need when I need it.

4. Now I have my life/work balance under control, I really enjoy holidaying with Anne and the children each year.

5. Actioning the plan that makes me financially secure now and for the rest of my life,   including retirement, gives me and my family an incredible sense of well-being.

6. I really enjoy selling my skills, experience and personal attributes well at interview.

7. I really enjoy extending my networking capabilities and reaping the benefits.

8. Now I have a minimum of £ _____ in the bank, the peace of mind is wonderful.

9. I love doing everything I need to do when I need to do it by.

10. The feeling of well being is exhilarating now I exercise until I'm breathless five times per week.

ThEmFee Affirmations

1.

2.

3.

4.

5.

6.

7.

8.

9.

10.

process. Follow the procedure and the rules I've shown you. Initially you shouldn't write more than 10 ThEmFee affirmations. Begin in the areas of life that are most valuable to you just now and, when you've done that, we'll get together and I'll explain how to imprint them into your subconscious in a way that nothing, and I mean nothing, will ever be denied you. Well, when I say nothing, I mean nothing that is for your highest good and the highest good of all concerned. The process only works for good. ThEmFee affirmations written with evil intent and not in your own and other people's best interests, will not work. Full stop.

"I've put together some simple step-by-step goal-setting master class guidelines for you to follow to help you with this process. You just need to fill in the gaps for this critical part of the process to be completed properly."

"You'll need a few days to decide on where you will start, so ring me when you've got your 10 affirmations written."

Paul, with enthusiasm and zeal, replied with, "I'll be in touch very, very soon."

Chapter Twenty-five

Paul couldn't sleep. He was in something close to a catatonic state for most of the night. However, between a blissful serenity, an unparalleled level of excitement and an awesome feeling of power and control, was a certain unease. The first three feelings he could understand. After all, he'd just been given the keys to the kingdom, but why the unease?

As he lay awake, he got closer and closer to the source of unease. It wasn't because he realised he had all the power in the universe at his disposal. It wasn't because of the responsibility that went with it. These were sitting quite easily with him, as he knew he would use the power for his highest good and the highest good of all concerned. It wasn't because he felt unworthy to receive all the good things the proper use of such power could bring. In fact, his unease was because he knew instinctively and intrinsically that he'd always had this power. He had not just suddenly been given it, or suddenly received it; he just now knew it at a different level of consciousness to the one with which he'd been living his life to date. His unease was rooted in the fact he hadn't managed to find for himself the truth he now so clearly understood.

The more he thought about it, the more he smiled wryly to himself as he lay in bed in the dark. 'It's so blindingly obvious, and yet I missed it,' he thought, 'It's like missing the 'Fs' in the sentence that Maya gave me at our first meeting.' His thoughts raced, 'Mind you, the reason I missed the 'Fs', and the reason I missed my unlimited potential and how to access it, were the same: my conditioning.'

Current day conditioning, all over the world, seems to disconnect people from this universal truth that Paul now understood so well. 'Why is it that we are conditioned so negatively: life's a struggle; life's a matter of chance; we're powerless; we're worthless; we're alone and isolated! Think pain, think suffering, think self!'

Paul now knew at the deepest level that there's no force, power or set of circumstances on the outside of human beings that's greater than the force, power or set of resources available to them on the inside. This is a true revelation in itself, enriched by the fact that this universal power is no respecter of persons: it's available to all.

He also realised, as he lay awake, that his feeling of unease was blocking his energy. All life is energy. When that energy is allowed to flow from an individual, which then opens up the gates for it to flow through them without any contradiction, without any friction, conflict or blockage, then that energy is boundless and endless.

It was just after 3 a.m. when he let go of all his unease, all of his doubts and all of his fears. He fell into the deepest, most peaceful sleep of his life. After 4 hours, he woke up bursting with energy, feeling the best he'd ever felt, and with a razor sharp clarity of thought. He was ready to write his ThEmFee affirmations.

With all the internal blockages removed, Paul could easily and simply answer the 'what do I want to be, do, see, have and share questions. The direction of his life in terms of career, health, wealth, relationships, happiness, lifestyle, etc., was now being determined.

After a few 'what if' exercises, the areas of his life that were most valuable and important to him and his family at that moment in time were identified. He found the writing of the ThEmFee affirmations relatively simple, following all the rules, apart from the odd temptation to 'future tense' them and to include the occasional 'I will be …' and 'I can be …' A quick review of the first draft of his affirmations resulted in only minor adjustments in order for them to follow all the rules. This removed any self-generated obstacles in the way they'd been written that might have prevented the affirmations from turning into a reality. He even plagiarised some of Maya's examples from the written guidelines she'd given him because they seemed to fit so well with his current wants and desires.

Paul initially wrote 34 ThEmFee affirmations and then whittled them down to 10 he was going to share with Maya for her feedback. Hopefully, he would obtain her assurance that they followed all the rules. He could hardly wait to ring her to arrange the next meeting. He was desperately keen to learn how to imprint his affirmations deep into his subconscious mind, but decided to wait 24 hours before doing so, in case his choice for his top 10 changed after he'd thought about them some more. As it turned out, the top 10 didn't change. However, it wouldn't have mattered much if they had done, their eventual outcome would still have been a certainty.

The big thing he concentrated on in the time between writing his ThEmFee affirmations and ringing Maya to arrange the next meeting, was whether he could really see and feel the desired outcomes as if they'd already happened in his mind, at a level beyond any doubt. He found that the more he thought about how the outcomes looked and felt, the more certain he was in his mind's eye that they already existed. He was learning to claim the future, to ordain his destiny. He tingled with excitement and anticipation as he phoned Maya.

"Hi, Maya, this is Paul," he announced calmly, "I've got my 10 ThEmFee affirmations all ready, so when can we get together?" Maya suggested the following evening at their usual place. Paul said "OK", qualified with, "I'm not sure I can wait that long without bursting at the seams with excitement." Maya laughed before replying, "All that pent-up excitement will do you no harm, providing you've got rid of all those conflicts, doubts and blockages." Paul was flabbergast, "How did you know about my unease?" She replied, "Paul, it's not your unease, it's humankind's collective unease. As your consciousness is freed and develops, so will humankind's. There may be 6.2 billion individuals on the planet, but we all share the same consciousness. On the journey to liberation and enlightenment, we must all cross that bridge. Otherwise, we become trapped in an illusion of individual limitedness." Paul reassured Maya, "All my conflicts, doubts and blockages have been exorcised completely. So, shall we meet tomorrow at 7 o' clock?" Maya said that would be perfect.

The time flew, and as Paul constantly reappraised his top 10 ThEmFee affirmations he became more and more reassured that he was starting with the right ones. His confidence and his sense of expectation grew. He knew he wouldn't be disappointed.

Chapter Twenty-six

They arrived at The Old Fox more or less together and met in the car park. Maya observed Paul's demeanour and said, "Hello, Paul! It's great to see you again. It's doubly great to see that all your conflicts, doubts and blockages are gone."

As they walked towards the entrance together, Paul asked, "Can you actually see that?" Maya nodded and said, "I can see it clearly, although I've felt it since about 3 o'clock in the morning yesterday." Paul queried this, "What do you mean? How can you have felt it then?" Maya replied, "When people allow the full creative and intelligent field of energy to flow from them and through them, you can feel it. I don't know how, you just can. You've just got to tune into it. It's like the mother of a new baby sensing all is well, or otherwise, when she and the baby are sleeping in different rooms. These matters defy conventional understanding and measures such as time and space. Some people call it remote sensing.

"The important thing is that you're now ready to learn how to project your consciousness through the fabric of space and time and claim the future events as defined by your ThEmFee affirmations. I'm as excited about this as you!"

Comfortably settled at their usual table, Maya began, "So you've got the 10 ThEmFee affirmations you want to begin with?" Paul nodded and she continued, "Well, we'd better take a look at them to see if they follow the rules I talked to you about." Before showing them to Maya, Paul began to explain why he had selected the areas in his life on which he'd written his ThEmFee affirmations but Maya stopped him, "There is no need for you to explain or justify where you are starting this process. I respect and honour whatever decision-making process you've been through, and I'm totally non-judgmental regarding the outcomes you wish to claim via your ThEmFee affirmations. All I want to do is check that you have written them properly, and that they follow the rules, because, if they don't, they will become difficult, slow or impossible to turn themselves into their physical equivalent."

Paul looked embarrassed as he realised his misunderstanding regarding why Maya wanted to discuss his ThEmFee affirmations with him. Maya pressed the point, "Paul, you must never, ever try and justify or explain your affirmations to anyone; you're the only person that you need to satisfy in relation to this. So long as they reflect your best and genuine desires, and are for your highest good and the highest good of all concerned, they will be perfect for you at this moment in your life.

"In fact, while we're on this topic, let's discuss this a little further. Who do you think should see your affirmations?" Paul thought very deeply on this one. At first he thought it should be anyone the affirmations involved, and anyone who could help them come about. Then he thought it should only be close family and friends. In the end, he confessed to Maya that he was confused and couldn't decide on an answer.

Maya fully understood his confusion, "This is a tough one because affirmations are usually so personal. However, the general consensus of advice is to tell no one! Share them with no one! Only share them with people who fall into this category: people who you know really well and 100% love you, 100% unconditionally. If there's the tiniest shadow of a doubt that a person's love for you is not 100% and is not totally unconditional, don't share your affirmations with them!" Paul was taken aback with Maya's depth of feeling as she gave this advice.

She continued, "Don't be concerned if you're now thinking that the only one you can share your affirmations with is your dog!" Paul laughed and replied, "Well, I wasn't quite thinking that, but it does cut the number of possibilities down considerably." Maya leaned forward and asked, "Why do you think the advice is to only share your affirmations with people you know 100% love you 100% unconditionally?" Paul knew the reason, "Because if you share them with someone who doesn't 100% love you unconditionally, they can put doubts in your mind about whether you're worthy of achieving your desires. They could easily create obstacles in your mind, because they're not sure of the impact that achieving your affirmations might have on them, or their relationship with you."

Maya said encouragingly, "That's right, and it goes even further than that because, as we've discussed already, the world is full of dream-stealers! They're all over the place. This can create a huge problem for so many of us, because some of the biggest dream-stealers in our lives are the people who are closest to us!

"Just this last week I must have met a dozen people who've told me about their mums, dads, brothers, sisters, best mates, life partners even, pouring cold water over their dreams. A male friend of mine was toying with the idea of getting his weight under control after years of being 30 lbs too heavy. He knew it was going to take a lot of discipline and commitment on his part. He also knew it would be a huge advantage if his wife bought into the idea, seeing as they lived together, ate together and so on.

"This idea never made it to becoming an affirmation because she convinced him that he was alright as he was. He knew that the reason his wife was not supporting him was based on her own insecurity. She'd commented a number of times that no other woman could ever be attracted to someone so overweight. Her world and all the low self-esteem and jealousy that went with it would be threatened if he lost the weight! This is a classic dream-stealer situation."

Paul commented, "I can see that. I'm not quite sure I understand and appreciate the sentiments, but I can see how such situations occur."

Maya continued, "Another classic example is a female friend of mine who decided to give up smoking. She did turn this desire into an affirmation, but made the mistake of telling all her friends about it. The smokers amongst these friends then hung her out to dry! They taunted her, mocked her, ignored her and did all they could to undermine her and her dream.

Paul interrupted, "Is that because, if your friend succeeded, it would create pressure on the others to give up as well? It is isn't it? They'd look bad if she succeeded, so they did all they could to stop them."

Maya went on, "I'm not saying that people are consciously aware of what they are doing, but they are effectively stealing your dreams by putting doubts, contradictions and blockages in the way.

"Another reason for not sharing your affirmations with many people is that, when others start noticing changes in your behaviour and circumstances, it's more than likely that they are seeing an affirmation or two that have become a reality. This means that the affirmations are turning into their physical equivalent. This will encourage you if you know they don't know what your affirmation is, yet they can describe it for you because they've seen the results! You'll know you're cooking on gas then, and that the universal force is really working for you."

Paul looked confused, "I can understand this, and it's all well and good, but you've asked me to show you my affirmations. Aren't you contradicting yourself here? Maya replied, "Definitely not. I want to see them to make sure you've followed the rules of writing them. I will not be passing any comment on what they are and, my very dear friend, you can rest assured that I 100% love you, 100% unconditionally! I only want the very best for you and I respect you enough for you to decide what that is, and I will help you, in any way possible, to achieve it, without being judgmental.

"I'm not in love with you; this isn't romantic or sexual. It's like the way I love and appreciate life, nature and all of creation. This includes the raw emotions and feelings that connect us with the field of creation that forms thoughts into their physical equivalents. The thought realm is eternal; the physical realm temporal. The door to happiness, peace, success, health, abundance, opens inwards, not outwards. Be very careful with whom you share your ThEmFee affirmations. Many people will unwittingly remind you of your separation, not your connectedness."

Paul felt whole. He felt omnipotent, "Let me now show you my affirmations, Maya", he said, with a reassured confidence. "I've started with the basics for my first 10, although I've written 34 in total. I decided to concentrate on five areas of my life, and I've written a couple of affirmations in each area. Here."

Paul handed over a piece of paper with the affirmations neatly arranged under a series of headings. Maya said, "Let me have a minute or two to read them through, and then we'll have a chat about them. Is that OK?" Paul nodded an assent.

Maya read:

My ThEmFee Affirmations, 9th May

Self

- Now that I know there is no force, power or set of circumstances on the outside of me that is greater than the force, power and set of resources inside of me, I really enjoy turning all my goals into reality.
- Being warm, sincere, genuine and honest in all my dealings with others, I have the foundation that brings me incredible success and happiness.

373

Other people

- ✓ I love doing helpful and worthwhile things for others.
- ✓ I love being full of life, enthusiasm, creativity and fun and, as a result, other people like being around me because of how good I make them feel.

Health

- All my thoughts and actions create health, energy and vitality within me.
- It is fun and easy weighing 12st 12lbs (180 lbs) and having the energy to complete all my daily tasks at work, home and play.

Home

- ✓ Now I am earning more than £100,000 per year, I really enjoy the lifestyle I give my family, and they love it too.
- ✓ Now that all the children have graduated from university, the sense of achievement the whole family feels is electrifying.

Work

- Pressure is exciting and stimulating to me; I do an even better job when I'm under pressure.
- Because of my inspirational leadership skills, the teams I am responsible for always exceed their objectives and, as a result, my career is flying.

Paul Adams

374

Maya looked up after carefully reading and studying what Paul had written. At regular intervals as she was reading, she had closed her eyes for a few seconds, before she opened them again and continued. Paul couldn't contain his curiosity and asked, "Well … well … what do you think? Are they written OK? Have I followed the rules?"

Maya nodded, "They are very, very good, Paul. I don't think I've ever seen anyone's first set of ThEmFee affirmations written so well". Paul then asked, "What were you doing when you closed your eyes as you were reading through them?" Maya explained her actions, "With any ThEmFee affirmations, no matter who's written them, when I've read the words, providing there are no glaring errors like 'I will be …', 'I can be …' or 'when I'm 50 years old ….', I like to close my eyes and concentrate fully on seeing the picture the words I'm reading generate in my mind, and feeling the feeling in my heart and body. I work on the simple basis that if I can see it and feel it, then you certainly can, because the affirmation is yours not mine. I then know that the future outcome you desire is on its way to you. All the forces in the universe have been commanded to unify and deliver into your world the desired outcome.

"I managed to do this with every one of your affirmations. Well done! There's just a couple of things I need to understand, and my comments are only because I know what you're like as a person." Paul was intrigued and Maya went on, "Under the heading of 'Other people' you've written 'I love doing helpful and worthwhile things for others'." Paul immediately interjected, "Yes, you know that doing good works for others is really important to me, it always has been. That's why it's in my top 10!" Maya continued, "I know that, and I also know that you are really uncomfortable when people make a fuss; you really dislike it." Paul replied, "Oh, you bet I do! It's horrible. I don't like the limelight or the attention." Maya continued, "I thought not, so why don't you make a little alteration that reflects that, and say something like 'I love quietly doing helpful and worthwhile things for others', because that way people won't know it's you that's behind it and, therefore, can't make a fuss. I just think that reflects more what you really would want to do, and how you want to feel as a result."

Paul thought for a moment, "I agree with you. If I attract attention as I start doing good things for other people, I just stop doing it! That's very astute of you, thanks!" Maya added, "The power we tap into, and the force we effectively instruct, will always deliver precisely the meaning of the words we use in our ThEmFee affirmations. We need to think through what it looks and feels like. Then, if there are potential blockages or obstacles to the sheer bliss and joy of the results, we can go back to the original words and adjust them accordingly." Paul was impressed with this.

Maya continued, "The other point I want to make relates to your work affirmations: 'Pressure is exciting and stimulating to me; I do an even better job when I'm under pressure'. Whether you realise it or not, this is a genius ThEmFee affirmation in terms of the way it's written. Most people wouldn't choose a weakness and turn it into strength via an affirmation." Paul was slightly embarrassed because he hadn't realised that he'd done that! Maya went on, "I know that you've struggled with stress in the past, and it has caused you to have long spells off work. I know it was the pressure you were put under that caused the problem. You've actually done a bit of mental judo here, using the power and force of your opponent to your advantage. Did you realise that?"

Paul thought for a few seconds, "Er … erm… in a way I suppose I did. My thinking was that there are no jobs these days with no pressure. The higher I've climbed up the corporate ladder, the more pressure there's been. I realised that pressure can either grind me into the ground and make me ill again, or I can use it as a springboard for my ever-increasing success. It's that simple."

Maya's face lit up, "Brilliant! Absolutely brilliant! Of course this style of writing ThEmFee affirmations can be used for so many things, such as shy people meeting new people for the first time, technophobic people becoming wizards at working with computers and other IT devices, people who have difficulty getting out of bed in the morning. It's very adaptable.

"Your affirmations are a credit to you. You have a true understanding of the rules regarding writing them. What impresses me most is your understanding of how they serve as a directional device that, when charged with the emotion that turns them into heart-felt feelings, changes and positively affects the unseen forces around us. The forces, as you know, then respond by transmuting those feelings into reality. When thoughts, emotions and feelings, ThEmFees, come together as one, we can, as most people would perceive, work miracles! Now, would you like to know how to imprint them in a way that 100% guarantees that they will manifest themselves in our real world?" Paul nodded vigorously.

"Once you've got this," Maya emphasised, "You have got everything you need to take control of your life in the full belief and faith that you can have every right and proper desire without limit. The process of imprinting, like everything else you've learned about, is not easy but it is simple. What you need to do is this: first thing in the morning and last thing at night, you need to dedicate 3 or 4 minutes to do the affirmations I've shared with you, plus your own ThEmFee affirmations." Paul frowned his lack of understanding.

Maya clarified, "To do your affirmations means find a quiet place, first thing in the morning and last thing at night, take out the paper upon which they are written, and then, one by one, read the words, see the pictures, charge the pictures with emotion, then feel the feelings with all your heart and soul and drive them into your very being. Make that feeling go deep into your subatomic structure. Let your DNA sing to its tune. Feel it until it oozes out of every pore of your body and remember: you're not wishing for something, you're not asking for something. You, in your mind, are there, you have it. The heart-felt feeling of how good it is, now you've got it, or become it, is the non-verbal language that projects itself into the field of creation, where all possibilities already exist, in a way that claims the future outcome you've chosen. All the forces in the universe then conspire and work together to manifest it, to make it real.

"Do this, with the same level of intensity and certainty of outcome, with the affirmations I gave you and each of your 10 ThEmFee affirmations. Just remind me of the ones I gave you."

Paul responded automatically, "I believe in the power within my grasp. I am finding, feeling and using the power within my grasp. My thoughts are an integral part of the power that is the unseen universal force that is the field of creation."

Maya continued, "Three or 4 minutes each morning and each evening will allow you to do them all, probably two or three times over. The reason I suggest you start with 10 of your own is because 3 or 4 minutes is a relatively short period of time that won't be an imposition on your daily schedule. If you were to do all 34 of your ThEmFee affirmations, it would take 10 or 15 minutes to do them properly. That's quite a lot of time, and it would put you off concentrating hard enough because you would probably start worrying about external things, such as whether the kids are ready for school, or whether the traffic is building up, etc.

"You should do your ThEmFee affirmations first thing in the morning and last thing at night because that is when your brain is naturally in what is called the alpha state. Normally, during the day, the brain operates in the beta state, which means it vibrates and oscillates at around 20 cycles per second. Twenty cycles per second is associated with being active; it's the mode you are in when you get things done. The alpha state means that the brain vibrates and oscillates at around only 10 cycles per second and is related to programming; it's the mode where you're most susceptible to subconscious suggestion. This is the perfect time to imprint your goals, via your ThEmFee affirmations, into your inner subconscious. First thing in the morning and last thing at night is when your mind is naturally at its most receptive for the instructions to be imprinted and accepted.

"If you can meditate, and proper meditation is often called 'going to alpha' or 'going to level', which means slowing your brain cycles down to around 10 per second, you can effectively imprint ThEmFee affirmations at any time of the day. If you can't meditate, it doesn't really matter, because as I've said you're at the alpha level naturally first thing in the morning and last thing at night. So you can take maximum advantage of it.

"It's important to do your ThEmFee affirmations twice a day, for a couple of reasons. Firstly, constant repetition is required to build and maintain beliefs. Secondly, it refuels the desire, and the thoughts, emotions and feelings generated, that keep us directly connected with the field of creation. This connectivity with the forces that surround us ensures that what we have chosen to become and have in our minds is mirrored back to us in the real world in the shortest possible timescale.

"If, for whatever reason, you don't manage to do your affirmations one morning or one evening, don't think that the process is irrevocably broken, because it isn't. Just make sure you continue the imprinting process as soon as you can. Missing the odd occasion to imprint the ThEmFee affirmations is OK. Doing your ThEmFee affirmations on the odd occasion, say once a week, isn't! OK?! Paying lip service to the process renders it totally ineffective and useless. If you're not willing to commit to the morning and evening discipline, don't bother starting!"

Paul answered in amazement, "Why would anyone not want to do their ThEmFee affirmations every morning and every evening? That beggars belief when you understand the power and control that doing it gives you."

Maya nodded, "I know, it's a strange thing that so many people can't be bothered, even after they've learned what you've now learned. It's probably to do with their conditioning. It's so much more comfortable for people to blame everything and everyone else for their situation in life, rather than taking responsibility and being in control by building a life that works for them.

"It's also amazing how people start off so well and achieve what they thought was impossible by using this process, and all the forces it harnesses, and then they stop! Feelings of not being worthy are mainly to blame for this. It's not easy believing in yourself totally, in the negative world in which we live. You need to be incredibly focused to maintain the discipline to have your every right and proper desire.

"One of the other reasons people don't utilise all the forces in the universe at their disposal is that often the wrong emotions are driving the ThEmFee affirmations. For instance, a good friend of mine had been guided and had used all this to wonderful effect and achieved incredible things. But he nearly gave up doing his affirmations because the one thing he wanted to achieve more than anything eluded him. It just simply would not manifest itself."

Paul asked, "What was it? What is some really big affirmation, like having 10 million pounds in the bank or something?"

Maya continued, "No, no, nothing like that, but it was the big one for him. It was about his perfect partner showing up in his life. This desire was translated into a brilliantly written ThEmFee affirmation, and a very disciplined imprinting process was actioned. However, the desired outcome didn't materialise. All the other affirmations he was doing at the time manifested themselves really quickly. But not this one. Another guide was telling me how he went to her for guidance and they then uncovered the blockage in no time.

"What they discovered was that his desire to meet his perfect partner was 100% but, when he examined the emotion with which he was charging his affirmation, it was fear not love! He didn't want to find his perfect partner for all the joy, happiness and wonderful things they could share together. He wanted to find his perfect partner because if he didn't he'd be on his own for the rest of his life! That fear, the sheer emotion of being alone all his life, then fuelled feelings of unworthiness, a kind of 'who the heck would want somebody like me?' feeling. Rather than life-enhancing feelings making his DNA dance, they were life-defeating feelings he was projecting, and the field of creation, as we know, always responds to our feelings and reflects back into the physical realm our heart-felt choices. He was, unwittingly, keeping his perfect partner at bay, out of his life, because of his misguided feelings and emotions.

"He didn't need to change the ThEmFee affirmation he'd written, because it was perfect. But he did need to change the emotion with which it was charged from fear to love. When he did this it changed the feeling from being unworthy to being totally worthy. He met his perfect partner 4 weeks later!"

Paul understood what Maya was saying. He explained to her that he had in fact evaluated whether his affirmations, the emotions with which they were charged, and the feelings they generated, were 'aligned', during the time between writing them and calling Maya to have their meeting to review them.

Maya concluded, "Well, Paul, you've now got the lot! You've got everything you need to live the life you've always wanted, and to have anything you desire without limit. You now need to put it into practice in totality. There is only one more piece of advice. As you begin to do your affirmations, you'll experience urges and intuitions to do certain things. The advice is very simple, and that is to do them, and do them straight away! If your chatterbox or self-talk says to you 'Oh, we really need to cut down on the amount we eat' take heed and do it immediately. Don't put it off. If an invite comes through the letterbox to go to a party hosted by someone you don't know very well, go! I can almost guarantee that you will meet someone who knows someone, or something, that will help you to realise one of your affirmations. Trust your instincts! Go with the flow. Infinite intelligence is sending us messages all the time regarding what to do to turn our thoughts into things. Listen to it, act on what it tells you to do and say. There is a saying 'success occurs when desire and opportunity meet'. People who don't understand this call it luck but, as we have already discussed, there is no such thing as luck.

"We have powers that we don't understand. Well, not consciously or rationally. And we don't need to understand how they work; all we need to know is that they do work. As we've said before, let other people study the roots, while we pick the fruit! Your guidance from me has ended for now. Go and put all this into dynamic and positive action for the benefit of yourself and all humankind. To make the world a better place, especially your world and the worlds of those close to you. Keep me up to date with what happens in your life as you master the powerful principles and practices. If at any time you become unsure of anything, do call me for a chat, because I'd be delighted to help. You shouldn't need to, but ..."

Paul gently interrupted her, "I know, I know: you'll be there. I can't tell you how grateful and appreciative I am that you chose to guide me, to share the insights and truths that were shown to you."

Maya added, "One last thing: don't try and explain the process or techniques you've learned to other people just now. It's a specialist subject. Becoming a guide yourself and explaining it to others is something you'll be able to do in time, initially under my supervision and eventually on your own. For now, just focus on mastering the principles and practices for yourself."

Paul said with intense emotion, "A thousand thanks; no, a million!"

Maya rose from her chair, "Paul, no more thanks please. Just go and do wonderful things with what you've learned. That's all the thanks I need". They kissed each other on the cheek and left the pub.

Chapter Twenty-seven

Paul was exhilarated. His energy, vitality and creative spirit were awesome and never dwindled. As he practised the lessons Maya had taught him, his command over all the circumstances and situations life presented him became fully developed.

He realised that the affirmations Maya had given him to repeat from their early meetings were designed to connect him and all humankind to the universal and infinite forces at his disposal. He was now beginning to work up through the gears and reach full power, yet it was effortless as he followed Maya's guidance.

His achievements were astonishing. He was humbled by his new-found knowledge and soon realised that success at anything in life comes not from the knowing, but from the doing. He had a mighty determination to do everything his guide had asked of him to the utmost of his ability.

He saw many gifted and talented people straining, striving and struggling to succeed in life but, because they didn't know what he knew, the harder they tried, the worse it got for them. They became disillusioned and demoralised as they scattered and diffused their life force. They didn't understand the basic principles involved in harnessing the limitless universal forces to deliver anything they desired in life. If people only knew that the key to success, achievement and abundance is to start with the end in mind, the possibilities would be boundless.

He found he didn't need any further guidance from Maya. Her instructions were clear, simple and memorable. He was positive in his approach and removed all elements of doubt that had been lurking in the corners of his mind. He met Maya on a regular basis after his guidance had finished. Their meetings initially focused on appreciation and gratitude for the new-found gifts and talents they'd learned to master and how they were used to benefit everyone.

Paul had quickly realised that to try and discuss and explain the powerful principles and practices with others was dangerous. It was dangerous because, as he was still an apprentice learning this new craft, trying to explain to others would diminish his connectedness and effectiveness. Explanation would have sapped his power, especially with people who already reckoned they knew everything. He remembered a quote: 'it's what you learn *after* you know everything that really counts'.

He smiled wryly to himself, realising that anyone approaching such dynamite teachings with doubt, scepticism or resistance of any kind would benefit very little. 'They're too blind to see that what stops them receiving what they want is their unbelief! Maybe that's why this way of thinking and doing has never taken root? All the 'clever' people want proof of infinite intelligence and hard evidence of why all this works, before giving it a try. What a waste', he thought.

The reality is that all you need is the belief that it works and the courage to try it out for yourself. Doing that provides all the proof you need.

Success, happiness, health, wealth, joy are available in bucketfuls on demand. How good can life get?! Paul recalled a quote from the Bible that explained it all. Christ said: 'Therefore I tell you, whatever you ask for in prayer, believe that you have received it, and it will be yours'!

Paul transformed his life and that of his family through his support, encouragement and success at work. He'd begun the process with personal and material objectives, and quickly moved on to community and humanitarian ones.

As his mastery grew, he knew the time was right for he himself to become a guide. Maya would supervise him before he started flying solo. The thinking revolution had started. The world shook in positive and eager anticipation.

Notes

Notes

Notes

Notes

Notes

Notes